The New Germany

For my parents

The New Germany

A HUMAN GEOGRAPHY

ALUN JONES

University College London, UK

JOHN WILEY & SONS
Chichester • New York • Brisbane • Toronto • Singapore

Copyright © 1994 Alun Jones

Published in 1994 by John Wiley & Sons Ltd
Baffins Lane, Chichester,
West Sussex PO19 1UD, England

Telephone National Chichester (0243) 779777
International (+44) (243) 779777

Other Wiley Editorial Offices

John Wiley & Sons, Inc., 605 Third Avenue,
New York, NY 10158-0012, USA

Jacaranda Wiley Ltd, 33 Park Road, Milton,
Queensland 4064, Australia

John Wiley & Sons (Canada) Ltd, 22 Worcester Road,
Rexdale, Ontario M9W 1L1, Canada

John Wiley & Sons (SEA) Pte Ltd, 37 Jalan Pemimpin #05-04,
Block B, Union Industrial Building, Singapore 2057

Library of Congress Cataloging-in-Publication Data

Jones, Alun.
    The new Germany: a human geography/Alun Jones.
    p. cm.
    Includes bibliographical references and index.
    ISBN 0-471-94929-9 — ISBN 0-471-94932-9 (pbk)
    1. Germany—History—Unification, *1990.* 2. Human geography—
Germany. 3. German reunification *(1949–1990).* 4. Germany—
Economic integration. 5. Germany (East)—Economic conditions.
I. Title.
DD257.25.J63 1994
943.087'9—dc20   94-9545
                                                           CIP

British Library Cataloguing in Publication Data

A catalogue record for this book is available from the British Library

ISBNs 0 471 94929 9 (Cl)
      0 471 94932 9 (Pr)

Typeset in 10/12pt Sabon by
Mayhew Typesetting, Rhayader, Powys
Printed and bound in Great Britain by Biddles Ltd, Guildford, Surrey

Dieses neue Deutschland ist nicht die alte Bundesrepublik oder eine grossere Bundesrepublik nur durch den Beitritt der ehemaligen DDR. Es ist in der Tat ein neues Deutschland, was die uberwiegende Zahl der Menschen in den alten und neuen Bundesländern so noch nicht zur Kenntnis nimmt.

Dr Berndt Seite, Ministerpräsidenten, Mecklenburg-Vorpommern in *Das Parlament*, (36), 3 September 1993, p. 3

This new Germany is not the old Federal Republic nor an expanded Federal Republic through the admittance of the former DDR. It is in fact a *New Germany* that the overwhelming majority of people in the old and new *Länder* have not yet acknowledged.

(Author's translation and italics)

Contents

Photographs

Figures

Tables

Preface

The unification of Germany in 1990 represents one of the most significant events in the post-war history of Europe. Due to its geographical location, economic strengths and trade interests in both Western and Eastern Europe, the new Germany can be expected to play a crucial role in the future development of the continent. However, German unification was a huge economic, political and social experiment whose results could not be predicted. This book provides an up-to-date account of the process of German unification and its impact in the new states (*Länder*) of Eastern Germany. It is not a text on West Germany or on East Germany; rather it is one that emphasises the difficulties of bringing together two countries with two very different post-war histories.

The book is divided into seven chapters. Chapter 1 looks at how, after 1945, two German states emerged with contrasting economic, social, and political systems. Chapter 2 traces the development of the German Democratic Republic (GDR) between 1949–89 and demonstrates that despite its small territory, poor resource base, severance from traditional markets in the West, and strict reparations imposed by the USSR, the GDR became one of the most successful economies in Eastern Europe by the 1980s. Chapter 3 examines the spectacular economic developments in West Germany over the same period and shows that despite certain economic difficulties the country had become a major global economic power by the 1980s, with its citizens enjoying a high standard of living. Chapter 4 chronicles the events leading up to the unification of the two Germanies in 1990 and considers the pressures for unification, the mechanisms to achieve this both internally and externally, and the optimism surrounding the process. Chapter 5 examines the ways in which unification has fashioned a new human geography of Germany with the creation of new spatial patterns of employment, population distribution and composition, infrastructure, urban centres, and regional income inequality. Chapter 6 provides a detailed account of how the new *Länder* are being modernised, the financial costs involved, and the progress made since 1990. The chapter demonstrates that the tasks facing the German authorities are considerable and that the privatisation process has led to major job loss throughout much of the economy in the east. Chapter 7 focuses upon how the new Germany was integrated into the political and economic structures of the European Community and considers Germany's changing relationship with Eastern

Europe and the former USSR in terms of trade, economic assistance, and efforts to restrain population migration. In addition, the choice of capital and seat of government of the new Germany in a new Europe is also discussed.

Much of the recent material for this text is derived from official sources, periodicals, and newspapers, and I have made use of additional reports, journals, statistical publications in German, not specifically cited. I realise that events in Germany are unfolding rapidly, and I have tried to present the most recent available data (1992–3). I have included suggestions for further reading at the end of each chapter, and more extensive material, both in English and German, may be found in the bibliography. Throughout the text I have used German spellings for cities and states within Germany but anglicised versions for places outside of the current German borders.

I am grateful to a number of people for their help in the preparation of this book. In the Department of Geography at UCL Richard Munton provided me with a sabbatical term during which most of the text was written, Hugh Prince and Hugh Clout both read the manuscript kindly giving useful advice, and Tim Aspen devoted a great deal of time to the drawing of the figures.

Elsewhere in London, thanks are due to the librarians at the German Historical Institute, staff of the German Embassy, Goethe Institute, and Lufthansa, and, of course, my publisher, Dr Iain Stevenson.

In Germany I am indebted to many people too numerous to mention, though I would like to single out the following for special thanks: Professor Wolf Gaebe (Stuttgart), Professor Heinz Heineberg (Münster), Drs Ferdinand Fasterding and Rainer Plankl (FAL Braunschweig), Dr Christof Ellger (Berlin), Andi Kellick (Sachsisches Staatsministerium für Wirtschaft und Arbeit, Dresden), and Dr Pia Zdrahal (Treuhandanstalt, Berlin).

Finally, my greatest thanks are to my wife, Jackie, for all her support and understanding during the writing of this text.

1 The emergence of the two German states 1945–9

The ravages of war had reduced Germany in 1945 to the conditions described by Willy Brandt in his memoirs, a chaos of

> craters, caves, mountains of rubble, debris-covered fields, ruins that hardly allowed one to imagine that they had once been houses, cables and water pipes projecting from the ground like the mangled bowels of antediluvian monsters, no fuel, no light, every little garden a graveyard and, above all this, like an immoveable cloud, the stink of putrefaction. In this no man's land lived human beings. Their life was a daily struggle for a handful of potatoes, a loaf of bread, a few lumps of coal, some cigarettes (quoted in Craig, 1982, p.35).

The war's end had been greeted with a range of responses among Germans, as Fulbrook (1991) notes, 'on the whole, the political attitudes of most Germans may be characterised in terms of apathy, a weariness in relation to "politics" and what it brought with it, and an overriding concern with sheer physical survival from day to day' (p.134). Not only was Germany ruined and occupied, but the crimes committed by Germans in the name of the German nation added shame and confusion to the overwhelming trials of daily existence (Bark and Gress, 1989). Without taking this as a reference point it is easy to take for granted the achievements of both West Germany and East Germany in the post-war period. Fewer and fewer Germans remember the formidable process of political, social and economic reconstruction that faced Germany at the end of the war.

Not only the future political-ideological division of the country but also the different socio-economic paths of development of the two Germanies were set out during the years of Allied control after the war. Plans for the defeated Germany were elaborated during the course of the war, with all sides agreeing that the whole of the country should be occupied, that German economic potential should be reduced and that reparations would be paid by Germany for damages inflicted. The defeated Germany would be divided into Allied zones of occupation both for purposes of demilitarisation and reparations. Germany was in fact to be divided into three zones, while the Yalta conference in 1945 agreed that a fourth zone should be created for the French out of the British and American zones (Dickinson, 1953). The

Soviet zone would remain unchanged. In addition German territory east of the Oder and west of the Neisse Rivers would become part of Poland in compensation for the land acquired by the Soviets under the Stalin–Hitler Pact in 1939 (see Figure 1.1). Some ten million people who were registered as living in these areas in 1939 would be expelled, representing a clear attempt by the Soviet Union and new communist governments to eliminate the problem of minority populations (Fritsch-Bournazel, 1988). East Prussia, the whole of Silesia and parts of Pomerania and Brandenburg, an area of over 44 000 sq. miles and inhabited by German peoples for over 500 years, were lost to Poland in one stroke of a pen. These decisions not only increased the geographical distance between Germany and Russia but also ensured for the Poles the anger of many Germans, thereby protecting Russia from any future German–Polish deal at its expense (Balfour, 1982).

The American zone of occupation extended over much of southern Germany. It comprised the state (*Land*) of Bayern and an expanded territory of Hessen. The need to provide the French with a zone led to the northern parts of Baden and Württemberg being separated from the south, while some former territory of Hesse was combined with former Prussian Rheinland to form the new *Land*, Rheinland-Pfalz. The enclave of Bremen formed a fourth *Land* and became the main American port of entry into occupied Germany (Mellor, 1978).

In the British zone four *Länder* were established. Schleswig-Holstein and Hamburg were historical political units, while a new *Land* of Niedersachsen was created from several former duchies and kingdoms, while the *Land* of Nordrhein-Westfalen was set up in 1946 through the merger of two former Prussian provinces. This *Land* was the most populous and also the most devastated since it contained many industrial cities important in the German war effort. For example, 72% of the buildings in Köln were destroyed and 90% of the city of Düsseldorf was uninhabitable as a result of Allied bombing.

The Soviet zone was initially divided into five *Länder* comprising Sachsen, Sachsen-Anhalt (following a merger of these two former provinces), Brandenburg, Thüringen and Mecklenburg. Berlin presented particular problems for the Allies. The city would be jointly occupied even though geographically it was firmly located within the Soviet occupation zone (Elkins, 1988). The north-eastern sector of the city was to be under Soviet control, the north-west under British and the southern sector under American administration. A French sector of the city was also later created. Access to Berlin for the Western allies was by designated land and air corridors through the Soviet zone, thereby placing the Allies in a strategically vulnerable position should relations between the Soviet Union and the Western Allies deteriorate.

The political factors that determined Germany's fate in 1945 were

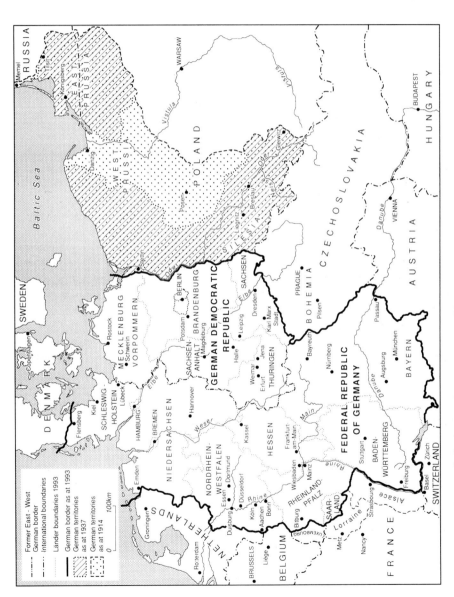

Figure 1.1 *Territorial change in Germany 1914–90*

primarily the character, aims and policies of the USSR, the United States of America, Great Britain and to a lesser extent France. In 1943 the US and British war aims were unequivocally the destruction of German power, the dismemberment of Germany and the assumption of full political authority on German territory by the Allied powers. It was believed that the occupation of Germany would be the only way to ensure that the country would never again be able to reconstitute a unified and potentially aggressive state (Bark and Gress, 1989). Germany's natural resources plus its strategic position in the heart of Europe rendered it a valuable prize were it to fall under the total control of either the Western Allies or the USSR. Despite plans for the territorial division of Germany and their subsequent realisation after 1945, little thought had been given to how the zones of occupation would be administered. Even between the Western zones there were major differences in the nature of administration, not least because of the difficulties of communication between the zones. Nevertheless, one observer quoting German reactions to Western occupation has stated that 'the British like us, but don't always notice that we are there; the Americans like us but treat us like badly behaved children; the French hate us on equal terms' (Balfour, 1992, p.84).

The Potsdam conference of July 1945 and its aftermath reflected the growing differences of opinion, particularly between the Western Allies and the USSR, on whether the defeated Germany should be stringently punished, stripped of its economic resources and industrial equipment or reprieved from total economic dismantling. The Western powers came to realise that the long-term goal should be to strive for a prosperous Germany because European, and ultimately international, economic recovery would be dependent upon it. The USSR, having demanded considerable reparations from Germany, held a different view of the country's future. Germany's economic destitution would be a positive step towards eventual communist acceptance there. The Russians, therefore, insisted on removing plant from their occupation zone and demanded reparations from the other Allied zones which were regarded as having greater productive resources. The Russians requested some $20 billion in reparations from the defeated Germany.

The zonal division of Germany fundamentally affected the country's human geography. Not only did the various occupational strategies of the victors influence the processes of economic and political development, but division itself had far-reaching effects upon trade patterns, population movements, the separation of key economic centres from their traditional hinterlands (for example Hamburg from the Elbe basin) and the loss of important territory with vital natural resources (for example Silesia's coalfields to Poland).

While the Potsdam conference agreed a balanced economic development in post-war Germany through the equitable distribution of essential commodities among the occupation zones, this did not happen in practice for several reasons. First, there were differences in the severity of the problems facing the Allies in each zone. Britain was hardest hit by the division, since its zone, particularly the Ruhr industrial region, had been most badly damaged by Allied bombing and faced severe housing problems. In addition, the zone contained industrial equipment subject to dismantling under reparations agreements. The Soviet zone, which accounted for over one-quarter of pre-war agricultural output (Dickinson, 1953) was faltering on the distribution of food to the Western zones hence compounding food shortages there. To overcome this situation, both the British and American governments were footing high food-import bills for their zones, while at home the British population was facing serious food shortages and rationing.

The massive number of refugees and expellees flooding into the Western zones in search of food and shelter compounded the difficulties facing the Allies. For example, some 25 000–30 000 refugees from former German lands in Eastern Europe were drifting through Berlin each day in August 1945 (Berghahn, 1987). In total, around 10 million Germans were uprooted as a result of Nazi Germany's defeat (Balfour, 1982).

On the industrial front, control over levels of production of key industries, the loss of output caused by reparations and the loss of territory in the east, combined with growing demands from a population swollen by refugees, began to convince Western administrations of the need for policy change. In 1946, US Secretary of State James Byrnes speaking in Stuttgart gave a clear indication that Germany must not be allowed to become the 'poor house' of Europe; a speech that is regarded as one of the turning points in post-war German history and one that sealed the fate for the future division of the country.

The Americans proposed that their zone should be combined with the other zones in order to permit more efficient administration. The British government agreed to merge their occupation zone with that of the US to create a 'Bizone' but the French initially resisted any territorial grouping. The Soviets, meanwhile, regarded the US suggestion as a dangerous move that would lead to greater American domination and could give rise to German nationalism being rekindled. The creation of Bizonia in 1947 was indeed more than an administrative convenience; it represented the first formal step towards the partition of Germany (Leaman, 1988).

The extra harsh winter of 1947 further crippled the German economy giving rise to serious shortages of coal and food, with Germans in the Western zone facing famine with only 1000 calories of food per day (one-half of pre-war levels). In some cities such as München hunger demonstrations were organised by student groups, while throughout the country the black market had become an essential sector of the economy.

Worried by the possible increase in social unrest in Germany caused by starvation, the new US Secretary of State, General Marshall, announced a European Recovery Programme at a speech in Harvard in 1947. Provided that the countries of Europe could collectively formulate a recovery plan, the US would be prepared to finance it. It was hoped that this programme would stimulate the economic recovery of Germany and of the rest of the continent. This announcement was followed by a meeting of representatives of 16 European states in Paris in the summer of 1947. It was obvious to the Western Allies that Bizonia would have to be included in the recovery programme and that the French zone, despite initial French protests, would have to join it too in order to benefit from what was to be termed 'Marshall Aid'. The French were in fact not in a position to administer their zone of occupation without Marshall Aid (Balfour, 1982). For the USA there were several motivations, both of a political and economic nature, for proposing the Marshall Aid programme. First, it would enable free-trade conditions to prevail, thereby benefiting US exports. Second, by ensuring the maintenance of capitalism it would stave off communist expansion in Western and Central Europe which would have threatened American strategic and economic interests.

The Russians, angered by what it regarded as American imperialism in Europe, walked out of the Paris talks and instructed the Polish and Czech representatives to do the same. With the others agreeing to go ahead with the recovery plan this effectively meant that the economic development of Germany would take two different paths; whereas the Western zones would benefit from Marshall Aid, the Russian occupied zone would not be included in the programme. This represented a second major step towards the emergence of two German states. The division of Germany was therefore the inevitable result of the interaction of the Allies' views on two post-war problems: the future of Europe and the future of Germany (Sowden, 1975). For the Americans the outcome of the Paris meeting represented a valuable strategic victory since the Western zones of Germany contained the industrial centres of the Ruhr and Rhein basins (Leaman, 1988). Economic growth in these areas would overshadow the economically impoverished Soviet zone of Germany which contained less than one-quarter of pre-war industrial production (Dickinson, 1953). Perhaps as important for the Americans was the fact that the Paris meeting revealed the strength of political influence they held over other Western countries particularly Britain and France, an issue which is important in understanding subsequent events.

Developments in the Western zones of Germany after the Paris meeting were closely linked to the political division of the country (Fulbrook, 1991). Two major events are worthy of note: first, the successful attempt at achieving price stability through a currency reform involving a new Deutschmark to replace the Reichsmark in the Western zone in 1948; and second, the attempt by the Russians in the same year to isolate Berlin from the Western zone by cutting off road, rail and water routes to the city across the Soviet zone. Communication with Berlin was maintained by the airlifting of over 10 000 tons per day of food, fuel and other essential items from bases in the Western zones at great financial and human cost (Elkins, 1988). After almost 11 months the Soviets eventually lifted the blockade, though the city had become the battleground between two competing ideologies. It meant that West Berlin would become firmly associated with the emerging state of West Germany and that East Berlin would remain under the control of the Russians. Western and Russian disagreements over the future of Germany had therefore created the Berlin dilemma.

The creation of Bizonia, the decision by France to add its zone to what was becoming an emerging political state combined with continued concern in the US about the threat of communist expansion in Europe led to moves to constitutionalise the Western zones of Germany. This process reflected the strong influence of US views over those of the British and French in deciding the future political nature of West Germany. In 1948, a parliamentary council comprising 65 representatives from each of the newly established *Länder* in West Germany was asked to convene in order to draft a 'constitution' for the Western zones. The British view was that the West German state should be centralised with a parliamentary rather than presidential government, while the French, anxious to avoid the potential threat of a strongly centralised Germany, preferred the US position that West Germany should be a federation with a weak central state. It was the US position that held sway, with the parliamentary council being requested to draw up a constitution to create a federal government for the Western zones.

Despite major disagreements in Germany between parties on the left and right of the political spectrum over federalism and the wish to keep open the possibility of reuniting the two Germanies, a Basic Law (*Grundgesetz*) rather than constitution was formally passed for West Germany by the parliamentary council on 8 May 1949 (Merkl, 1989).

The vitally important Basic Law was designed to provide a temporary organisation for a temporary state, pending the reunification of Germany and the ultimate incorporation of the entire country into a European union. The Basic Law was drafted in the name of the entire 'German people'. Article 116 of the Basic Law bestows automatic citizenship on all who were citizens of Germany before its division, or who were admitted to its 1937 territory as refugees of 'German stock' or who were the wives or dependents of such persons. This includes those who were defined as German but living in former German lands which were part of Polish or Soviet territory (Edinger, 1986). The number of people who could therefore qualify for German citizenship under this definition was considerable, and the possible future political and economic consequences of this decision had certainly not been evaluated thoroughly given the range of pressing issues facing West

Table 1.1   *The contents of the Basic Law*

Chapter	No. of Articles	Subject
1	19	Human Rights
2	18	Federal–Regional Government relations
3	12	Role of Lower House (Bundestag)
4	4	Role of Upper House (Bundesrat)
5	8	Role of Federal President
6	8	Role of the Chancellor and Ministries
7–11	77	Legislation, justice, finance

Germany at this time. (This point was to be of great significance following the reunification of Germany in 1990.)

The Basic Law draws on the experience of the Third Reich, the Weimar Republic and Imperial Germany and sought to define in considerable detail both the general principles on which the new state was to be based and the methods by which it was to be governed (Johnson, 1983). A useful discussion of its content is provided by Balfour (1982). Table 1.1 summarises the main points.

The Federal government (*Bund*) has responsibility for issues relating to foreign affairs, defence, nationality, freedom of movement, currency, customs and trade agreements, air travel, railways, post and telecommunications and commercial law. The states (*Länder*) in turn have almost exclusive responsibility for cultural affairs, education, radio and television, environment and local government and planning. 'Concurrent powers' are those where the *Bund* has a prior right to legislate, leaving the *Länder* to do so where it has not taken up its option—including civil and criminal law, road traffic and labour law. The situation is further complicated by the fact that the *Länder* have the task of administering Federal laws within their borders, thereby providing them with considerable scope to interpret Federal law broadly according to regional situations.

A set of procedures for raising and sharing out revenue between the *Bund* and the *Länder* was also devised. Proceeds of certain taxes, for example sales tax, go to the *Bund*, while revenue from other taxes such as those on property and beer go entirely to the individual *Länder*. Other tax revenue (from income and business taxes) is shared out between the *Bund* and the *Länder* according to agreed proportions. All tax legislation is formulated by the *Bund* and applies uniformly throughout the country, in order to avoid imbalances in the tax burden (Ardagh, 1988).

To even out differences in wealth between the relatively rich and relatively poorer *Länder* as a result of these revenue-raising measures, a compensation arrangement or equalisation scheme (*Finanzausgleich*) was also devised whereby no *Land* is left with a tax revenue 5% above or below the Federal average. The Basic Law therefore is strongly committed to ensuring equal standards of living across all West Germany.

With Berlin under four-power occupation and located in the heart of the Soviet zone, the search for a temporary capital for West Germany was begun. The choice of capital for the new West German state occasioned the use of geography to support political argument. Not only was there a need to choose a city that would reflect the Federal democracy of the new state but would also be provisional in nature and centrally placed to respond to the political ambitions of West Germany in Europe. The case for individual towns and cities was taken up by both politicians and academics. Berlin's role as a symbol of aggressive Germany, its occupation by the four Allied powers, its geographical location in the heart of the Soviet zone and in a Middle European belt which was most at threat from Soviet influence ranged against its selection. Others argued for the construction of a new city to house the capital functions which would be located in the central part of West Germany near the town of Fulda. The town of Celle, and Frankfurt-am-Main were also proposed, though there was much opposition to the latter with many fearing an American domination of West German affairs given the city's location in the US occupation zone. The eventual short list saw the addition of Bonn-Bad Godesberg and Karlsruhe. There was great debate over the eventual selection of the small town of Bonn as the provisional capital of West Germany (Pommerin, 1989).

In the Soviet zone, the heavy burden of reparations and the arbitrary nature of the dismantling process aroused widespread resentment against the Russians. Furthermore, the blame for the loss of German territory to Poland was firmly placed in the lap of the Soviet occupiers (Dennis, 1988). Considerable debate has taken place over the process by which Germany came to be divided into two states. Some authors, such as Krisch (1985), hold the view that long before the creation of the German Democratic Republic (GDR) in 1949, the Soviets had undertaken measures that were designed to project Soviet political power across Germany ensuring at the same time that the social, economic and political arrangements of the Soviet zone conformed to the Soviet model. These activities, it is claimed, prepared the ground for the formation of the GDR as a Soviet-style state. Others, such as Dennis (1988), cast doubt over whether the Russians wanted to impose a Soviet system on their zone.

What is clear, however, is that the Soviets wished to establish an anti-Fascist regime in their zone and remove the socio-economic preconditions of militarism and Fascism. Socialism was regarded as the antidote to capitalism since fascism was viewed as intrinsic to the latter. Between 1945–9 the Soviets carried out a series of measures in their zone to break up the social and economic structure of Hitler's Germany and of Imperial and Weimar

Germany as well. These radical measures included land reform (1945), the reform of schools (1945–6), the nationalisation of industrial property belonging to Nazis and war criminals (1945–6) and the restructuring of the judiciary and police (Childs, 1983). Land reform, for example, led to the expropriation of over 2.5 million hectares of land without compensation from over 7000 land owners (each owning over 100 hectares) and redistributed to half a million peasant farmers and labourers.

The deteriorating political relationship between the USSR and the West which was displayed in disputes over reparations, access to Berlin, the Marshall Plan and currency reform rapidly reduced the prospect of a united Germany. The rationale behind Soviet policy towards the West and the future of Germany during this period is difficult to discern. Many authors have attempted an interpretation (e.g. Adomeit, 1982; Keiderling, 1982; Dennis, 1988). Adomeit (1982) best summarises Soviet objectives towards Germany, focusing upon Soviet hesitancy and lack of a clear prescription for the country's future political and economic status. Both a neutral united Germany with possible economic leanings to Western Europe and the USA or a divided Germany with an impoverished economically unviable Russian zone had major disadvantages for the USSR. The drafting of the Basic Law in West Germany accelerated the process of Germany's division. The creation of a 330-member People's Council (*Volksrat*) in the Soviet zone in 1949 led to the preparation of a constitutional draft for the founding of the German Democratic Republic which formally came into being on 7 October 1949, some five months after the foundation of the Federal Republic of Germany. The constitution of the GDR bore strong similarities to the West German Basic Law—upper and lower parliaments, a *Länder* structure, multi-party representation and the question of German reunification remaining open. However, within a short space of time divergences between the West and East German constitutions emerged as political and economic realities in the GDR demanded particular responses on the part of the East German authorities.

Apportioning blame for the division of Germany has received a great deal of attention from writers both within and outside Germany. Fulbrook (1991) provides a useful summary of the main issues: the possibility that the United States over-reacted to the fear of Russian designs on Western Europe; that the Marshall Aid Programme was deliberately drawn up in a way that the Russians could not accept and which would require particular political institutions in the Western zones to administer it; the transformation of the Russian zone according to socialist principles thereby leading many Western governments to believe that Russia had an expansionist strategy for the continent.

The two Germanies were therefore drawn into two contrasting political, economic and ideological systems from 1949 onwards. For West Germany

Photograph 1   *US Troops: Kitzingen, Bayern, 1988.* British, American and French forces were garrisoned in West Germany

this meant cooperation with her Western European neighbours: at first in terms of the setting up of the European Coal and Steel Community (ECSC) which led to the coal and steel resources of six countries (including West Germany) being placed under the authority of a European Commission (see Jones and Budd, 1991); in 1955 full membership of the US-backed North Atlantic Treaty Organisation (NATO) and in 1957 of the European Economic Community (EEC). Membership of NATO and the EEC therefore locked West Germany into military and economic arrangements which would prevent her from acting unilaterally. Large numbers of British, French and American troops stationed on West German soil served to reinforce this message (see Photograph 1).

The GDR also entered into a broadly similar set of economic and military alliances created by the USSR. In 1950 East Germany became a member of the Council for Mutual Economic Assistance (COMECON), a grouping comprising the USSR and its emerging economic and political satellites in Eastern Europe. Indeed within two years some three-quarters of the GDR's trade was with members of COMECON. On the military front too the GDR was by the mid-1950s an integral member of the Warsaw Pact, the defence structure for the Eastern bloc and had massive Soviet forces based on its territory.

West and East Germans therefore stood in opposing camps, living under different economic structures and organisational forms and protected by military arrangements based upon ideological suspicion and mistrust. The decision by the GDR authorities in May 1952 to deepen the division of the country by converting the demarcation line between East and West Germany into a fortified border (see Photograph 2) thus sealed the fate of the German people. The post-war division of Germany was therefore complete. The following chapters chart the economic developments and achievements of both East and West Germany after 1949.

SUGGESTED READING

Backer, J. (1978) *The Decision to Divide Germany.* Duke University Press, Durham, USA.

Bark, D.L. and Gress, D.R. (1989) *A History of West Germany. Volume 1. From Shadow to Substance 1945–1963.* Basil Blackwell, Oxford.

Fulbrook, M. (1991) *The Fontana History of Germany 1918–1990. The Divided Nation.* Fontana, London.

Mellor, R.E.H. (1978) *The Two Germanies. A Modern Geography.* Harper and Row, London.

Merkl, P. (1963) *The Origin of the West German Republic.* Oxford University Press, Oxford.

Milward, A.S. (1984) *The Reconstruction of Western Europe 1945–1951.* Methuen, London.

Turner, H.A. (1987) *The Two Germanies since 1945.* Yale University Press, New Haven.

2 Economic development in the German Democratic Republic, 1949–89

INTRODUCTION

The division of Germany and the loss of German territory to Poland and the USSR had a marked effect upon the human geography of Central Europe. Division brought with it economic dislocation, increased population mobility, the emergence of new political structures and the forging of new trading links. The two German states that emerged as a consequence of Allied disagreements over the future of the country as a whole were profoundly different in their territorial configuration, organisation and resource base.

The German Democratic Republic (GDR) was established without regard for natural, historical, political or cultural factors (Krisch, 1985). The border between the two Germanies, which in May 1952 was heavily fortified (see Photograph 2), took no consideration whatsoever of the economic and human landscape, breaking up lines of communication and separating towns and villages from their hinterlands. The territory of the GDR encompassed 108 910 sq. kilometres, slightly less than half the area of the Federal Republic of Germany and only one-fifth of the Germany of 1937. In the north it comprised parts of the north German plain and Baltic coastal regions, while in the south it included the industrial region of Sachsen. However, the GDR was badly disadvantaged from the loss of the large coal reserves of upper Silesia and the severing of links with the port of Hamburg. Compared with West Germany, the GDR was poorly endowed with natural resources. Its only significant source of fuel was brown coal which was open cast and upon which its domestic and industrial energy requirements were based. The area encompassed by the new boundaries of the GDR accounted for only one-quarter of German agricultural and industrial production in the years preceding the Second World War. The GDR was also seriously hindered by the USSR's policy of dismantling East German industry as reparation for war damage to its own industry—a policy which was to last well into the 1950s (see Chapter 1). Factories, machinery, equipment, railways and rolling stock were commandeered for use in the USSR. Having

Photograph 2 *The inter-German border in the Harz mountains.* Barbed-wire fences,
watch towers and guard-dog patrols prevented cross-border
movement

lost its traditional markets and suppliers in the West another, significant
problem for the GDR was that it was forced to reorientate its trade towards
the USSR and Eastern Europe—new markets which were neither sufficiently
large nor a reliable basis upon which to foster economic development. In
particular, the USSR's ability to meet both the energy and raw material
demands of the GDR was in doubt from the outset (Schnitzer, 1964).

The division of Germany, therefore, not only created a territory in the
East with an inadequate food, industrial and energy base but also adversely
affected the prospects for its economic recovery and ultimately influenced the
direction its economic development would take. This chapter examines the
economic development and organisation of the GDR between 1949–89 and
demonstrates how, despite these inauspicious beginnings, by the 1980s it had
become a major industrial nation with the highest per capita income and
living standards of all the COMECON countries.

TERRITORIAL ORGANISATION

Between 1945–52 the territorial organisation of East Germany was based
upon five *Länder*—Mecklenburg, Brandenburg, Thüringen, Sachsen-Anhalt
and Sachsen. In 1952 these were replaced by 15 new districts (*Bezirke*),

Table 2.1 *Total population and area of GDR Bezirke, 1955*

	Population (thousands)	% of total area GDR
Berlin	1139	0.4
Cottbus	799	7.6
Dresden	1941	6.2
Erfurt	1302	6.8
Frankfurt	666	6.6
Gera	740	3.7
Halle	2055	8.1
Karl Marx Stadt	2218	5.5
Leipzig	1582	4.6
Magdeburg	1445	10.6
Neubrandenburg	686	10.1
Potsdam	1208	11.6
Rostock	850	6.5
Schwerin	651	8.0
Suhl	548	3.6
	17 830	

Source: *Statistiches Jahrbuch der DDR*, 1988.

including East Berlin, modelled upon the Soviet system with each *Bezirk* named after its principal town or city. Table 2.1 shows that in 1955 the three largest *Bezirke* in terms of population were Halle, Dresden and Karl Marx Stadt while Potsdam, Magdeburg and Neubrandenburg were largest in area. Although there was considerable size range between the *Bezirke*, for example Suhl and Potsdam, some attempt was made to try to equalise populations (Mellor, 1978). The *Bezirke* were sub-divided into 27 urban districts (*Stadtkreise*) and 191 rural districts (*Landkreise*). The districts were also further sub-divided into over 8900 local communes (*Gemeinden*).

A main feature of the territorial arrangement of the GDR was that each *Bezirk* possessed a distinctive set of economic resources or activities. For example, it was possible to distinguish between those *Bezirke* which were either industrially or agriculturally oriented, for example Neubrandenburg (agriculture) and Halle (industry) and, on a finer level, to identify those which were specialised to varying degrees in particular industrial sectors. This regionally based specialisation in economic activity persisted throughout the brief history of the GDR. For example, the *Bezirk* Cottbus specialised in the mining and processing of brown coal and accounted for two-fifths of the GDR's production in this economic sector in 1987, the *Bezirk* Karl Marx Stadt produced half of the GDR's textiles in the same year, while the *Bezirk* Halle accounted for some two-fifths of the country's chemical production (*Statistisches Jahrbuch der DDR*, 1988).

THE TRANSFORMATION OF THE GDR INTO A SOCIALIST
INDUSTRIAL ECONOMY

Changes to the legal and administrative systems, in education, land ownership and industry during the period of Soviet occupation of East Germany
marked the beginning of fundamental changes in the economic and social
structure of the country. Under the influence of the Soviet occupying forces
the Socialist Unity Party (SED) took over in East Germany under the
leadership of Walter Ulbricht and was eager to launch the country's
economic development along Marxist–Leninist principles. The planning and
control of the GDR economy was to be characterised by central decisions on
output, prices fixed by the State, obligations on the part of enterprises to
produce planned quantities and a State monopoly of foreign trade
(Strassburger, 1984). The GDR economy was also to be linked to the
economies of the Soviet bloc, and this was achieved through the GDR
joining the COMECON trade grouping in September 1950. Within one year
over three-quarters of all GDR trade was with the Socialist bloc, and
dramatically, less than one-tenth was with West Germany.

The first economic plan for the GDR was implemented in 1949 for a
duration of two years and was intended to restore industrial production,
particularly in the heavy industrial sectors, in order to provide the East
German population with consumer goods and to meet Soviet reparation
requirements (Dennis, 1988). A second economic plan was implemented in
January 1951. The main features of the plan were to chart the desired
development of the GDR economy, taking into account the availability of
material and human resources, anticipated technological progress, foreign-
trade potential and the need for regional improvements in the standard of
living of the population (Bradley Scharf, 1984). The expansion of industrial
output was the cornerstone of this five-year plan, with the target of raising
industrial production by 90% of the 1950 level by the end of the plan. In
addition, living standards were expected to improve substantially, national
income to expand by 60%, labour productivity in the industrial sector to
grow by 72% and the farm sector to increase its output by 25% (McCauley,
1986). Within the plan emphasis was once again placed upon the expansion
of basic industries (brown coal, iron and steel) in order to supply the
chemicals and investment goods industries.

However, the concentration of effort upon the expansion of the heavy
industrial sector in the GDR was at the expense of consumer goods.
Throughout the duration of the plan most consumer goods were in short
supply and rationing still existed for a range of basic products. Discontent
among the East German population was great and many left in search of a
better life in West Germany (see below). The centralisation of planning
under the socialist system, in particular the fixing of wage rates by the State,

also greatly infringed the rights of workers at factory level. The State's failure to recognise the disaffection of large sections of its population and at the same time continuing to demand further increases in industrial output sparked major demonstrations throughout many East German cities in June 1953 which were violently suppressed by the authorities with the support of Soviet troops (McCauley, 1983). While many of the plan's output targets for basic industries were reached (for example, brown coal output including briquettes had risen from 174 million tonnes in 1950 to 250 million tonnes in 1955), the failure to improve the availability of consumer goods prompted the GDR leadership to announce in 1953 that there had been some mistakes in its economic planning and that it had not been possible for the State to overcome some of the handicaps of the GDR economy that were described above. After the June demonstrations, therefore, the State attempted to chart a 'new course' for economic planning encompassing a reduction in the growth of heavy industrial output, the switching of investment into light industry and greater subsidisation of food prices in an effort to quell sources of discontent. These policies were facilitated by the end of reparation payments and by an increase in Soviet credit (Dennis, 1988). Despite pressures from opponents to introduce policies which recognised the particular needs and economic reality of the GDR, the Ulbricht regime still clung dogmatically to Stalinist principles of economic management (McCauley, 1986). The haemorrhage of population to West Germany continued unabated, further adding to the woes of the East German economy (Childs, 1983).

By the mid-1950s, State control and ownership of all key economic sectors in the GDR had largely been achieved. The socialisation of agriculture was also gathering momentum and by the end of the decade had to all extent and purposes been completed (see below). While the 'new course' for the East German economy was abandoned in 1955, the second five-year economic plan (1956–60) did try to reconcile the need to expand heavy industrial output and raise standards of living. The scenario for the GDR economy as outlined by Ulbricht was that the principal goal of the plan was to catch up and even overtake West Germany's per capita consumption of most consumer goods and foodstuffs by the end of 1961. This was a highly ambitious goal which proved to be unattainable despite a steadily increasing growth rate in the national economy from 7.9% in 1957 to 12% in 1959. By 1960, however, growth in the GDR economy had slowed to a level of 4%, and the country stood a long way behind West Germany which had experienced sustained economic growth in a period described as the 'economic miracle' years (*Wirtschaftswunder*) (see Chapter 3). The renewed surge in the migration of many young people and skilled workers from the GDR (over 350 000 people left between 1960–1) reflected the severity of the crisis confronting the country. To prevent the collapse of the GDR economy as a result of further large-scale population movements to the West, the East German authorities severed the border between East and West Berlin in August 1961. The temporary boundary of barbed wire was progressively transformed into a wall that cut the city in two and, behind it on the East Berlin side was a whole defence in depth, with alarm wires, floodlights and watch towers (Elkins, 1988).

By the beginning of the 1960s the East German economy was characterised by low levels of investment, delays in production and installation of new capacities and supply deficiencies in raw materials and intermediate products which lowered the use of those facilities that did exist. It became obvious to the East German authorities that economic planning to date had not been successful and that new planning methods would be required to meet the needs of what was hoped would become a progressive industrial economy (Schnitzer, 1964). The reasons for the failure in economic planning in the GDR up to 1963 can be attributed to three factors (Strassburger, 1984):

- quantitative planning ignored economic factors and led to investment mistakes;
- the rigid price system in operation brought distortions in the price structure which led to the waste of raw materials and other supplies and delays in adopting new technological innovations;
- the bureaucratic and centralised decision-making structure of economic management in the GDR obliged enterprises to meet targets which soon became economically irrational.

The seven-year plan was consequently dropped in 1961 and formal discussion of economic reforms began in early 1983. Later that year a 'New System of Economic Planning and Management' (NES) was adopted which, it was hoped, would suit the special economic conditions of the GDR (McCauley, 1986).

The NES reforms consisted primarily of greater transference of economic decision making from the State to the production enterprises themselves and the steering of their production by the State through a series of financial instruments including price reform and credit schemes, as well as financial incentives to those enterprises generating profits. Greater technological improvement in GDR industry was seen to be a major way of resolving the difficulties that the country faced in its labour supply. Under the reform programme, each branch of industry was to be managed by Associations of State-Owned Enterprises (*Vereinigungen Volkseigener Betriebe*, or VVBs), which were responsible for planning, coordinating and controlling the production of all the enterprises in a particular industrial branch. Improving the quality of output and ensuring the more economical use of resources in the particular industrial branch were the principal tasks of the VVBs. Profit was to be the main criterion of enterprise performance, with financial incentives accruing to business managers and workers in those sectors where this was achieved. This contrasted greatly with the situation in the 1950s where incentives to industry were often tied to overall output targets rather than quality criteria, or to the value of trade turnover, which in this latter case prompted enterprises only to produce those articles which involved using the most costly raw materials (Schnitzer, 1964). The NES reforms were initially applied to a selection of key industrial sectors including chemicals, energy and electrical engineering. Later in the decade they were extended to several other sectors, including agriculture.

Despite early economic successes (economic growth per annum varied around 4.9–5.2% between 1965 and 1968) and a strengthening of the reform measures in 1967–8, the GDR economy was showing signs of serious economic dislocation towards the end of the decade. Those industrial sectors which had been given privileged positions in the reform programme found that not only had they surged ahead at the expense of other sectors but that their sustained development was being hampered by log-jams in supplies from non-priority sectors in the economy and from the irregularity in supplies of raw materials etc. from other countries in the COMECON trading bloc. These factors, combined with a recentralisation of political and economic power throughout Eastern Europe as a result of upheavals in Czechoslovakia in 1968, led to the reform programme being laid to rest with none of the fanfare that had greeted its inauguration (Fulbrook, 1991).

A worsening economic situation in the GDR by the early 1970s, coupled with Ulbricht's unease with West German overtures towards a normalisation of relations between the two Germanies, led both domestic critics and the USSR to remove him from power and to be replaced in May 1971 by Erich Honecker.

Economic policy in the GDR under Honecker aimed primarily to remove the powers of decision that had been accorded to the VVBs, to eliminate the economic imbalances caused by the NES, to improve the GDR's domestic energy and raw materials situation, to expand the technical infrastructure of the economy and to reduce the country's trade debt through increasing exports. The five-year economic plan (1971–5) set rather modest growth targets: national income to rise by 26–8% over the five-year period and industrial production to increase by 6% per year. Importantly, the plan also embraced a range of social measures aimed not only at easing the entry of women into the labour force but also including higher pensions and the announcement of a major building programme to improve housing availability.

As a result of the 1971–5 plan almost all of the economic targets were achieved or in some cases surpassed. Significantly, too, increases in the

Table 2.2 *Ownership of selected consumer durables in the GDR, 1965–75 (number per 100 households)*

	1965	1970	1975
Cars	8	16	26
Radios	87	92	96
TV sets	49	69	82
Fridges	29	56	85
Washing machines	28	54	73

Source: Statistisches Jahrbuch der DDR, 1976.

production of consumer durables (for example, the number of cars produced increased by 33 000 and the number of television sets by 128 million over the plan's duration) led to per capita increases in ownership (see Table 2.2). However, the success story was not prolonged, and the GDR economy soon began to experience serious problems as a result of its poor resource endowment and the increasingly unstable international economic environment brought about by the Arab–Israeli war in 1973–4.

The GDR's growth over the previous two decades had been dependent upon large-scale imports of essential fuels and raw materials, particularly from the USSR. In 1975 the GDR economy was plunged into further difficulties by the Soviet decision to increase the price of its raw materials traded within the COMECON bloc. The GDR was, therefore, not only running up a trade deficit with Western countries, which had been accounting for a steadily increasing share of GDR imports from the mid-1960s onwards, but also with the USSR, its principal trading partner in COMECON. The GDR's foreign-debt situation therefore reached a critical state by the late 1970s, with its export prices less than half its import costs. With 40% of the GDR's imports in 1981–2 made up of fuels, minerals and metals, and a further 16% of imports accounted for by other raw materials (German Embassy, *Facts and Figures*, 1985), the country's national debt reached a peak of $11.6 billion in that year, second only to Poland among the COMECON states (Dennis, 1988). The GDR therefore began the 1980s in economic and political gloom (Osmond, 1992).

The Honecker regime did not succumb to these grave difficulties by undertaking major reform of its economic policies; rather it implemented a scheme for the reorganisation of production in the GDR. Whereas previously the VVBs had been the link between the central state ministries and the individual production units, this organisational structure was replaced by 'Kombinats'. Each *Kombinat* comprised between 20 to 40 production units (all within the same industrial branch) with a total workforce of between 2 000 to 70 000 employees. In addition, the *Kombinat* included supply industries and research centres linked to the particular production branch. Like the former VVBs, the *Kombinats* were directly responsible to the State ministries though they were granted much greater scope for local management decisions. The 130 *Kombinats* were expected to secure and expand production where necessary to meet the requirements of the State's economic plans, to develop new products, to organise themselves in a way that would enable the most efficient use of new technologies and cut costs and to seek ways of improving the general work conditions for the labour force.

The GDR economy was able to ride the economic storm of the early 1980s and the authorities able to report in 1985 that growth in the economy had been at the level of 5.5% in the previous year. However, from the mid-1980s onwards the economic situation deteriorated rapidly with national growth rates falling to 4.3% in 1986 and to 3% by 1988 (Fischer Welt Almanach, 1990). The falsification of accounts by the East German authorities could not hide the very obvious economic problems being faced or indeed the serious environmental condition of large tracts of the country which had been brought about by almost four decades of absolute neglect. With the provision of consumer goods still largely insufficient and the economy plagued by high levels of indebtedness, the scene was set for the culmination of what McCauley in 1986 had rightfully predicted would be 'a difficult decade' (p.194).

INDUSTRIAL CHANGE IN THE GDR

The industrial sector in the GDR was by far the most dominant and by the late 1980s accounted for almost three-quarters of the country's national product. Its importance can be further gauged by the fact that it provided employment for almost half of the GDR's workforce in 1988. This share had remained relatively constant over the previous decades and reflected the lack of development of a service-based economy in the GDR.

Industrial production in the GDR was largely concentrated in four *Bezirke*, namely Halle, Leipzig, Karl Marx Stadt and Dresden. By the late 1980s some 43% of East German industrial output originated in these four *Bezirke*, with Halle being the most important. Over 40% of the GDR's chemicals production, 22% of its metallurgical output, 21% of its building materials, 10% of its machine tools and 11% of its processed food were produced in the *Bezirk* Halle in 1987.

Industrial development in the GDR was dependent upon imported fuels (largely oil, gas and hard coal from the USSR) and the domestic production of brown coal. Open-cast brown-coal production is largely concentrated in the Cottbus and Halle–Leipzig regions which together accounted for almost two-thirds of East Germany's brown-coal production by the late 1980s.

Table 2.3   *Employment in industrial sectors in the GDR, 1970–88 (%)*

	1970	1980	1988 Empl. (000)
Fuel and energy	6.2	6.7	7.1 (229)
Chemicals	11.6	10.8	10.3 (335)
Steel	4.3	4.2	4.2 (138)
Construction materials	3.2	3.0	2.9 (94)
Mech. engineering/cars	28.7	29.4	29.9 (970)
Electronics	12.9	13.7	14.3 (463)
Consumer goods (exc. textiles)	16.0	15.5	15.2 (492)
Textiles	8.8	7.2	6.7 (216)
Food	7.7	8.7	8.5 (277)
			(3240)

Source: European Parliament (1990), 'The Impact of German Unification on the EC', *Working Document, 1*, Luxembourg.

Domestic brown-coal production was increased from the mid-1970s following price increases in energy supplied by the USSR. From the late 1970s onwards, therefore, around 70% of the GDR's energy demands were met by domestic brown-coal output with catastrophic consequences for the environment.

Over half of all industrial employment in the GDR in 1988 was accounted for by three industrial sectors—mechanical engineering (29.9%), electronics (14.3%) and chemicals (10.3%) (see Table 2.3). These three sectors employed 1.76 million workers and were responsible for 50% of the value of industrial production. The mechanical-engineering industry was East Germany's most important source of exports to the COMECON group and accounted for almost half of the country's total exports in the mid-1980s. Within this production sector the construction of heavy machinery and machine tools was particularly pronounced, and regional concentrations were to be found in the *Bezirke* of Leipzig, Halle, Dresden, and Karl Marx Stadt. The degree of sophistication in this industrial sector was, however, particularly poor, thereby making it difficult for the sector to penetrate Western markets. The technological backwardness of East German industry was perhaps best seen in the car industry where productivity at the main plants of Zwickau and Eisenach was, even by the late 1980s, only 40% of that of the West German car industry.

The electronics, precision-engineering and optical-goods industries employed 463 000 workers in 1988, some 14.3% of the industrial workforce. It became a key sector for the modernisation of other branches of the GDR economy, and this was recognised by several pronouncements in the State's economic plans from the 1960s onwards. State investment in this regionally

Table 2.4   *Ten largest Kombinats in the GDR, 1989*

Kombinat	Workers	Industrial sector
Baumwolle, Karl Marx Stadt	70 000	Textile/Clothes
Robotron, Dresden	69 000	Electronics
Mikroelektronik, Erfurt	59 000	Electronics
Fortschritt Landmaschinen, Neustadt	58 000	Agric. Machines
Mansfeld Kombinat, Eisleben	47 000	Metals/Steel
GasKombinat Schwarze Pumpe	37 000	Energy/Chemicals
Edelstahl Kombinat, Brandenburg	34 000	Steel
Petrochemisches Kombinat, Schwedt	30 000	Mineral Oil
Leuna-Werke, Leuna	30 000	Chemicals
ChemieKombinat Bitterfeld	30 000	Chemicals

Source: European Parliament (1990), 'The Impact of German Unification on the EC', *Working Document, 1*, Luxembourg.

scattered sector, particularly in micro-electronics, resulted in the GDR catching up considerably with West Germany by the mid-1980s. Two important micro-electronic *Kombinats* were established, one at Erfurt and the other in Dresden. These employed over 120 000 workers and represented two of the largest *Kombinats* in East Germany by the late-1980s (see Table 2.4).

The chemicals industry employed 335 000 workers in 1988 and contributed 20% of the country's national product. The GDR occupied a crucial position in the COMECON group for chemicals production. The industry was chiefly located in the Halle–Leipzig–Bitterfeld and in the Frankfurt-an-Oder regions and was initially based upon the use of locally-mined brown coal. However, from the late 1960s much of the industry's energy needs were met by imports of oil from the USSR. The increase in price of this energy source from the mid-1970s resulted in large *Kombinats* such as that at Leuna expanding their use of brown coal. Productivity in the sector remained well below the West German level throughout the 1980s.

The organisation of East German industry into *Kombinats* failed to overcome the problems of the command economy in the GDR. Some of the most serious problems stemmed from the inaccuracy of planning in the industrial sector, in particular, the sheer difficulties of managing such large enterprises. Planning reports for various industrial sectors soon became outdated as supply and other business conditions quickly altered. The centrally-planned system not only led to the inefficient use of raw materials—for example, the GDR had one of the highest per capita energy consumption rates in the world, higher in fact than the USSR and the other Eastern European COMECON states—but also of labour. The SED leadership placed great stress on winning the loyalty of East German workers. Employment was guaranteed, and workers were rewarded for meeting and surpassing production targets. However, pitting factories aginst each other in 'socialist competitions' designed to raise production proved to be of only limited effectiveness in the face of low morale among East German workers caused by low wages and chronic shortages of consumer goods (Turner, 1987).

Without the discipline of foreign competition the protectionism afforded by the centralised trading system permitted East German industry to resist technological change. In addition, the command economy neglected infra-structural investment in financial and marketing institutions, telecommunications and data processing and in the transport system. In this latter case the division of Germany led to the closure of over 35 of the 40 pre-1945 rail routes across the border with West Germany, the reorientation of the East German rail system away from West Berlin and the alteration of the rail system's technical and operational structure in order to make it compatible with that of Eastern Europe and the USSR.

THE AGRICULTURAL SECTOR IN THE GDR

Some 6.2 million hectares in the GDR (58% of the total land area) were used for agricultural purposes by the late 1980s, and approximately 11% of the workforce were employed in the agricultural sector. Over three-quarters of agricultural land was used for arable production, with cereals and winter grains being the most dominant crops. Livestock production was also deliberately increased in order to achieve domestic self-sufficiency in both meat and milk products.

There were several key phases in the development of GDR agriculture along socialist lines (Immler, 1971). The first took place in 1945 when the Soviet occupiers of what was to become the GDR introduced a hard-hitting land reform programme. All land holdings over 100 hectares were confiscated as were those holdings and property belonging to reputed war criminals and Nazis. The land was subsequently reallocated to agricultural labourers or managed as State farms (known as *Volkseigenen Gutern* (VEG)). The land reform programme operated between 1945–9 and led to over 2.25 million hectares of agricultural land being redistributed, some 35% of all agricultural land in Soviet-occupied Germany.

The second phase of socialist transformation of the farm sector occurred between 1949–54 when not only were holdings over 100 hectares broken up but also initially those over 50 hectares and later those over 20 hectares. Some 47% of land in the GDR changed ownership in this period. In addition, the setting up of agricultural production cooperatives (*Landwirt-schaftliche Produktionsgenossenschaften* (LPGs) in 1952–3, with farmers gaining certain concessions from joining, marked a clear step towards Soviet-style collectivisation of GDR agriculture. Three types of LPG were established:

- type-1 LPGs had the arable land in common tillage though machinery remained in private ownership;
- type-2 LPGs not only had common tillage but also communal possession of machinery;
- type-3 LPGs had all arable and pasture land in communal use as well as livestock and field boundaries reorganised in order to benefit from scale economies.

It was this last type of LPG that became the most dominant in GDR agriculture after 1960, with the state exerting greater pressure upon farmers to join collectives. This radical reorganisation of the farm sector contributed significantly to the massive exodus of East Germans to West Germany throughout the 1950s until the building of the Berlin Wall in 1961. The 1970s onwards saw the increasing specialisation of the LPGs along livestock or arable lines in order to increase total output and achieve the desired East German goal of food self-sufficiency. By the mid-1980s East German agricultural self-sufficiency had reached over 90%, and for some products output often surpassed national requirements: for example, milk and milk products, meat products, eggs, sugar beet and potatoes. However, for cereals (especially animal feed) and fruit and vegetables the GDR remained a net importer. Throughout the 1980s it imported between one and two million tonnes of cereals per year largely for feed for the livestock sector.

Despite these overall production achievements, the socialisation of East German agriculture was not without serious problems. From an economic point of view, many difficulties stemmed not from the lack of production capacity but rather from the means by which production was organised, especially the intermittent availabilty of necessary farm inputs and their often inappropriate application in terms of quantities, combinations or time period. This was particularly the case with regard to farm labour. A second major problem was caused by the emphasis of the farm system upon output rather than market and the poor flexibility of the production unit. The top-down plans compelled farms to operate production programmes that were not sensible, with meeting the targets of the plans becoming the overriding criteria for the farm business. The frequent failure of farm equipment, the low availability of technical investment and the obvious delays incurred meant that many production units failed to meet their output targets. The spatial concentration of production and the division of crop and livestock production units served to increase transport and time costs for farm inputs, while, in addition, the maintenance of livestock production required bulky imports of animal feed. An insufficient and/or not continuous supply of animal feed created further difficulties for the sector.

The centrally-planned system not only involved long delays caused by excessive bureaucracy but also prevented individual production units from having much scope to influence the organisation and development of the farm business. Within the production unit itself, the scale of the business operation resulted in high administration, control and organisational costs. The lack of motivation among farm workers became a major problem faced by the State, while coordinating the plans of individual production units in order to meet overall output targets presented even greater headaches.

The socialist agricultural system in the GDR also created a range of serious environmental problems including water pollution and soil erosion. Specialised intensive livestock production plants led to problems of liquid manure disposal, while specialised arable units overused mineral fertilisers. For example, lime use per hectare was 123% greater in the GDR than in West Germany, potash 30% greater and nitrogenous fertiliser almost 20% greater (Bundesministerium für Landwirtschaft, 1992).

East German rural areas also suffered from poor road and farm networks, and inadequate water supplies and sewage purification facilities. The absence of comprehensive rural development plans meant that many rural areas, especially those furthest removed from the location of the LPGs, became increasing desolate.

POPULATION CHANGE IN THE GDR

One of the most serious hindrances to the development of a socialist state in the GDR was the population issue. In 1939 the area that later became the GDR had a population of 16.7 million. By 1946 this had increased to 18.5 million as many Germans fled from former German lands in Eastern Europe (Berghahn, 1987). However, many of these migrants later headed west along with other East Germans. By 1950, therefore, the total population of the GDR had fallen to 18.4 million having reached its peak in 1948. As the socialisation of the GDR progressed, the outflow of East Germans increased steadily. By 1955 total population had fallen by 600 000 from its 1953 level. The decision in 1961 to stem these migration flows came after almost one million East Germans had fled to the West during the previous decade. By 1965 the total population stood at 17 million, some 1.4 million inhabitants fewer than when the GDR was founded. By the 1970s a trend of population stagnation caused by a low rate of natural increase had set in, so that East Germany's population remained below 17 million throughout that decade and the 1980s. By contrast with West Germany, where foreigners accounted for over 8% of the total population by the end of the 1980s (see Chapter 3), the GDR allowed entry only to a relatively small number of foreign workers and their families. This usually took place as a result of various labour contracts signed with countries supportive of the GDR's socialist regime (for example Vietnam, Cuba, Angola and Mozambique). By the end of the 1980s the foreign population of the GDR totalled only 191 000, of which almost one-third were Vietnamese.

Shortages in the labour market caused by the out-migration of young skilled people and a low level of natural increase presented the GDR authorities with very severe difficulties. These were partly resolved by improving the qualifications of the labour force and by actively encouraging as many women as possible to participate in the production process. This was achieved by the creation of a network of institutional, financial and material provisions enabling women to combine full-time employment with their family responsibilities (Alsop, 1992). By the end of the 1980s, therefore, almost half of the East German workforce was female. However, female participation did not of course diminish gender inequalities in the labour market, since not only did many women occupy the lowest paid jobs but they were also under-represented in managerial positions.

The key condition for ensuring that women participated in the labour market was the provision of child care facilities by the State. While in 1965 crèches were provided for only 16.5% of children under three, by 1980 this figure had increased to 60%. Similarly the availability of kindergarten places was sufficient to accommodate 92% of children between three and six in 1980. In Ost Berlin in 1986, for example, kindergarten places existed for 98% of all children between three and six (*Statistisches Jahrbuch der DDR*, 1988).

Pro-natal policies were another means by which the GDR authorities attempted to rectify the imbalances in the population structure. Generous maternity benefits were introduced by the Honecker regime, including preferential allowances for those full-time working mothers with two or more children. Throughout the greater part of the 1970s deaths continued to exceed births in the GDR, but by 1978 the pro-natal policy was beginning to affect the trend in natural increase.

In terms of population, the GDR remained much smaller than West Germany. In 1950, its population was only 36% of that of the Federal Republic, and by the mid-1980s this figure had dropped to 27%. East Germany has always been less densely settled than West Germany, while its population distribution not only reflected geographical contrasts of pre-war origin but also processes of industrial and agricultural change, the emphases of various State economic plans and socialist housing policy since 1950 (Mellor, 1978). In general terms, the northernmost regions of the GDR were always the most sparsely populated, while the bulk of the urban population lived in the Berlin region and in southern districts. Between 1950 and 1989 changes in population totals at *Bezirk* level could be generally attributed to one of four factors:

- outmigration caused by collectivisation of the countryside;
- Soviet reparations policy (early 1950s);
- expansion of industry and mining according to State economic plans;
- the growth of the capital East Berlin and surrounding regions.

Socialisation of East German agriculture encouraged many farmers to leave for the West. The northern, largely agricultural, *Bezirke* of Schwerin and Neubrandenburg were particularly hit by out-migration. Between 1955 and 1960 the population of Schwerin fell from 650 000 to 620 000, dropping even further throughout the 1960s to a level of only 590 000 by 1970. Similarly, the population of Neubrandenburg fell from 680 000 in 1955 to 650 000 in 1960, dropping to only 630 000 by 1970.

The dismantling of East German manufacturing production by the Soviets in the 1950s also caused out-migration in particular industrial regions. The *Bezirk* Karl Marx Stadt, for example, witnessed a fall in total population of 100 000 between 1955 and 1960. By contrast, the emphasis by the GDR authorities upon heavy industry and mining as the basis for economic growth led to several *Bezirke* experiencing population increases. The *Bezirk* Cottbus, for example, in which large reserves of brown coal are located, saw its population grow from 790 000 in 1955 to 860 000 by 1970 and to over 880 000 by 1987 (*Statistisches Jahrbuch der DDR*, 1988).

East Berlin, while losing population throughout the 1950s (60 000 people left between 1955 and 1960), experienced a steady increase in population after the building of the Berlin Wall. The city became the site for many large residential developments (see below) and new industrial activities. Consequently, the population of Ost Berlin grew by 190 000 between 1960 and 1987 to reach 1.26 million. Some 7.5% of the GDR's population were therefore living in the capital by the end of the 1980s.

URBAN PLANNING AND CHANGE IN THE GDR

The housing situation in East Germany in the immediate post-war years was more favourable than in West Germany, though the average size of dwellings was greater in the West than the East. The East German housing stock totalled 5.1 million dwellings in 1950 (the same as the 1939 figure) although population had increased from 16.7 million in 1939 to 18.4 million in 1950. The exodus of East Germans to the West throughout the 1950s generally resulted in the State according low priority to the housing market

Photograph 3   *Central district of Magdeburg, Sachsen-Anhalt.* Soviet-inspired city planning has created wide streets, high skylines and few shops in many of East Germany's urban centres

compared to other sectors of the GDR economy. The condition of many dwellings was therefore allowed to deteriorate for the greater part of the first two decades after 1945.

The role of the state in urban policy began tentatively with the partial redevelopment of those cities that had suffered most at the hands of Allied bombers. Chief industrial cities such as Ost Berlin, Magdeburg, Leipzig and Dresden, as well as coastal centres such as Rostock and Wismar received notable attention. Most of the work focused upon the reconstruction of inner-city areas, for example the Altmarkt in Dresden and the Rossplatz in Leipzig.

Major residential developments in the 1950s were concentrated in the largest East German cities, particularly the capitals of the *Bezirke*. In addition, new towns were built at Eisenhüttenstadt and Neu-Hoyerswerda, and a model residential development for 4000 people was built in Bad Durrenberg/Mersburg (Sinnhuber, 1965). Urban planning reflected socialist principles, with many towns and cities exhibiting common features such as monotonous architectural design, geometric street plans, few shops and high-rise buildings strung along overwide streets to achieve, as in the USSR, 'the big-city effect' (Mellor, 1978) (see Photograph 3, Magdeburg).

In the 1960s, new residential developments all took a standardised

Photograph 4 *Apartment block, Magdeburg, Sachsen-Anhalt.* Improving housing
conditions for East Germans was one of the main goals of the
Honecker regime. Many of the apartment blocks constructed were
badly designed and poorly equipped

building form with many system-built housing estates being constructed in
both the larger cities and medium-sized urban centres. However, despite this
wave of housing development some 1.2 million East Germans were in 1970
still living in homes that were built *before* 1870 (Jeffries and Melzer, 1987).

The Honecker regime regarded the improvement of living conditions for
GDR citizens as a vital means to increase economic production. Housing
policy became the cornerstone of this newly adopted 'social policy'. In 1973
it was announced that housing would be given investment priority, and that
for the period 1976–90 2.8–3 million new dwellings were to be constructed
and the living conditions of all East Germans were to be improved
substantially. Between 1976 and 1980 750 000 dwellings were planned, and
a further 100 000 existing homes were to be modernised. Construction
exceeded its target with some 813 000 dwellings built betwen 1976 and
1980 and over 200 000 homes renovated. Much of the emphasis was on
large-scale development of apartment blocks (*Gross Siedlungen*), usually on
the periphery of the city. Some 40 *Gross Siedlungen* were constructed in East
Germany in the 1970s and a further 13 in the 1980s. Six *Gross Siedlungen*
were built in East Berlin after 1971. The estates at Berlin-Marzahn (59 200
dwellings), Berlin-Kaulsdorf-Hellersdorf (42 400) and Berlin-Hohenschon-

hausen (37 100) represented the largest *Gross Siedlungen* in East Germany. Elsewhere, large estates were built in Rostock-Nordwest (37 400 dwellings), Leipzig-Grünau (34 000), Halle Neustadt (32 700) and in Chemnitz-Fritz Heckert (31 500). The Leipzig-Grünau estate, for example, was, by the mid-1980s, housing roughly one-fifth of the city's population. Each estate contains a range of amenities including crèches and kindergartens, though the apartments themselves are generally small and provided with the most basic of facilities (see Photograph 4). Occupants, however, enjoyed highly subsidised rents and heating bills. Outside of the estates, much property remained in generally poor condition with brown-coal-stained exterior walls masking the dilapidation of property interiors (see Photograph 9, Leipzig-Plagwitz).

The housing situation in the GDR by the late 1980s, then, was one where significant building programmes had been completed. One in four East Germans lived on one of the large residential estates, and in some cities such as Rostock the figure was as high as one in two. There was, however, great regional variation in housing quality and age compared to West Germany. In the smaller urban centres and in those more rural *Bezirke*, housing was often in a serious state of disrepair. East Germans did not enjoy either the same amount of living space as West Germans or the range of home comforts, no matter how basic.

CONCLUSIONS

Despite the very real failings of the command economy one must not be too dismissive of the achievements of the GDR between 1950 and 1989. It is important to recognise that the GDR was considerably more disadvantaged economically as a result of Germany's division than was the Federal Republic. It had a smaller land area and total population compared to West Germany and equally significant, a poorer resource base. It did not receive Marshall Aid and experienced strict Soviet reparations. Its economy was cut off from traditional suppliers in the West, and its links to West German ports were severed. Moreover, the country experienced a loss of over one million inhabitants within the first 10 years of its existence. That East Germans survived this turmoil and that by the 1980s the country could achieve global status as a major industrial nation is testimony to the considerable economic achievements that had been brought about by 40 years of socialist planning. However, one must be careful when assessing the economic performance of East Germany in taking statistical data published by the GDR authorities at face value. The East German leadership often exaggerated the achievements and glossed over the failings of the command economy.

While a comparison of the economic profiles of East and West Germany

Table 2.5   *Emploment profile in West Germany (1965) and East Germany (1988)*

	% total workforce	
	1965 West Germany	1988 East Germany
Manufacturing	37.6	38.0
Service sector	22.2	24.4
Trade	12.4	10.0
Agriculture	10.7	10.8
Construction	9.2	6.8
Transport	5.4	7.7
Energy	2.4	3.0

Source: Statistisches Bundesamt (1992), Wiesbaden.

Table 2.6   *Relative wealth of Central and East European Countries, 1975–85 (GDP per capita US$)*

	1975	rank	1980	rank	1985	rank
Bulgaria	3167	6	5535	5	7474	3
Czechoslovakia	4048	2	6588	2	8153	2
Hungary	3610	3	5881	3	7431	4
Poland	3233	5	5241	6	6441	6
Romania	2739	7	4623	7	5852	8
Yugoslavia	2675	8	4555	8	6022	7
GDR	4258	1	7050	1	8993	1
Soviet Union	3485	4	5847	4	7328	5
West Germany	4875		8137		10 411	

Source: EC (1992), 'Socio-economic situation and development in the regions in the neighbouring countries of the Community in Central and Eastern Europe', Brussels.

in the late 1980s starkly reveals the economic superiority of the latter: for example, an employment sector profile in East Germany in 1988 almost identical to that of West Germany in 1965 (see Table 2.5), this overlooks the accomplishments of the GDR in relation to its partners in the COMECON trading group. Although one must tread cautiously when dealing with official GDR statistics, an analysis of trends in industrial output between 1950 and 1987 reveals some staggering results. Using the base year 1950 (index=100), GDR energy output in 1987 was 449, chemicals 1457, machinery and cars 1760, electronics 4956 and metallurgical products 1270 (*Statistisches Jahrbuch der DDR*, 1988). As a result, East Germany by 1975 was the most wealthy country in COMECON and held this position up until 1989 (see Table 2.6).

SUGGESTED FURTHER READING

Berentsen, W. (1981) 'Regional change in the GDR', *Annals of the Association of American Geographers*, 71(1), 50–66.

Childs, D. (1983) *The GDR: Moscow's German Ally*. George Allen and Unwin, London.

Childs, D. (1985) *Honecker's Germany*. George Allen and Unwin, London.

Dennis, M. (1988) GDR. *Politics, Economics and Society*. Pinter, London.

Jeffries, I. and Melzer, M. (ed.) (1987) *The East German Economy*. Croom Helm, London.

Krisch, H. (1985) *The GDR. The Search for Identity*. Westview, Boulder.

McCauley, M. (1983) *The GDR since 1945*. Macmillan, Basingstoke.

Von Beyme, K. and Zimmerman, H. (eds) (1984) *Policy Making in the GDR*. Gower, Aldershot.

3 Economic and social developments in West Germany, 1949–89

Between 1949 and 1989 West Germany achieved the status of one of the world's economic leaders. Only Japan could match Germany's spectacular economic performance over this period. The development of a modernised industrial economy with a strong currency and international standing brought many material advantages to most West Germans. However, it would be wrong to assume that West Germany did not have its share of economic difficulties during these years. Industrial restructuring and its regional impact, labour shortages, rural decline, and indeed problems in some localities brought about by economic success itself have all required policy responses. This chapter cannot hope to address all these points in depth but, instead, highlights the key issues that have affected the development of West Germany since 1949 to provide a broad picture of the country's post-war experience.

TERRITORY AND ADMINISTRATION

The Federal Republic of Germany covered an area of over 248 000 sq. kilometres and accounted for some 58% of the (1937) population of the pre-war Reich, 51% of its agricultural production and just under two-thirds of its industrial output. West Germany contained the Ruhr coalfield and associated iron, steel, chemicals and engineering industries, the great ports of Hamburg and Bremen on the North Sea coast and the highly urbanised areas of the Rhineland axis. It therefore possessed the economic 'jewels in the crown' of the former German Reich. For example, in 1938 the area that was to become West Germany produced 98% of Germany's hard coal and 95% of its iron ore. The division of Germany therefore worked largely to the advantage of West Germany.

Administratively West Germany was divided by the Western Allies into regional states (*Länder*), though without prior consultation with the German population. The *Länder* varied in area, population size and economic resources. The Allies had carved the *Länder* from the territory of their respective zones of occupation. Only three of the *Länder*—Hamburg, Bremen and Bayern—had any historic continuity (Kloss, 1976). It soon

Table 3.1   *West German Länder: area and population, 1950*

Länder	Area (km²)	Population (thousands)
Schleswig-Holstein	15 675	2594
Hamburg	753	1605
Niedersachsen	47 407	6797
Bremen	403	558
Nordrhein-Westfalen	34 044	13 207
Hessen	21 110	4323
Rheinland-Pfalz	19 837	3004
Baden-Württemberg	35 749	6430
Bayern	70 546	9184
Saarland	2567	955
West Berlin	480	2147
West Germany	248 576	50 808

Source: Mellor (1978).

became clear that differences in size between the *Länder* were too great, and provisions were made within the Basic Law to allow changes to *Länder* boundaries to be made according to local wishes. In 1951, the *Länder* of Baden, Württemberg-Baden and Württemberg-Hohenzollern were merged and later renamed Baden-Württemberg. By 1953 there were nine *Länder* in West Germany excluding West Berlin which, although separated territorially from the rest of the country, was legally part of the Federal Republic (this was contested by the GDR and Soviet authorities) and was its most populated city (Elkins, 1988). In 1957, following a referendum, Saarland became the tenth state of the Federal Republic, adding to West Germany a further 2570 sq. kilometres of territory with sizeable coal deposits.

As Table 3.1 shows, by far the largest *Land* of the Federal Republic in terms of population was Nordrhein-Westfalen which contained 13.2 million inhabitants in 1950, over one-quarter of the Republic's total population. This *Land* included not only the industrial cities of Duisburg, Essen and Bochum in the Ruhr but also the large Rhein cities of Düsseldorf and Köln, as well as the Republic's capital Bonn. Bayern was the largest state in terms of area (twice that of Nordrhein-Westfalen) and Niedersachsen the second largest.

Since the mid-1950s no changes in *Länder* boundaries have occurred, though in the early 1970s considerable debate took place on a possible reorganisation of the country's *Länder* structure. Several proposals were made including the merger of Hamburg, Schleswig-Holstein and Niedersachsen to create one northern *Land* and the transfer of parts of Rheinland-Pfalz to the neighbouring *Länder* of Hessen and Nordrhein-Westfalen. In this latter case, the proposal was rejected by the local populations in 1975 referenda.

WEST BERLIN AND INTER-GERMAN RELATIONS

The division of Germany led to the former Reich capital Berlin being centrally located in the heart of GDR territory. The eastern part of the city which had been occupied by the Soviets was to become the capital of the new GDR state under the official title, 'Berlin, Haupstadt der DDR', while the western districts of the city which had been under the control of the Western Allied powers were to become part of the territory of the Federal Republic of Germany. There was fundamental disagreement between the GDR, the USSR and the West over this arrangement. While Ost Berlin was regarded by the GDR as an integral part of its territory and national capital, the East German authorities contested the incorporation of West Berlin into West Germany and the demands by the West to be given access to it across East German territory. Berlin therefore became the focus of confrontation between two ideologically oppposed power blocs.

The Western Allies agreed that West Berlin would be a constituent *Land* of West Germany where the Basic Law and West German financial policy would apply, though the Allies would retain control over defence matters and emergency powers for the city, and special arrangements would be made for the election of West Berlin representatives to the West German parliament.

The geographical separation of West Berlin from the rest of West Germany presented a host of difficulties: how to ensure the economic functioning of the city and secure access to it across East Germany; how to maintain the city's population and encourage its development; and how best to solve the practical problems of communications, heating, water supply and sewage disposal for West Berliners. The USSR's attempt at blockading West Berlin in 1948 by the closure of land access routes and the tremendous airlift undertaken by the Allies in response demonstrated the determination of the West to protect West Berlin, although ensuring the city's long-term survival was much more problematic.

Rail, road and air connections between West Germany and West Berlin were restricted to a limited number of corridor links (see Figure 3.1). Rail traffic, for example, was restricted to four transit lines, on which only a specified number of trains per day could run (Elkins, 1988). On the roads, East German speed restrictions and border hold-ups meant passage from West Germany to West Berlin was often slow. The economic prospects for resident and prospective companies in West Berlin under these conditions were therefore particularly bleak. Consequently, from the early 1950s, the Federal Government implemented various schemes and incentives to assist

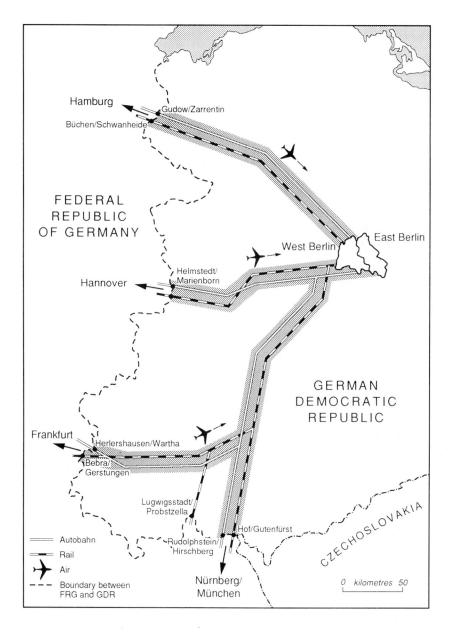

Figure 3.1 *Permitted routes to Berlin*

the city in a effort to prevent standards of living from falling below those in the rest of the Federal Republic. Tax preferences, government subsidies and credits were offered to those establishing businesses and wishing to settle permanently in West Berlin, postal and telephone services were generously funded and direct financial assistance was given to the city to assist its budget. Over half of the city's budget, even up to the mid-1980s, was derived from West German financial transfers.

These commitments angered the East German authorities, and the growing numbers of East Berliners settling in West Berlin prompted the construction of the Berlin Wall in 1961 which served to segregate the city's two communities. The division of Berlin led to a deterioration in relations between West Germany and the GDR and increased the level of insecurity felt by West Berliners about their own future. West Germany, however, was determined to mitigate the impact of West Berlin's isolation, though the GDR authorities continued to harass the transport links from the city to West Germany throughout the 1960s. This aggravated further the severe geographical handicaps that faced West Berlin.

A change in political leadership in West Germany in the late 1960s brought with it new directions for inter-German relations (Blacksell, 1981). The Eastern policy (*Ostpolitik*) of the SPD–FDP coalition government under the Chancellorship of Willy Brandt resulted not only in an improvement in relations between West Germany and the USSR and Poland but also with the GDR. An easing of restrictions of movement to West Germany for some East Germans, greater access to the West German market for GDR goods and financial transfers from West Germany to the East German authorities, in part to maintain communications links to West Berlin, were the main practical results of this policy (Turner, 1987).

The West Berlin economy, however, remained disadvantaged. Its growth was restricted by high energy costs, political insecurity, severance from traditional markets and suppliers and loss of East German labour following the building of the Berlin Wall. In an effort to overcome these difficulties, oil was transported to the city from West Germany by rail, agricultural produce was brought in by road and labour was recruited from the Mediterranean region (see below). Financial assistance to West Berlin companies was also stepped up. The GDR authorities, motivated by a desire to acquire hard currency, also sold brown coal and heavy machine goods to West Berlin and agreed arrangements for water supply and sewage disposal.

By the 1980s, therefore, the West German authorities were not only spending vast amounts of money in supporting West Berlin but were also guaranteeing bank loans to prop up the ailing GDR economy. For example, interest-free credits were provided to East Germany for the purchase of West German goods, and at the same time East German goods were granted duty-free access to the West German market. In 1984, for example, the West

German banks with the Federal government acting as guarantor agreed a loan of DM950 million to East Germany. Increasing the level of contact between West and East Germans and providing financial help to the GDR regime was seen as the most effective way of improving the conditions of those Germans who had to live under socialism and, in turn, in keeping alive the German unification question.

THE WEST GERMAN POPULATION

In 1989 West Germany's population stood at 61.8 million, compared to 61.5 million in 1980, 60.6 million in 1970, 55.4 million in 1960 and 50.8 million in 1950. These figures, however, say little about the dynamics of population change in the Federal Republic since 1949. The influx of refugees and expellees in the 1950s, the arrival of a large number of immigrant workers in the 1960s and their families in the 1970s, a declining birth rate among the resident German population giving rise to a natural decrease in population and a foreign population that not only made up 7.5% of the country's total population but also accounted for almost 12% of all births in West Germany by the end of the 1980s have been the main components of population change over the period. Each of these components has been well documented (see, for example, Mellor, 1978; Wild, 1979; SOPEMI, 1990).

Between 1950 and 1965 West Germany experienced a population increase of between 500 000–750 000 people each year. Natural increase offers only a partial explanation for this population growth. Immediately after the Second World War the West German birth rate was very high and stood at 16.8 births per 1000 in 1949. Although the rate fell to 15.5 in 1953, it soon began to rise as the economic situation in the country began to improve. Between 1956 and 1963 the birth rate increased from 16.1 to 18.3, coinciding with the economic miracle in West Germany (see below). The onset of the first post-war recession in West Germany also affected the birth rate, so that in 1967 the rate stood at 17 births per 1000 and remained on a downward spiral thereafter. By 1970 it had fallen to 13.4, while a decade later it had fallen further to a level of 10.1. Throughout the 1980s the birth rate hovered around the 9.5–10.2 level, thus placing West Germany in the lowest league in comparison with her Western European neighbours. Several reasons are often cited for the fall in the birth rate in West Germany, and these include a disinclination to marry (for example, in 1961 out of 1000 men aged 27 years 221 were married, while a similar survey in 1982 showed that the figure had fallen to 118), a divorce rate that tripled between 1949 and 1986 and greater concern with self-advancement rather than the burdens of parenthood. While the West German birth rate has fallen quite significantly, the death rate, oscillating around 11.5 deaths per 1000, has remained relatively constant since 1949. For the first time, in 1972, the country recorded a natural decrease in population—a situation that remained unchanged throughout the remainder of the 1970s and 1980s.

In-migration has therefore been a very influential component of population change in West Germany since 1949. Between 1949 and 1973 some 13 million refugees, expellees and guest workers entered West Germany, and their arrival coincided with a period of high birth rates in the country, so that between 1945 and 1974 West Germany's total population increased from 44 million to 62 million, i.e. a 40% increase.

Refugees arriving in West Germany not only included those from the GDR but also Germans forced out of former German Reich territory in Poland and the USSR (see Chapter 1) as well as those who had been part of minority German communities in Czechoslovakia, Hungary and the USSR (Hamilton, 1975). By 1961, therefore, 13.5 million refugees and expellees had settled in West Germany, and nearly one in every four West Germans had either themselves been born east of the Iron Curtain, or had refugee–expellee parents (Wild, 1979). There remained, however, an estimated four million Germans living in Eastern Europe and the USSR: some in areas where they had originally settled and others in regions to which they had been dispersed by forced resettlement and deportation schemes (see Chapter 7 on population movements and for German cultural programmes). Furthermore, these ethnic Germans have experienced the suppression of their mother tongue, have been denied certain rights or sometimes had their very existence ignored.

The decision to stem the flow of migrants from the GDR by the construction of the Berlin Wall created very real labour-supply shortages in West Germany. Sustaining economic growth in West Germany became dependent upon the recruitment of overseas labour, particularly from the Mediterranean basin. In the early years of the 1960s most guest workers (*Gastarbeiter*) were from Italy, Spain and other EEC countries, though by the early 1970s Turks (24% of all guest workers) and Yugoslavs (21%) represented the largest guest worker communities. However, the onset of recession in West Germany in the first half of the 1970s led in 1973 to a virtual ban on new labour recruitment from countries outside of the European Community (*Anwerbstopp*). Whereas most of those guest workers who arrived in West Germany in the 1960s were single men, after 1973 many had been joined by their families wishing to settle in the country. By 1975, therefore, there were over four million guest workers and their dependents in West Germany with almost one-quarter of them under 16 years old. The Federal and *Länder* governments' response in 1977 was to outline the overall aims of policy towards immigration and resident foreign populations, in particular, further tight controls on immigration, the integration of existing foreign workers and their families into West German

Table 3.2 *Entry of ethnic Germans into West Germany, 1980–9*

Year	Total	From		
		Poland	USSR	Romania
1980	52 071	26 637	6954	15 767
1981	69 455	50 983	3773	12 031
1982	48 170	30 355	2071	12 972
1983	37 925	19 122	1447	15 501
1984	36 459	17 455	913	16 553
1985	38 968	22 075	460	14 924
1986	42 788	27 188	753	13 130
1987	78 523	48 419	14 448	13 990
1988	202 673	140 226	47 572	12 902
1989	377 055	250 340	98 134	23 387

Source: SOPEMI, 1992.

society and the offer of financial assistance to those wishing to return home (*Rückkehrhilfen*). Of greatest concern to the Federal authorities has been the fact that the native German population account for the greatest natural decrease, while high birth rates among West Germany's foreign population has meant that by the end of the 1980s this group comprised over 7% of the country's total population.

The migration into West Germany of East Germans (*Ubersiedler*), ethnic Germans (*Aussiedler*) and asylum seekers has also been important. West Germany's liberal asylum laws have led to a large number of applications from asylum seekers. For example, in 1980 over 107 000 asylum applications were received by the Federal authorities, 12% of which were recognised. Throughout the 1980s the number of applications fluctuated greatly (only 19 737 in 1983 yet 99 650 in 1986). However, in the last few years of the 1980s West Germany became more popular as a target country for asylum seekers, and the number of applications rose steadily, with the largest number of applications received from Polish, Turkish and Yugoslavian nationals.

The entry of ethnic Germans into West Germany has also fluctuated greatly (see Table 3.2). In the first part of the 1980s, between 35 000 and 70 000 arrived each year; as the decade progressed and emigration restrictions became more relaxed, the number of *Aussiedler* entering West Germany rose sharply as an exodus momentum took hold. Consequently, over 202 000 ethnic Germans arrived in West Germany in 1988, followed by a further 397 000 the following year. Their arrival has caused considerable difficulties for local, regional and Federal authorities (see Chapter 7).

The emigration of East Germans to West Germany took place at the

mercy of the East German authorities. In the early 1980s some 11 000–
15 000 East Germans each year were granted permission to emigrate. In
1984 the authorities officially sanctioned a much larger number of
emigrations (almost 41 000), and after this date the level remained much
higher than in the earlier part of the decade. Consequently, some 26 000
East Germans emigrated to West Germany in 1986, and a further 39 800 in
1988. The massive exodus of people from East Germany that occurred in
1989 is discussed later.

A declining birth rate combined with a relatively constant death rate in
West Germany has led to an increase in the country's elderly population (i.e.
those over 60 years). In 1961 28.8% of West Germany's population were
under 20, while 55.1% were aged between 20 to 60 years and 16.1% were
over 60. By the mid-1980s, this situation had altered quite significantly, so
that only 24.6% were under 20 years, 55% were aged between 20 and 60
and 20.5% were over 60.

The distribution of population in West Germany has developed in clearly
discernible stages since 1949. Between the end of the war and the early
1950s the large influx of refugees from East Germany and Eastern Europe
created major disturbances in the overall pattern of population distribution.
Those *Länder* bordering East Germany, such as Schleswig-Holstein,
Niedersachsen and Bayern, experienced the greatest influx of refugees,
compounding existing economic problems in these regions. Eager to spread
the burden of refugees across all parts of its territory, the Federal government introduced a refugee resettlement programme in 1949 which led to
almost half a million refugees being transferred. Nordrhein-Westfalen, for
example, was requested to take over 450 000 refugees under the resettlement
programme.

The 1950s saw a sharp rise in the country's urban population as housing
programmes and reconstruction got under way, and the expansion of the
industrial sector offered great attractions to former rural workers. The
Rhein–Ruhr, Rhein–Main and Rhein–Neckar regions therefore experienced
the largest increase in population over this period and set the trend for an
ever-widening gap in population growth between the western and eastern
parts of the country (Wild, 1979).

The 1960s were characterised by several important processes: in
particular, the growth in population in the south and south-west of the
country, notably Baden-Württemberg, Rheinland-Pfalz and Bayern as these
regions became more attractive as investment locations; and a general out-
migration of Germans from the inner areas of most West German cities and
their replacement by large numbers of immigrant workers. On a regional
level, high concentrations of foreign populations in West Germany were to
be found in the industrial conurbations and chief cities of Nordrhein-
Westfalen, Baden-Württemberg, the Rhein–Main–Neckar region, as well as

in Hamburg and West Berlin. This trend continued throughout the 1970s and 1980s, so that by 1989, 23% of West Germany's foreign population were located in Hamburg and West Berlin, and a further 29% in the main cities of Nordrhein-Westfalen, Baden-Württemberg and Hessen. For example, by the late 1980s the city of Offenbach (Hessen) had 235 foreigners per 1000 residents, Frankfurt 234, München 210, Stuttgart 200, Mannheim 174 and Düsseldorf 158. Within West German cities the foreign population is often spatially segregated, for example in the Kreuzberg district of West Berlin, Kalk in Köln and Ludwigvorstadt in München. The highest district concentration of the foreign population in West Germany is found in the Bahnhofsviertel in Frankfurt where in 1989 the foreign population comprised well over 80% of all residents.

The 1970s not only saw the decline in population in the older industrial regions of the country but also a continuation in population growth in parts of southern Germany and an acceleration of the process of rural sub-urbanisation. Many West Germans sought properties outside of cities, leading to a tremendous growth of commuting. For example, between 1970 and 1987 the number of people commuting into Düsseldorf for employment purposes increased by 67% (Glebe, 1994). Similarly, more than one-third of the 800 000 workforce in München by the late 1980s were commuters, with one-quarter of them commuting distances in excess of 40 kilometres from their home to workplace (Helbrecht and Pohl, 1993).

The changes in population growth and distribution since 1949 have had a marked effect upon urban development and planning policies in West Germany (Heineberg, 1988). Four phases in post-war urban development in West Germany are generally recognised (Hadju, 1983): post-war urban reconstruction, increasing suburbanisation and green-field housing developments, growing environmental consciousness in urban planning and finally renewed interest in the historic urban fabric. The most important aim of urban planners in the immediate post-war years was the speedy construction of accommodation to overcome the housing shortage brought about by war devastation. The arrival of large numbers of refugees increased the urgency of this task. However, by the mid-1950s housing problems became more acute as people began to drift into towns and cities from the country's more rural regions.

The growth in the West German economy throughout the 1950s, however, resulted in increased affluence and the desire to live in more spacious accommodation away from the inner cities. Zones of low density housing sprawl on the urban–rural fringe thus characterised a great deal of urban development from the late 1950s to the mid-1960s. Not all development was uncontrolled, with many city authorities having to coordinate urban growth. In many cases this was done through the development from the 1960s onwards of new satellite towns (*Entlastungsstädte*) designed to

Photograph 5   *Pedestrianisation: Central München.* Traffic restriction and
pedestrianisation schemes were introduced into most West German
cities from the 1950s onwards. City centres have therefore taken on a
very similar appearance

house between 20 000 (for example, Mannheim-Vogelsang) and 60 000 (for
example, München-Perlach and West Berlin-Gropiusstadt) people. The main
type of housing constructed in the satellite towns was high-rise apartment
blocks, which soon became the setting for a range of social, economic and
architectural problems (Heineberg, 1988). The 1950s and 1960s also saw
the transformation of the central areas of most West German cities into
large-scale retail and business centres accessible by car. This led to problems
of congestion, noise and pollution, especially in the historic centre (*Altstadt*)
of cities. From the late 1960s, therefore, the planning of central city
development was given much more thought with emphasis placed upon
pedestrianisation schemes (*Füssgängerbereiche*) of which 32 were created in
West German cities between 1967 and 1974 (see Photograph 5 of
Neuhauser-Kaufingerstrasse in München), public transport networks,
restricted car access, increased entertainment facilities (cafes, restaurants,
street artists, informal stalls, etc.) and the protection of historic urban
features from commercial development. In Münster, for example, the
Altstadt has been protected by a variety of traffic schemes, pedestrianisation
and strict control over all planned developments likely to impair the visual
profile of the city (see Photograph 6). In the 1980s continued emphasis was
placed upon the conservation of the historic centre of towns and cities in

Photograph 6   *Historic centre of Münster, N.R. Westfalen.* Conservation schemes became a principal element of urban planning in West Germany from the 1960s. In Münster strict controls are imposed over all new building developments in the historic quarters

West Germany. Federal, *Länder* and local authority monies have been poured into town renewal and development schemes (*Städtebauförderung*) across West Germany. Comprehensive programmes for conserving buildings and monuments without stifling urban development have been introduced in many of West Germany's oldest towns and cities. In Braunschweig, for example, the merchant quarter surrounding the *Altstadtmarkt* has been the subject of a detailed conservation scheme involving the restoration of building façades, traffic control measures and the improvement of access for pedestrians to homes and shops.

THE WEST GERMAN ECONOMY

In almost all respects West Germany's economic performance after 1949 was outstanding. By the mid-1970s, despite the economic problems caused by oil price rises following the Arab–Israel war in 1973, West Germany had the most powerful economy in Europe and had become the world's second-largest trading nation after the United States. To understand this rapid rise of prosperity it is convenient to distinguish several key periods in the country's economic development (Hennings, 1982). These can be summarised as follows:

- Economic reconstruction (early 1950s);
- Export-led growth through West Germany's integration into Western European and world trading system (1950s);
- Slower more cyclical growth (mid-1960s);
- Recession and structural change in the West German economy (1970s);
- Problems of West German international competitiveness (1980s).

The West German economy was based upon social-market principles (*Soziale Marktwirtschaft*) which attempt to steer a middle course between unrestrained capitalism and the regimentation of the centrally-planned economy. In addition, considerable economic powers were given to the *Länder* which enabled them to pursue, within limits, their own policies. A central bank (Bundesbank) was empowered to act to safeguard the value of the Deutschmark. These were, then, the principal components of economic management in West Germany from 1949 onwards.

American aid under the Marshall Plan combined with currency reform were the catalysts for economic recovery in West Germany. The construction of new factories, housing and the rebuilding of cities generally changed the outlook of the German population and motivated them to improve their own personal situation. The system of *Soziale Marktwirtschaft* gave full scope to those who were willing to work hard and take risks for the sake of high profits (Childs and Johnson, 1982).

In the 1950s West Germany witnessed unprecedented economic growth, with per capita income almost doubling, housing becoming more freely available and shops displaying an increased variety of consumer goods. In economic terms, unemployment had been sharply reduced, inflation brought down to a very low level and exports, particularly of manufactured goods, enabling very favourable Balance of Payments figures to be achieved. This period in West Germany's economic development is universally regarded as the 'economic miracle' years. The reasons for the 'economic miracle' are many and it is difficult to attribute one factor above any other for the remarkable success of the West German economy in this period. Balfour (1982) provides a useful summary of the main points:

(i)   West Germany is often considered to have benefited from the fact that her economy was not burdened until the mid-1950s by any defence expenditure of her own but only by the costs of her occupiers;

(ii)   the rearmament programme set in motion by the Korean War which broke out in June 1950 led to an increase in demand for finished manufactured goods, and in particular, for modern machinery. West German industry was in a very good position to supply these needs;

(iii)   while refugees and expellees from the East had initially been a serious liability, as the West German economy began to grow rapidly during the 1950s they provided a valuable source of labour both because of their numbers and skills. The labour supply in West Germany during the period was plentiful and flexible, with not only refugees but also former farm workers and the unemployed swelling manpower supplies;

(iv) the integration process in Western Europe, symbolised by the creation of the European Economic Community in 1957, provided a major market for industrial goods on West Germany's doorstep. Export-led growth was therefore fundamental to West Germany's recovery;

(v) patriotism, unemployment and lack of funds all served to keep the trade unions from making exorbitant demands. In addition, the rights accorded to workers in the management of industry (known as *Mitbestimmung*) resulted in relatively harmonious employer–worker relations, with demands for wage increases remaining moderate and production not halted by frequent strikes. With most West Germans wishing to rebuild their personal finances only a relatively small proportion of personal income was spent on consumption. The rate of saving was high and the profits of firms were ploughed back into the company rather than distributed as wages or as dividends to shareholders;

(vi) government tax policies also encouraged overtime working and gave considerable incentives to savers and companies to invest. Tax exemptions and various other methods also favoured the retention of profits by companies;

(vii) German banks also played a crucial role in providing capital investment for industry and became an important source of both short- and long-term credit for the industrial sector.

The economic miracle in West Germany was therefore based upon a range of factors which came together at a time when world demand for industrial goods was high. West Germany was extremely well positioned to take advantage of this situation and was therefore able to experience annual growth rates of around 8% between 1950 and 1960, rates far outstripping those of its Western European partners. By 1960, therefore, West Germany had become a very prosperous capitalist society.

The West German industrial sector was dominated by a relatively small number of large concerns with a high degree of financial and technical concentration which operated globally. In 1954 the ten most important industrial enterprises in West Germany accounted for almost one-third of the country's industrial turnover, while by the mid-1980s the figure was fast approaching one-half (Table 3.3).

West German industrial activity was also concentrated geographically. Most industrial employment was located in a region extending along the

Table 3.3 *Leading West German companies, 1986*

Rank	Company	Turnover (DM billion)	Employees (thousands)	Industrial sector
1	Daimler	65.4	319	Automobiles
2	Volkswagen	52.7	281	Automobiles
3	Siemens	47.0	363	Electronics
4	B.A.S.F.	43.0	131	Chemicals
5	Bayer	40.7	173	Chemicals
6	Veba	40.1	69	Petrochemicals
7	Hoechst	38.0	181	Chemicals
8	Thyssen	31.9	127	Steel
9	R.W.E.	28.7	70	Energy
10	Bosch	21.7	147	Electronics
11	Ruhr Kohle	20.9	132	Energy
12	Klockner	19.7	72	Steel

Source: Lebeau, 1989.

Rhein axis between the Ruhr and Neckar tributaries. Consequently, over half of West Germany's industrial turnover by the 1980s derived from just two *Länder*, namely Nordrhein-Westfalen and Baden-Württemberg.

West German economic growth in the 1960s was less rapid than that experienced in the 1950s though it remained export led. Much had changed since the early years of the 'economic miracle'. Workers who had tasted the pleasures of the affluent society grew more eager for the money and leisure time needed to make more of them, and their desires were translated into more vociferous demands from trade unions (Balfour, 1982). Imports rose alarmingly and the country was faced with a balance of payments' crisis. By the mid-1960s the West German locomotive appeared to be running out of steam as in 1967 the country experienced its first post-war recession.

One of the main reasons for the lower level of growth in the West German economy in the 1960s was caused by the changing quality of labour supply. The building of the Berlin Wall in 1961 effectively stemmed the flow to West Germany of qualified East German labour and forced West German companies to recruit foreign workers to fill gaps in the labour market. Bilateral agreements between West Germany and a series of countries in the Mediterranean basin were subsequently signed throughout the 1960s in an effort to formalise labour supply arrangements (Spain and Greece, 1960; Turkey, 1961; Morocco, 1963; Portugal, 1964; Tunisia, 1965 and Yugoslavia, 1968). In 1960 only 250 000 foreign workers were employed in West Germany; by 1970 their number had increased to 1.8 million (almost 7% of the West German labour force). By 1972 the number had further increased to 2.3 million. The majority were less skilled and required more training than the East Germans who had come before 1961 (Hennings, 1982).

Recession aroused exaggerated fears and worries in West Germany, especially with some of the country's leading industrial concerns facing serious difficulties. Government response to the crisis included a major programme of investments in infrastructure projects including roads and railways with the hope of knock-on effects throughout the West German economy (Leaman, 1988). Reorienting the transport network to take account not only of the division of Germany but also West Germany's growing economic and political links with the countries of the European Economic Community were the principal goals. By mid-1968 the West German economy had picked up with growth rates reaching 7% and exports up by 13%.

Changes in political leadership in West Germany in 1969 brought new economic concerns and priorities. The distribution of the benefits of economic growth across all sections of West German society became the watchword for the SPD–FDP coalition government. However, the oil crisis in 1973–4 threw the West German economy into serious recession, though it is important to note that West Germany coped better than most of its European partners. Unemployment shot up to unprecedented levels, and West German industry further suffered from declining competitiveness on the international scene as a result of the emergence of newly developed economies in the Far East and Asia. The West German economy therefore only managed to grow by 2.5% per year between 1976 and 1980 and unemployment continued to hover around one million. The younger age groups of the labour force were particularly hit by the recession. Over 40% of all those unemployed in West Germany in 1979 were under 30.

Within the West German economy there were important changes between 1976 and 1980. Of key significance was the fall in employment in the primary and secondary sectors. For example, in 1976 6.5% of the workforce were employed in the primary sector, though by 1980 the figure had dropped to 5.4%. The importance of the service sector both as an employer and as a creator of wealth increased sharply in West Germany in the second half of the 1970s (Leaman, 1988) (Tables 3.4 and 3.5).

West Germany's third and most severe recession began in 1981. While the unemployment rate went up to 4.7% in 1975 following the aforementioned oil crisis, a second wave of oil price rises in 1979 placed a considerable burden upon the West German economy which resulted in unemployment soaring to 7.5% in 1982 and further increasing to 10.5% by 1985. The self-confidence of *Modell Deutschland* (the German Model) that had been developed in the halcyon period of the 1950s had given way to uncertainty about the economic prospects for the country (Dyson, 1989). Great debate took place under the heading *Standort Deutschland* (Location—Germany) on the nature of the economic problems of West Germany. Compared to its

Table 3.4   *West Germany: index of gross wealth creation, 1970–80 (1970 = 100)*

	1975	1976	1977	1978	1979	1980
Industrial sector	105	111	114	116	122	123
Energy	115	120	121	127	133	134
Motor vehicles	103	119	128	133	na	na
Construction	100	103	104	107	114	119
Electro-technical	123	132	145	144	na	na
Chemicals	113	134	137	140	na	na
Service sector	124	130	136	143	150	156
Banking	128	136	147	156	168	174
Insurance	131	137	140	142	151	157
Health	144	149	151	154	159	na

Source: Leaman, 1988.

Table 3.5   *West Germany: contribution of economic sectors to GDP, 1970–83 (%)*

	1970	1975	1977	1979	1981	1983
Primary	3.8	3.4	3.1	2.6	2.5	2.4
Secondary	58.2	54.4	52.9	52.7	51.2	49.3
Tertiary	38.0	41.8	43.9	44.7	46.2	48.2

Source: Leaman, 1988.

main competitors, West German labour costs were very high as a result of extremely generous social security and paid leave arrangements. For example, the legal entitlement for holidays increased from an average of 16.7 days in 1960 to around 30 days in 1983 (Berghahn, 1987). Consequently by the mid-1980s West German labour costs were the second highest in the world after Switzerland. In addition, hours of work in West Germany were both inflexible and short. For example, compared to the Japanese who worked 2138 hours per annum, the average West German employee worked only 1716 hours.

Despite these concerns the West German economy was still very strong compared to its European partners. By the late 1980s West Germany remained the world's leading exporting country ahead of both the USA and Japan and had the second highest foreign-trade surplus after Japan. The power of the Deutschmark stemmed from the country's exporting prowess. It was against a background of trade surplus (DM135 billion in 1989), low inflation, strong currency and improved economic growth prospects (growth rate had increased to 4% in 1989) that decisions over German unification were taken in 1990 (see Chapter 4).

ECONOMIC POLICY AND REGIONAL CHANGE IN WEST GERMANY

Although the West German economy developed into Europe's strongest, economic growth was not uniform across all parts of the Federal Republic. Since 1949 successive West German governments, both at Federal and *Land* levels, have been confronted with a series of regional economic problems which have required various policy responses. Achieving similar living conditions in all areas of the country was enshrined in the West German Basic Law, and since 1949 great efforts have been undertaken to this end as governments have been forced to play a greater role in cushioning and remedying the effects of economic change. Government intervention in regional development in West Germany has been well charted, particularly for the period up to the late 1970s, when as we saw above, the German economy was thrown into its most serious economic crisis (Burtenshaw, 1974; Wild, 1979). In the 1980s, many West German regions continued to undergo major economic transformations in response to changes in the international division of labour. Heavy industrial regions such as the Ruhr and Saarland, on which the West German economic miracle of the 1950s and early 1960s had been largely based, experienced a significant decline in their manufacturing base and major job losses. The 1980s saw a wide range of policy measures introduced and funds from Federal, *Länder* and EC sources assigned to combat the structural crises faced by these regions. However, regional problems were not confined to declining industrial regions such as the Ruhr, but also those urban agglomerations such as München and Stuttgart where economic growth had rocketed from the 1970s onwards were also facing severe difficulties characterised not only by housing shortages, traffic congestion, and inflated land prices but also environmental conflicts brought about by uncontrolled urban and industrial development. Indeed by the late 1980s, München had reached the social tolerance limit of economic growth, with many authors declaring the city as being at a crisis point between further economic expansion and social collapse (Helbrecht and Pohl, 1993). Outside of the industrial and urban regions, fragile rural areas too were also bracing themselves for a further round of social and economic difficulties caused by changing agricultural policy (Jones *et al.*, 1992).

It is worthwhile summarising the changing picture of uneven economic development in West Germany and the main policy responses. War devastation and the division of Germany both created regional problems for the Federal Republic. Some of the greatest damage inflicted by Allied bombing was upon towns and cities in West Germany particularly in the Rhein–Ruhr region and the ports of Hamburg, Kiel and Bremen. In Kiel, for example, less than 20% of the housing stock was undamaged, while of the remaining 80% over half was totally destroyed. In Köln serious damage was inflicted upon over half of the city's housing, while the city centre was entirely destroyed. In total, around two million homes in West Germany were destroyed by Allied bombing (Hewitt et al., 1993). The border area with East Germany presented additional problems with the handicap of separation from historic markets and hinterlands aggravated by the influx of thousands of refugees from the East. Many of the country's most depressed rural areas also lay in these borderlands. It was not surprising, therefore, that the Federal Government was forced to intervene in spatial economic planning, and the Regional Development programme that was introduced in 1951 which designated almost one hundred Kreise as distressed areas (Notstandsgebiete) was the first major effort to this end (Wild, 1979). The fortified border ('Iron Curtain') separating the Two Germanies represented not only the political division of Germany but also its internal economic dislocation, and in 1953 a 40-kilometre wide strip of territory running the entire length of the West German border with East Germany from Schleswig-Holstein to Bayern was designated as a special development zone (Zonenrandgebiet) with preferential treatment offered for potential business investors.

The agriculture-dominated state of Schleswig-Holstein, far removed from the principal urban–industrial centres of the Rhein–Ruhr, and cut off from traditional markets in Mecklenburg-Vorpommern, was faced with severe difficulties. Consequently an area-based development plan was introduced for large parts of the Land from 1953 onwards. The plan, known as Programm Nord, focused on improving living conditions in the more depressed central and western districts, and included land reclamation schemes, reorganisation of farms, the construction of roads and village improvements. Similar area-based programmes, though with different objectives, were also introduced in other parts of West Germany including Emsland (Niedersachsen) and the Alps (Mellor, 1978).

By the late 1950s–early 1960s it became apparent that the fruits of the 'economic miracle' were not being enjoyed by citizens in all parts of the country (Mayhew, 1973). Not only were many rural regions experiencing problems brought about by out-migration and the decline of the farm sector, but several industrial centres such as Kiel, Wilhemshaven and Salzgitter were also encountering difficulties (Burtenshaw, 1974). Even in the Ruhr, West Germany's industrial heartland, the beginnings of an economic crisis were taking shape, especially in the traditional sectors of coal and steel. A more substantial government involvement in regional economic development was becoming increasingly necessary and the Regional Development Act of 1965 marked the determination of the Federal and Länder governments to reduce economic disparities across West Germany. The 1965 Act designated Federal Development Areas (Bundesausbaugebiete) based upon various socio-economic indices including population density, levels of industrial employment and out-migration, and income per head. The outcome of the application of these indices was that over one-third of the country was designated as development areas though only 13% of the West German population lived there. The *Bundesausbaugebiete* were, therefore, mainly rural regions characterised by poor farm structures, low levels of mechanisation and little opportunity for non-agricultural employment.

The economic recession in West Germany in 1966–7, which hit areas such as the Ruhr and Saarland particularly badly, resulted in a great deal of criticism of the 1965 Act which had tended to neglect those industrial regions outside of the *Zonenrandgebiet*. As a consequence a new regional programme was introduced in 1969, 'Joint Task: Improvement of Regional and Economic Structures'. Some 21 areas for the programme were designated and in total covered well over half of the territory of West Germany. Importantly, many of the country's declining industrial regions were included in the programme and Federal monies were available for a variety of development purposes. These included not only loans for the setting-up of new businesses or the expansion of existing ones but also a variety of subsidies for improving industrial sites and necessary infrastructure. The 1969 programme resulted in a substantial increase in government resources directed towards removing spatial imbalances in economic wealth across the country. While the 1969 programme was welcomed, and its results initially regarded by some as encouraging, the severe crises that rocked the West German economy in the 1970s and 1980s created critical problems for many regions. Federal, *Länder* and other government agencies were therefore forced to reevaluate their role in regional planning as a consequence (Stiens, 1988).

The 1970s saw very serious problems of economic adjustment in West Germany for those sectors and regions in weak competitive positions. Whereas regional policy in the 1950s and 1960s had been based upon creating equal living conditions between urban and rural areas of West Germany, from the mid-1970s onwards areas with old-established manufacturing industries and traditional services emerged as the country's new problem regions. Imbalances in the development of regional economies led to the term north–south divide (*Nord–Süd Gefälle*) being coined to distinguish the 'dynamic' southern *Länder* from the 'rustbelt' northern *Länder* (Ardagh, 1991). Great debate took place in West Germany throughout the 1970s and 1980s on the nature of the *Nord–Süd Gefälle*. It was clear that marked interregional differences in economic development occurred in West Germany from the mid-1970s and that unemployment levels, patterns of job loss and the growth of new forms of economic activity and organisation varied tremendously between the northern and southern *Länder*. For example, unemployment levels in 1980 in Nordrhein-Westfalen, Bremen,

Table **3.6**   *Unemployment rates in West German*
              Länder, 1989 (%)

Bremen	13.6
Saarland	12.5
Hamburg	10.3
Nordrhein-Westfalen	9.1
West Berlin	9.0
Niedersachsen	8.9
Schleswig-Holstein	8.3
Rheinland-Pfalz	6.1
Hessen	5.4
Bayern	4.4
Baden-Württemberg	3.9
West German average	6.9

Source: Fischer Almanach, 1990.

Table 3.7   *Job loss in the West German manufacturing sector, 1970–85*

	1970	1985	% loss	% share of WG loss
West Germany	12 075 055	9 895 292	18	
Schleswig-Holstein	335 636	278 911	17	3
Hamburg	327 203	200 813	39	6
Niedersachsen	1 230 331	945 033	23	13
Bremen	132 029	99 556	25	2
Nordrhein-Westfalen	3 514 654	2 720 666	23	36
Hessen	1 076 860	871 582	19	9
Rheinland-Pfalz	593 454	522 287	12	4
Baden-Württemberg	2 154 375	1 905 012	12	11
Bayern	2 097 274	1 914 808	6	6
Saarland	217 860	180 603	17	2
West Berlin	395 374	256 021	35	7

Source: Nuhn and Sinz, 1988.

Saarland and Hamburg were almost twice as high as those recorded in the southern *Länder* of Bayern and Baden-Württemberg, and this remained the case throughout the 1980s. By 1989, therefore, the rate of unemployment in Bremen stood over three times that of Baden-Württemberg (see Table 3.6).

The contraction in manufacturing employment from the 1970s onwards was one of the major features of structural change in the West German economy. Between 1970 and 1985 the number of employees in the manufacturing sector in West Germany fell by 2.17 million, though there were considerable regional variations in job loss. Table 3.7 shows that the

Table 3.8 *Employment change in the Ruhr, 1981–91 (by sector)*

Agriculture, forestry and fisheries	−4%
Energy and mining industries	−18%
Manufacturing industry	−11%
Construction	+2%
Trade	+7%
Transport	+10%
Credit institutions and insurance	+21%
Producer services	+55%

Source: Dege and Kerkemeyer, 1993.

north German city *Länder* of Hamburg and Bremen lost 39% and 25% respectively of their manufacturing jobs between 1970 and 1985, West Berlin lost some 35% and Nordrhein-Westfalen 23%. Bayern, conversely, experienced only a 6% fall in manufacturing employment. If we consider the share of each West German *Land* in overall manufacturing job loss between 1970 and 1985, then Nordrhein-Westfalen accounted for well over one-third of all jobs lost in the manufacturing sector over this time period.

Problems of economic change in core regions of the West German economy are no better demonstrated than in the Ruhr region of Nordrhein-Westfalen (Dege and Kerkemeyer, 1993). Global processes of economic change have left their mark on the region, demonstrated by the fact that since the late 1950s, approximately 1.5 million jobs have been lost in the manufacturing and construction industries (Table 3.8).

With around 2.2 million workers, the Ruhr region (*Ruhrgebiet*) has one of the largest labour markets in Europe. In 1981 1.1 million workers (51% of the workforce) were employed in the manufacturing sector, yet by the end of the decade this figure had fallen to 950 000 (44%). However, the tertiary sector in the same period became the Ruhr's biggest employer accounting for 55% of all the jobs in the region by 1989. Some dramatic increases in tertiary employment were recorded in the coal and steel towns of the Ruhr. For example, only 41.3% of the workforce in Duisburg were employed in the tertiary sector in 1970, while by 1987 this had risen to 56.8%. In Essen, too, tertiary sector employment increased from a level of 50.4% to 71.7% during the same period.

Crisis in the coal and steel industries of the EC, especially from the mid-1970s, led to the *Ruhrgebiet* shedding thousands of jobs in both industries (Helm, 1989). For example, between 1979 and 1989 some 58 000 jobs were lost in the steel industry in the region. Although the Ruhr still produces 26% of the European Community's hard coal and 16% of its steel, the region underwent a considerable transformation in the 1980s especially with regard to the relative importance of the coal and steel industries as sources of employment and as contributors to regional wealth. By the late 1980s, therefore, the coal and steel sectors contributed less than one-quarter to regional wealth and employed only one-third of all workers in the region. The future of both sectors remains in jeopardy in the region.

Efforts to restructure the Ruhr economy away from its dependence upon heavy industry have been the chief aim of regional policy. Several regional institutions are working to achieve this goal. The '*ZukunftsInitiativ Montan*' specifically focuses upon the restructuring of the Ruhr economy away from coal and steel and is a cooperative venture between employers and local governments. The initiative also aims to promote the region among the European business community. The Kommunalverband Ruhrgebiet (KVR) is a key institution in the promotion of the region to potential investors. The KVR, which is based in Essen, represents the interests of the 15 cities and *Kreise* in the Ruhrgebiet. The KVR's promotion of the Ruhr has been based upon several factors. First, the geographical location of the region in the centre of the European Community and within easy access of the Community's Brussels–Luxembourg–Strasbourg institutional axis has been regarded as a major advantage. Indeed, within a 250-kilometre radius of the Ruhr is a market of 60 million people, representing around 20% of the EC's total population. Furthermore, the Ruhrgebiet itself offers a market of 5.4 million people and accounts for 8% of the total wealth created in West Germany.

Second, not only is the Ruhr workforce highly qualified, but a commitment on the part of *Land* and local authorities as well as large industrial concerns to vocational training has enabled labour to be retrained in line with prospective changes in the Ruhr economy. For example, the large steel company, Krupp Stahl AG, based at Duisburg-Rheinhausen, has set up training programmes in metal working and electrical industries and in commercial and office management (KVR, 1992, *Ruhr the Driving Force of Germany*).

Third, the KVR is trying to capitalise on the explosion in property prices in those cities and regions of southern Germany such as Frankfurt, München and Stuttgart. Land prices in München are more than ten times higher than in the Ruhr, while in Frankfurt they are twice as high. The reclamation of old industrial sites in the Ruhr for new building projects has been a top priority for many towns and cities, which have been assisted in this task by the Landesentwicklungsgesellschaft Nordrhein-Westfalen (LEG), a semi-private development agency based in Düsseldorf. The reclamation of sites for the development of science and technology centres or leisure parks has been a preferred option. For example, in Duisburg the former Thyssen steel plant at Meiderich is the setting for an ambitious leisure/theme park within which the former steel works will serve as monuments to the region's past economic glories (Stadt Duisburg, 1991).

Research and technological transfer has also been a vital element in the efforts to diversify the Ruhr's economic structure. The first technological centre in West Germany was set up in Dortmund in 1984 and incorporates 120 enterprises and employs over 3000 people. A further 20 similar institutions were established in the Ruhr in the second half of the 1980s. The 15 universities and polytechnics in the Ruhr, many of which were set up in the 1960s, have also emerged as important focal points for research in the natural sciences, engineering and economics with strong links with new businesses in the region.

The traditional image of the Ruhrgebiet as a landscape of mines and iron and steel plants, of ravaged nature with acute environmental pollution, low availability of cultural and educational facilities and poor quality of life has been one that has been difficult for the region to shake off in its quest to attract new investors. The KVR was empowered with the responsibility of improving the region's image both at home and overseas, and since the mid-1980s has carried out major publicity campaigns to promote the Ruhr as an investment location (KVR, 1992). While a reduction in the level of environmental pollution and an increase in the number of green open spaces has been achieved in the Ruhr over the last 15 years, the attractions of the southern Länder remain strong. There is no doubt that the economy of the Ruhrgebiet went through a major phase of structural change in the 1980s, the negative consequences of which are still very much in evidence. Unemployment levels in the Ruhr cities are acute and well in excess of the national average. For example, Gelsenkirchen recorded an unemployment rate of 13.1% in 1990, Duisburg 12.2%, Essen 12.5%, Bochum 12.1% and Oberhausen 10.2%. Long-term unemployment remains a problem, with 38% of the unemployed in the Ruhr having been so for over a year and 23% longer than two years. The Ruhrgebiet's experience of structural change, of entire industries closing, of unemployment and social deprivation and of economic restructuring may be an experience which can be drawn upon in the new Länder, though one must not forget with all the attention focusing upon the problems of the east (see Chapter 6), that west Germany, as the Ruhrgebiet demonstrates, also has its own particular regional crises to resolve.

The Federal government's constitutional commitment to ensuring equal living standards across all parts of the country also involves sizeable financial transfers from the richest to the poorest Länder (known as Finanzausgleich). These transfers increased from DM1.72 billion in 1970 to DM3.56 billion in 1980 and reached DM6.18 billion in 1989. Hamburg, Nordrhein-Westfalen, Hessen and Baden-Württemberg and Bayern are net contributors, while Schleswig-Holstein, Bremen, Niedersachsen, Saarland, and Rheinland-Pfalz are net recipients.

Problem regions in West Germany have also received assistance from the

European Community's structural funds (European Regional Development Fund (ERDF), European Social Fund (ESF), and the European Agricultural Guidance and Guarantee Fund (EAGGF)). Two types of region have benefited from this financial aid: declining industrial regions (known in EC terms as Objective 2 areas) and depressed rural regions (Objective 5b areas). Emsland, western Schleswig-Holstein, Eifel-Hunsruck, Harz and eastern Bayern are all designated as Objective 5b areas, and development programmes have been drawn up by the various *Länder* for EC funding. Objective 2 regions in West Germany include the Ruhr, Bremen, Saarland, Emden and Braunschweig-Salzgitter.

EC assistance to Bremen is designed to diversify and modernise the industrial sector, in particular to restore industrial sites and offer investment aid to small and medium-sized businesses (SMEs); to improve services to businesses, in particular advice on export markets; to undertake environmental improvements especially the decontamination of former industrial sites and to advise on the disposal of toxic wastes. EC aid in Saarland has been spent largely in the capital Saarbrucken and the *Kreis* of Saarlouis. The decline of the coal and steel industries in the region has required the use of funds for the promotion of SMEs and labour retraining. In addition, EC monies have also been used to encourage cooperation between local businesses and those in neighbouring France and Luxembourg. Such transnational cooperation is favoured by the European Commission and other examples in West Germany include the Aachen region in Nordrhein-Westfalen and its cooperation with the Liège–Maastricht area in Belgium–Netherlands.

Several West German problem regions have also been eligible for assistance under other specific EC schemes. For example, the port of Lubeck in Schleswig-Holstein has received grant aid from the EC's Renaval programme for the renovation of the harbour and former industrial sites, while Braunschweig-Salzgitter has been assisted under the Community's Resider programme, and funds have been used for the development of business parks and for encouraging the setting up of SMEs (EC, 1992b).

Combining trends in population growth with economic change allows a comprehensive picture of regional characteristics in West Germany to be drawn. Six types of socio-economic region had emerged in West Germany by the late 1980s (Stiens, 1988) (see Figure 3.2). Type-1 regions are attractive investment locations characterised by comparatively low levels of unemployment, a highly developed service sector, high wages and salaries and accounting for an increasing proportion of West Germany's Gross Domestic Product (GDP). Such regions have also experienced high levels of sub-and counter-urbanisation since the 1960s, brought about by inflated land prices and lack of housing space. Type-1 regions include much of the Rheinlands (Rhein-Main and Rhein-Neckar), the Stuttgart and München agglomera-

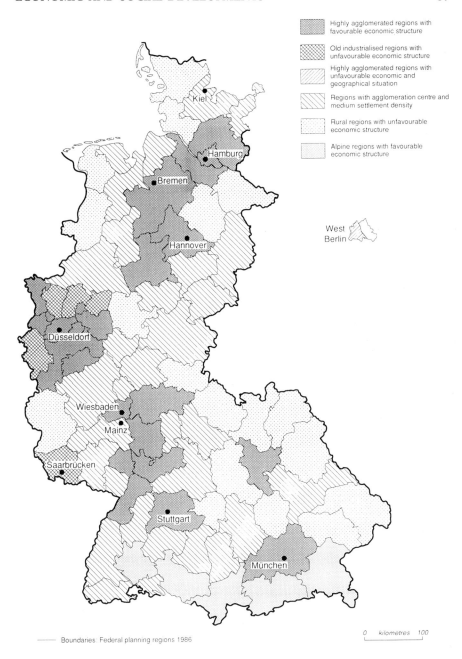

Highly agglomerated regions with favourable economic structure

Old industrialised regions with unfavourable economic structure

Highly agglomerated regions with unfavourable economic and geographical situation

Regions with agglomeration centre and medium settlement density

Rural regions with unfavourable economic structure

Alpine regions with favourable economic structure

West Berlin

Kiel

Hamburg

Bremen

Hannover

Düsseldorf

Wiesbaden

Mainz

Saarbrücken

Stuttgart

München

———— Boundaries: Federal planning regions 1986

0   kilometres   100

Figure 3.2 *West Germany: socio-economic regions (Source: Stiens, 1988)*

tions and a broad belt of territory stretching from Bielefeld–Hannover–Hamburg. Type-2 regions are those heavy industrialised areas undergoing economic restructuring away from mining and steel, having high levels of environmental pollution, few open spaces and contributing a decreasing proportion to the country's GDP. Type-2 regions have also experienced a negative population growth as a result of out-migration, although they retain a large foreign population. The *Ruhrgebiet* and Saarland fall into this category. West Berlin due to its unique spatial location and political status is defined as a Type-3 region (the only example in West Germany), characterised by a high population density and unfavourable demographic and employment situation. Type-4 regions are those with a lower level of population density and a smaller total population. They include medium-sized urban centres and their hinterlands: e.g. Kiel, Marburg, Freiburg, and Regensburg, and they have experienced lower levels of population decline since the 1970s. They offer great potential for economic growth especially as a result of congestion in the Type-1 regions. Type-5 regions are rural with a declining agricultural workforce, high levels of out-migration and a poorly developed infrastructure. Opportunities for non-agricultural employment are few, and consequently these regions present some of the greatest challenges to planners. The Eifel-Hunsruck, Emsland, much of Western Schleswig-Holstein and eastern Bayern fall within this regional type. The final category is Type-6 regions which are located in both southern Baden-Württemberg and Bayern. These Alpine foothill regions have become important not only for tourism and second homes but also as increasingly attractive locations for investment (Ruppert, 1982). They stand in contrast to the Type-5 rural areas described above.

AGRICULTURAL AND RURAL CHANGE IN WEST GERMANY

Unlike in the GDR, farmers in West Germany did not experience the major upheavals of land reform and new forms of agricultural organisation imposed by the State. Successive West German governments adopted a vigorous support policy for the farm sector which recognised not only the variety of natural conditions under which farming was practised in the Federal Republic: for example, the open moraine landscape of northern Germany, the hill lands extending across middle Germany and the high mountainous areas of the German Alps, but the government also attached great social value to the preservation of the family farm. Indeed, it has been the family farm which has served as the guiding image for West German agricultural policy since 1949 and this is reflected in the West German Agricultural Act of 1955, in the terms of West Germany's support for the EC's Common Agricultural Policy (CAP) and more recently in the fierce

Photograph 7 *Small farmstead near Weilheim, Bayern.* Successive West German governments have adopted a vigorous support policy for the farm sector. The focus for this support is the family farm which has been the guiding image of German agricultural policy

debates over agricultural policy reform in the world trade talks under the General Agreement on Tariffs and Trade (GATT).

The basic objectives of West German agricultural policy up until the 1980s were to increase agricultural productivity, to guarantee a satisfactory standard of living for the agricultural population, to stabilise agricultural markets and to guarantee a food supply to consumers at reasonable prices. To achieve these objectives the agricultural sector was substantially supported by both Federal and *Länder* governments. Ehlers (1988) suggested that West German agriculture went through three different phases of development since 1949 and these were:

(i)   the phase of consolidation and agricultural modernisation after the war (1949–60);
(ii) the phase of agricultural integration into the EEC market (1960–72);
(iii) the phase of permanent pressure for agricultural adjustment within the framework of the CAP (since 1972).

In the early years following the creation of the Federal Republic there were considerable pressures not only upon the agricultural sector to provide enough food to feed West Germans, but also upon rural areas to cope with the heavy influx of refugees and expellees from the east. Several regional plans were introduced to deal with areas (for example, in Schleswig-Holstein and southern Bayern) experiencing particular difficulties. Over 15% of the West German workforce were employed in agriculture throughout the 1950s, although the sector was characterised by a preponderance of small undermechanised farms. In 1949, for example, some 52% of farms in West Germany were under five hectares in size, while over 76% were under 10 hectares. It was obvious then that a substantial modernisation of the farm structure and layout was required. In addition, a high level of investment in farm machinery and equipment, combined with an overall improvement in living conditions in rural areas were also needed. The Land Consolidation Act of 1953 and the Agricultural Act of 1955 were clear attempts at tackling these issues.

Industrial growth in West Germany in the 1950s accelerated the process of change in agriculture as many farm labourers left farming in search of employment in other economic sectors. It has been estimated that more than 40% of those working in agriculture in 1950 had left the sector by the early 1960s (Ehlers, 1988).

Formation of the EC coincided with a period of major transformation of the West German farm sector. Of particular importance was the further drastic reduction in the number of holdings and people employed in farming (the total number of farms in West Germany fell by over 350 000 between 1960 and 1970) and the increase in average farm size. The capitalisation of the farm sector led to impressive increases in levels of production particularly for those products which were generously supported by the EEC's Common Agricultural Policy (CAP): for example wheat, barley and livestock products. The West German agricultural landscape reflected these processes with the extension of field boundaries, the removal of hedgerows and economic specialisation being the order of the day.

By the early 1970s difficulties at the EC level, in particular the high budgetary costs of storing and disposing of agricultural surpluses, prompted a reappraisal of the operation of the CAP. Ways of reducing surplus production and at the same time maintaining farm income levels dominated EC agricultural debates from the 1970s. The concentration of production on increasingly fewer farms in the EC was also a feature of agricultural development in West Germany from the 1970s. Between 1976 and 1986 the total number of farms in West Germany fell by 20% from 889 000 to 707 700. While in 1976 some 54% of farms were under 10 hectares, a decade later the figure had fallen to 49%. Farms over 20 hectares in size had accounted for 22.4% of total farms in 1976 yet by 1986 this figure had risen to 28.7%. The average farm size in West Germany therefore increased considerably from 11.6 hectares in 1970 to 16.8 hectares in 1986. The CAP aggravated the income situation between smaller and larger farms in West

Germany to the extent that by the mid-1980s 10% of West German farmers controlled almost one-third of total farming income, while conversely, the lower 40% of farmers accounted for less than one-fifth of total farming income.

Faced with increasing costs and reduced support many West German farm businesses sought off- or on-farm non-agricultural sources of income. By 1988 over 41% of West German farms were being run on a part-time basis with non-agricultural earnings providing the greatest source of income.

By the late 1980s West Germany had achieved an important position in EC food production, accounting for 21% of its milk, 20% of its beef, 26% of its pork, 14.5% of its wheat and 26% of its sugarbeet (Jones *et al.*, 1993). However, these achievements were set against considerable concern being expressed by a steadily increasing section of West German society about the environmental consequences of rising food output. Protection of the rural environment therefore became one of the new directions for West German agricultural policy from the mid-1980s (Jones, 1990). Extensification, nature conservation and set-aside policy soon became the committed goals of Federal and *Länder* agricultural policy (Jones, 1991). The improvement of living conditions in rural West Germany was the principal aim of the programme known as '*Verbessurung des Agrarstruktur und des Küstenschutzes*' ('improvement of agricultural structures and coastal protection'). Federal and *Länder* monies were used to improve various aspects of rural life including protection and creation of rural-based employment, environmental conservation schemes, village renewal (*Dorferneuerung*) and the expansion of cultural and social facilities in rural settlements. In Bayern, for example, an ambitious rural development programme was introduced in 1981 within which village renewal schemes played a significant role.

By the late 1980s, therefore, West German agriculture had been transformed by technological change and almost three decades of European Community agricultural policy. Farm size and output had both increased substantially over the post-war period, while employment in farming had been greatly reduced. Pressures for radical reform of the CAP by the late 1980s in order to curb spiralling EC expenditure and to avoid conflict with the EC's principal trading partners, particularly the US, sent shock waves throughout the farming community. West German farmers, especially those larger producers of grain, livestock and milk felt particularly threatened by these proposed developments.

WEST GERMANY IN THE EUROPEAN COMMUNITY

Over the course of the last 40 years, West Germany has emerged as the European Community's most important economic power and as an increasingly important political actor on the European stage. Full and active participation in the process of closer Western European integration has been a central tenet of West German foreign policy since 1949. Bulmer (1989) offers three reasons for this. First, the onset of the Cold War ended Germany's traditional role in Central Europe. Second, the division of Germany resulted in a major dislocation to former patterns of German trade, with new markets having to be found in Western Europe and elsewhere. Third, accommodation had to be found with France and other neighbours.

First attempts at healing the wounds with France came in the form of the Schuman Plan signed in Paris in 1950 which set up the European Coal and Steel Community (ECSC). Under this agreement, the coal and steel resources of France and Germany (and of Italy and the Benelux countries) were placed under supra-national control. The Ruhr, the Saar, Alsace and Lorraine regions formed the hub around which European integration through the ECSC was to be achieved (Simonian, 1981). In West Germany, the Schuman Plan proved to be a particularly contentious issue in some political quarters, with criticism focusing upon the negative impact upon prospects for German reunification, French designs to hold down Germany by espousing European integration and the belief that the ECSC had an insufficient democratic character (Padgett and Paterson, 1991). Others, however, saw the ECSC as a means by which West Germany could gain international acceptance particularly as an equal to France and for it to retain some control over its own coal and steel industries. As Feld (1981) remarks, 'West Germany saw in the unification of Western Europe a desirable and feasible means through which it might attain again respectability of her independence and equality by the West' (p.28). In addition, the integration of West Germany in a uniting Europe would provide a solution to both the economic and political aspects of the German problem.

Despite ill-fated attempts at creating a European Defence Community (EDC) in Western Europe, moves were afoot in the mid-1950s to establish a European Economic Community. In March 1957 six states including West Germany (i.e. those signatories of the ECSC) signed the Treaty of Rome which set up a common market of over 200 million inhabitants. Although it is often claimed that the Treaty of Rome represents a trade-off between West German industrial and French agricultural interests, the West German government also adopted a strong position over support for its farm-based population at the conferences, setting out the terms for German entry into the EEC (Hendriks, 1991).

While some observers have even suggested that a Franco–German axis exists in EC policy making (Morgan and Bray, 1986), it is clear from an analysis of the evolution of the EC that agreement between Bonn and Paris has been essential for the Community's development. There are many examples of cooperation between the two countries to propose new

Table 3.9 *West German trade with the European Community, 1984–90*

Trade with the EC as % of total West German trade

	1984	1986	1988	1990
West German imports	50	52.2	51.7	52
West German exports	49.9	50.8	54.2	54.5
Balance: DM billion	+26.3	+51.4	+80.8	+63.8

Source: Statistisches Jahrbuch 1991 für das vereinte Deutschland, Wiesbaden.

Table 3.10 *West German trade with France, 1987–90*

Trade with France as % of total W. German trade with the EC

	1987	1988	1989	1990
% Imports from France	22	23	23	23
% Exports to France	24	23	27	24

Source: Statistisches Jahrbuch 1991 für das vereinte Deutschland, Wiesbaden.

initiatives, to settle grievances of other Community members and to save the Community from political collapse. The EC has come to be more important for West Germany than its partners, and successive Bonn administrations have always held the view that West Germany has more to lose both economically and politically from stalemate or collapse of the EC than the other participants (Simonian, 1981).

Within the Community West Germany has upheld the principle of trade liberalisation and sought closer monetary union and careful economic management. It is regarded by some as having played a model role in the Community (Bulmer and Paterson, 1987), underlined by the fact that it is the largest contributor to the Community budget accounting for 26.5% of total contributions in 1987 (Shackleton, 1990).

It has been, however, the opportunities that Community membership offers West German manufacturing industry that fuels support for European integration. Table 3.9 shows that by 1990 well over half of West German trade was with the Community and that it has been able to sustain a very favourable balance of trade surplus amounting to some DM63.8 billion in 1990. Table 3.10 demonstrates that West Germany's trade with its EC partners is dominated by the strength of its economic ties with France, which is West Germany's most important EC and international trading partner, accounting for 12% of West Germany's imports and 13% of its exports.

During the course of its membership of the Community West Germany has played the diplomatic game very skilfully. Through its close political and

Table 3.11   *Nature of West German trade with the EC, 1990 (DM billion)*

	Imports from EC		Exports to EC	
		%		%
Food and drink	34.5	12	19.9	6
Energy products	18.7	0.4	0.4	1.2
Chemicals	33.2	11.5	44.1	12.6
Metals, steel, paper	55.3	19.3	66.1	18.9
Machinery	92.5	32.3	166.8	47.6

Source: *Statistisches Jahrbuch 1991 für das vereinte Deutschland*, Wiesbaden.

economic relationship with France it has been adept at putting forward a 'grand-design' for Europe through which it has been able to further its own national interests. West Germany has not tried to dictate policy in the EC, generally it has sought consensus, pioneering or developing initiatives in conjunction with other member states. Such flexible and adaptive behaviour has enabled it to overcome some of its particular geo-political vulnerabilities and it has been able to establish itself as a key pillar in the construction of a European political and economic architecture. Progress achieved towards European political, economic and monetary union has demonstrated beyond doubt the importance of West Germany in the shaping of the European Community.

CONCLUSION

By the late 1980s the West German economy had enjoyed several decades of growth, albeit irregular, and West Germans had been able to enjoy the fruits of this success measured either in terms of the possession of material goods, regular overseas holidays, short working hours or generous social provisions. However, there was growing discussion about whether West Germany would be able to sustain this economic growth in the 1990s. West German economic expansion in the post-war period was, as we have seen, based upon the production and export of high-quality manufactured goods, although technological change has severely reduced the numbers employed in this sector of the West German economy. Moreover, competition from Japanese and East Asian producers in traditional German overseas markets led to major contractions in manufacturing employment in West Germany from the late 1970s onwards. Despite this situation, many observers expected the West German economy to overcome these difficulties, with many citing the European Community's 1992 Single Market programme as an opportunity for the country to take full benefit of the opening of the Community market as a stimulus to further economic growth. It was also widely agreed that West Germany would be well placed to profit economically from political reform in Eastern Europe, thereby increasing German exports across the continent as a whole. Lebeau (1989) summed up the mood: 'for the immediate future the sky remains blue, but with a heavy dark cloud of unemployment and poverty looming' (p. 273).

No one, however, could predict the clouds that were building up on the distant horizon which would change momentously the course of West Germany's economic development.

SUGGESTED FURTHER READING

Berghahn, V.R. (1987) *Modern Germany*. Cambridge University Press, Cambridge.
Bulmer, S. and Paterson, W. (1987) *The Federal Republic of Germany and the European Community*. Allen and Unwin, London.
Childs, D. and Johnson, J. (1982) *West Germany: Politics and Society*. Croom Helm, London.
Dyson, K. (1989) 'Economic Policy' in G. Smith, *et al.*, *Developments in West German Politics*. Macmillan, Basingstoke, 148–64.
Elkins, T.H. (1988) *Berlin: The Spatial Structure of a Divided City*. Methuen, London.
Merkl, P. (ed.) (1989) *The Federal Republic at Forty*. New York University Press, New York.
Smith, E.O. (1983) *The West German Economy*. Croom Helm, London.
Wild, T. (1979) *West Germany. A Geography of its Peoples*. Longman, Harlow.

4 German unification: processes and timetable

THE TRIGGERS

Up to 1989 the German Democratic Republic had been a relatively stable and prosperous member of the communist bloc. However, by December of that year the country had witnessed millions of East Germans demonstrating for reform on the streets of its major cities, the dismantling of the Iron Curtain between West and East Germany and the breaching of the Berlin Wall. In July 1990 the two Germanies were joined in economic and monetary union and in October 1990 politically united under the same constitution. Many, both inside and outside Germany, were astonished at the speed of these events which were to reshape momentously the European political map.

It was a combination of events and circumstances, many of them external to Germany, that created the conditions for the collapse of the GDR state. These have been well charted (see Ardagh, 1991; Heisenberg, 1991; Osmond, 1992). It is worthwhile, though, examining the route by which the two Germanies came to be united, since, as Chapter 6 will demonstrate, not only has unification led to serious economic and social adjustment problems in the former GDR, but the pace at which unification was allowed to proceed is now coming under critical questioning from both West and East Germans.

In 1989 the GDR, although economically less powerful than West Germany, was nevertheless considerably better off than its communist neighbours and had established an important role for itself in the COMECON trading bloc. While East Germans did not enjoy the range of consumer goods that were available in the West, food shortages and queues on the scale of Polish experience were rare. Unlike Poland and Czechoslovakia, the GDR was politically stable, with dissent having little widespread support or foundation. Moreover, government programmes such as for housing were broadly accepted as genuine attempts at improving the well-being of East Germans.

One needs, therefore, to look at the wider political context in which the GDR was located in the late 1980s. Here, reforms in the USSR and a declared loosening of Soviet control over the destiny of its East European satellites paved the way for democratic pressures to be exerted throughout communist Eastern Europe. Democratic reforms in Poland and Hungary raised expectations among all East Europeans as a tide of optimism engulfed the eastern part of the continent.

It was, however, the decision by the Hungarian government on 10 September 1989 to dismantle the country's fortified border with Austria, thus breaking the Iron Curtain around socialist Europe, which allowed an exit to the West for East Germans. Some 25 000 East Germans, who had come to Hungary 'on holiday', left that way, prompting a ban by the GDR government on travel to Hungary and a series of crisis talks (25–29 September) between the foreign ministers of the USSR, the GDR, Poland, Hungary and Czechoslovakia in an attempt to find a solution to what was becoming a virtual haemorrhage of population (InterNationes, 1992).

As several thousand East Germans sought refuge at West German embassies in Bucharest, Prague and Warsaw, those who remained at home became increasingly restive. Discontent spurred the establishment of a broadly based pressure group in East Germany—'*New Forum*'—which sought wide-ranging political and economic reforms. Ironically, events also coincided with the planned official celebrations for the 40th anniversary of the founding of the GDR on 7 October which were to be attended by President Gorbachev, the Soviet leader. Several thousand people demonstrated against the SED governments and many were arrested. Two days later in Leipzig, 100 000 people took to the streets chanting 'we are the people' (*Wir sind das Volk*). Just over one week later, with pressure mounting, Erich Honecker, the SED General Secretary, resigned from office to be replaced by Egon Krenz.

Mass demonstrations continued unabated, despite a radical clearout of many key government officials. On 4 November in the capital East Berlin, the largest protest demonstration in the history of the GDR drew almost one million East Germans, while at the same time the flood of people to the West went unstemmed, now passing through Czechoslovakia.

With no possibility of preventing the exodus of people, coupled with public dissatisfaction and widespread demands for reform, the government resigned on 7 November. The wall that had divided the city of Berlin and that had become the symbol of an ideologically divided Europe was opened on 9 November.

MOVES TOWARDS GERMAN UNIFICATION, NOVEMBER 1989–JULY 1990

Once the Berlin Wall was opened and more crossing points between the two Germanies were created, hundreds of thousands of East Germans headed

West. While many returned to their homes in the East having satisfied their pent-up curiosity about conditions in the West, there were others who decided to stay in the West, thereby placing intolerable strains on social services (particularly housing) and adding to the problems of what was becoming an increasingly fragile West German labour market. Euphoria at the breaching of the Berlin Wall was rapidly turning to displeasure by mid-November as West Germans were faced with large numbers of East Germans seeking homes and jobs in West German cities. In East Germany, increased exposure to the trappings of capitalism, revelations about the squandering and double lives of SED government officials and new information about the condition of the East German economy and the environment led many to turn their back on their socialist past. '*Das Volk*' had now become '*Ein Volk*' (one people)—calls for German unity became the order of the day, as political turmoil threatened.

On 22 November Chancellor Kohl delivered a statement before the European Parliament in Strasbourg concerning events in the GDR, as Germany's European neighbours became more anxious about the country's fate. Six days later a more dramatic statement was delivered by the Chancellor in the German Bundestag on overcoming the division of Germany and Europe. His statement covered ten topics, representing a ten-point plan:

(i)   Immediate humanitarian measures to deal with the flow of East Germans to West Germany and the establishment of a currency fund to facilitate movement in both directions.
(ii)   Commitment to greater economic, scientific, technological, cultural and environmental cooperation with the GDR. Increasing telephone and transport links with the GDR to re-establish traditional East–West lines of communication in Central Europe.
(iii) Comprehensive aid and cooperation pledged on the condition of democratic reform and the dismantling of the centrally-planned economy in the GDR. (Kohl argued that these were not preconditions but simply the foundation needed for effective assistance by West Germany.)
(iv)   Creation of common institutions to deal with industrial, transport, environmental, science, health and cultural issues.
(v)   Development of confederative structures with a view to creating a *federation* after free elections in East Germany.
(vi)   Intra-German relations were to be developed in the context of international law and human rights.
(vii) Intra-German relations must be developed in the context of European integration. A trade and cooperation agreement between the EC and the GDR should be signed as soon as possible. The EC should broaden

its horizons to address with openness and flexibility the countries of Central and South-Eastern Europe.

(viii) New institutional forms of pan-European cooperation should also be sought.

(ix) Disarmament must keep pace with political changes.

(x) Reunification remained the political goal of the Federal government of Germany. The goal must be linked to pan-European developments.

Kohl's most controversial proposal was point five (Childs, 1991). The prospect of a united Germany strategically occupying *Mitteleuropa* caused considerable concern and prompted serious political discussions in the USSR, in NATO and in the EC in the closing months of 1989 (Ludlow, 1991). In his New Year's address, Kohl reiterated his earlier points and spoke of free elections in the GDR, improvement of economic conditions there and that German unification must take place in the context of European integration (Weiland *et al.*, 1991). Faced with mounting problems of housing East German refugees (known as *Ubersiedler*) in West Germany, pressures increased for the economic integration of the two Germanies. These became even more pressing when the Interior Ministry (*Bundesinnenministerium*) announced in early January 1990 that 343 854 *Ubersiedler* had sought permanent refuge in West Germany since September 1989—a figure equivalent to the population of the East German cities of Halle and Dessau combined.

In February, following a conference of foreign ministers of NATO and the Warsaw Pact (12–13 February), and the visit to Bonn by Hans Modrow, the new East German Prime Minister, it was agreed that negotiations over economic and monetary union between the two Germanies would begin after the free elections in East Germany which were to be held on 18 March. The nature and speed of unification, and the extent of commitment to it by individual political parties, was the basis on which the election was fought. The outcome was a decisive one in favour of the centre–right alliance (including Kohl's CDU party) which polled 47.79% of the vote. Their platform was for the most rapid unification of East and West Germany.

The external aspects of German unification were dealt with on the basis of what were termed the '2 + 4 talks' involving East and West Germany and the four Allied powers. The agenda included the status of Berlin, German sovereignty and political/military questions concerning a new European structure. Agreement was reached on five key points (Ludlow, 1991):

(a) territorial issues;

(b) non-aggression pledges of a united Germany;

(c) renunciation by Germany of the manufacture, possession and control of nuclear/biological/chemical weapons;

(d) withdrawal of Soviet troops from Germany;
(e) undertakings regarding German troops on GDR soil.

The '2 + 4 talks' addressed the entire range of complex issues comprising the German question. Not surprisingly, considering the damage inflicted by the German Reich between 1939 and 1945 (see Foucher, 1993), the country with the most immediate apprehension about German unification was Poland (Osmond, 1992). Great concern existed about those former German territories which since 1945 had been part of Poland. Despite Kohl's insensitivities to his Polish neighbour regarding this issue, particularly on his visit to Silesia in November 1989, the '2 + 4 talks' concluded that the united Germany would draw up an agreement with Poland recognising the inviolability of the Oder–Neisse line as the border between the two countries.

Also on the European front there was the question of how a united Germany could be accommodated within the European Community. Some authors have claimed that integrating Germany into the EC was more easily resolvable than some of the other issues facing the country (Fulbrook, 1991). However, the difficulties faced by the Community in incorporating what had been a centrally-planned economy with its integral links with the Soviet dominated COMECON trading block should not be underestimated. While Chapter 7 deals with this issue in more detail, here it is appropriate to consider how a united Germany could be integrated into the EC in an institutional sense. Spence (1991a; 1991b), Secretary to the Task force on German Unification which was set up within the European Commission, provides useful insights into the conditions and foreshortened timescale in which the EC was forced to work.

German unification implied integration of the GDR into the EC. For Germany, there were two constitutional ways of incorporating the GDR into a new German state. The first of these routes was that the GDR could become part of the Federal Republic of Germany by opting for membership of it under Article 23 of the Basic Law. This would simply enlarge the existing territory of the FRG. A second route was possible under Article 146 of the Basic Law whereby a new constitution could be drawn up following negotiations between West and East Germany. The first of these routes was chosen with two inter-state treaties (*Staatsvertrag* and *Einigungsvertrag*) paving the way for economic, monetary and political union. This decision had an important bearing upon the way in which the EC could handle the issue, since unlike previous EC enlargements, German unification would not involve the Community negotiating with the GDR but with the FRG, namely the existing member state. German unification was therefore very much a special case for the Community (Spence, 1991b).

ECONOMIC, MONETARY AND SOCIAL INTEGRATION OF THE TWO GERMANIES

Even before the free elections in March 1990, much political debate was taking place about how the two Germanies could be brought together in an economic, monetary and social union and the financial costs likely to be incurred in doing so. The campaigns of all the political parties in the election focused upon how best to secure electoral advantage through political manipulation of these issues.

For Chancellor Kohl sight was also to be kept on the all-German elections that were scheduled for later that year. Promises would have to be made to the East Germans that could be achieved realistically within a short time period and which would not damage the support of the West German electorate. The SPD party meanwhile took a different line, preferring to spell out more honestly the real costs that lay ahead. The East German electorate preferred the rash promises of Kohl that 'no one will be worse off as a result of unification' and that 'the landscape of the east will blossom' (Weiland *et al.*, 1991).

The crucial decision to be taken was the rate at which the East German Mark (Ostmark) would be convertible with the West German Deutschmark. On 1 April Karl Otto Pohl, President of the Bundesbank, recommended that the exchange ratio should be 2:1 except for personal savings up to DM2000. This view was based upon concern over possible inflationary consequences of setting the level more favourably, particularly as the black market rate had been over 5:1 (Ardagh, 1991). Some German economists had even estimated that the real value of the Ostmark was as low as DM0.23 (quoted in Jeffries, 1992). East German politicians, meanwhile, continued to argue for a 1:1 conversion rate between the two currencies.

On 23 April, the same day as citizens of Karl Marx Stadt chose to rename their town Chemnitz (Sachsen), the West German government declared that terms for conversion would be 1:1. In May more precise details were announced with the amount of money allowed to be converted varying according to citizens' age. For example, citizens over 60 years of age could exchange up to DM6000 at 1:1, those 15–59 years DM4000 and those under 15 years DM2000. Debts of East German industry were to be converted at the rate of 2:1.

In May, too, the West German government announced that a special four-year programme was to be set up to fund German unification. DM115 billion were assigned to it for the period 1990–4. Some 17% of the total (DM20 billion) would come from budgetary savings while the remainder, known as the *Fonds Deutsche Einheit* (German Unity Fund), was to be raised by borrowing on the international capital markets. Crucially, taxes were *not* to be raised to pay for unification.

The treaty establishing a monetary, economic and social union between the two Germanies was signed in Bonn on 18 May and was to come into effect on 1 July 1990. The treaty itself was divided into six chapters: (1) Basic Principles; (2) Monetary Union; (3) Economic Union; (4) Social Union; (5) Budget and Finance; (6) International Provisions.

Of course, not all Germans were in favour of German unification: for example, the celebrated German writer Günter Grass spoke out against the process of unification in 1990, arguing against a 'super-Federal Republic' in favour of a confederation that would 'point the way to a new, different, and desirable' Germany (Grass, 1990, p. 5). His words were not heeded by those responsible for drafting the treaty between the two Germanies. Instead, a social market economy based upon Germany's icon the Deutschmark and steered by the Bundesbank in Frankfurt-am-Main was to be the future for the united Germany.

Conditions for the development of market forces and private enterprise were to be created in East Germany. A trust agency, *Treuhandanstalt*, was to be charged with the privatisation of the GDR economy. Foreign trade, too, was to be progressively brought into step with that as practised by West Germany in line with its commitments within the EC. Controls and restrictions on intra-German trade were to be abolished, and a 'diversified, modern economic structure' was to be the objective of economic development in the former GDR (Article 14). Environmental law as applied in West Germany was to be the standard against which this economic development was to be allowed to take place (Article 16).

As regards the social union of the two Germanies, pension, sickness, accident and unemployment benefit schemes in East Germany were to be designed to match those in the West (Article 18). Special importance was attached to an active labour market policy including vocational training and retraining. Article 19 also recognised the importance of women in the East German labour market. Concern over the ability of East Germany to fund unemployment benefit schemes after unification prompted a special clause on temporary financial support to be included by the Bonn government. West German tax systems, other revenue-raising measures such as VAT, and budgetary procedures were also to apply in East Germany.

East Germany was therefore to be radically overhauled along West German lines. From 1 July, when the treaty came into effect, East German salaries and wages were paid in Deutschmarks and East German shops instantly filled up with West German goods, although at West German prices. In Ost Berlin, thousands queued at midnight outside a branch of the Deutsche Bank eager to convert their Ostmarks (Weiland *et al.*, 1991). The following day many splashed out on second-hand cars, new videos or furniture (Ardagh, 1991). Western goods were eminently more preferable than inferior East German ones, while for East Germany's trading partners in COMECON such inferior goods had now to be paid for in hard Deutschmarks.

POLITICAL UNIFICATION OF THE TWO GERMANIES

During the summer months of 1990 a flurry of activity took place in Bonn and Ost Berlin concerning moves to achieve a political union of the two Germanies. At the same time the desolate state of the East German economy was becoming more readily apparent, especially as the collapse of the COMECON trading block loomed. The technological gap between East and West Germany could be measured in decades. Antiquated machinery produced poor quality goods at high cost and with considerable waste. Labour productivity was only a third of that of West Germany (Schonfeld, 1992). Huge surplus capacities existed in the steel, chemicals, heavy engineering, shipbuilding and textiles sectors of the East German economy. Infrastructure was badly in need of repair, while pollution, caused by lignite-burning power stations, factories and households and an alarming neglect of environmental protection presented enormous clean-up problems. Currency union had offered little comfort. Against this background, Chancellor Kohl pressed for full political unification.

August and September 1990 witnessed several events that characterised the difficulties of uniting the two Germanies. For two days in August 250 000 East German farmers took to the streets demonstrating against marketing problems, falling prices and declining State support. Doctors also took to the streets on 22 August complaining that a second-class medical service existed in East Germany and that their salaries amounted to less than 70% of those received by doctors in the West. Two weeks later, it was announced that unemployment levels in East Germany had increased to over 350 000 since monetary union which led to Chancellor Kohl facing a hostile crowd on his walkabout in Halle, where he reacted angrily to being pelted with eggs and tomatoes. On the same day 40 guestworkers from Mozambique were attacked by a right-wing mob at a hostel in Potsdam. In September, with the economic picture becoming gloomier, 10 000 people demonstrated in West and Ost Berlin for the retention of certain social rights, particularly the right to abortion on demand in the first 12 weeks of pregnancy.

On 3 October a second treaty (*Einigungsvertrag*) between the two Germanies was signed—a treaty that owes more to the takeover of the East by the West rather than a political comprise. Five *Länder* in East Germany were reconstituted and the 23 boroughs of Berlin were grouped to form the state of Berlin (see Figure 4.1). Article 2 of the treaty stated that the capital of Germany was to be Berlin and that the question of the seat of parliament and government would be resolved at a later date.

Figure 4.1 *The new Germany: Länder*

Since 1990, therefore, Germany comprises 16 *Länder* including Berlin. The division of the former East Germany into five Federal states has received much criticism, especially from regional planners, who believe that the territorial division is neither the optimum for achieving effective planning nor for meeting the financial requirements of the *Länder* as laid down in the Basic Law (Rutz, 1991).

The *Einigungsvertrag* covered a range of political, legal and constitutional issues as well as provisions for servicing debts accrued by East Germany. The first all-German free elections for the Bundestag since 1932 were planned for 2 December. October and November saw campaigning begin in earnest, with Kohl's party, the CDU, hoping to perform well in the East having secured German unification in less than one year, despite the Federal Labour Office's announcement on 6 November that 538 000 East Germans were unemployed and a further 1.76 million were on short time. In West Germany, Kohl's success appeared less secure as *Länder* governments were being asked to commit more funds for the development of the East and at the same time to accommodate large numbers of *Ubersiedler*. On 22 November, for example, the Nordrhein-Westfalen government announced that 80 000 East Germans had arrived in the *Land* since monetary union in July. Only a few days later, the government of Mecklenburg-Vorpommern maintained that not enough was being done to aid development and requested more West German and EC financial assistance. Importantly, on 12 November the CDU leadership declared that German unification would be financed without tax increases. For the SPD campaign, Oskar Lafontaine, the party leader, warned of the dire economic, social and political consequences as a result of the way in which the two Germanies had been united. Several events lent support to his views. Only three days after the Interior Ministry announced that xenophobia was on the increase in East Germany, 90 neo-Nazis were arrested at an illegal demonstration in Cottbus (Brandenburg). That same week, it was also announced that production of the Trabant car—the symbol of East German manufacturing industry—was to be discontinued as from the end of the year and that between 40 and 45 former East German companies were also to close with the loss of a further 50 000 jobs.

The result of the Bundestag election on 3 December was a comprehensive victory for the champions of the unification process—Chancellor Kohl's CDU party (*Frankfurter Allgemeine*, 4 December 1990). Not suprisingly, the overriding concern of voters in the election was national unification. As Jeffries (1992) observes:

the election marks in one sense the culmination of the formal unification process . . . and at the same time, the starting point from which the practical process of managing the fusion of two economies and two societies with widely divergent characteristics would be launched. The election therefore represented an opportunity for the electorate both to look back and give its verdict on the events of 1990, but also to look ahead and mark out its vision of the future of Germany (p.127).

Kohl's CDU party secured 36.7% of the German vote (35.9% in the West and a convincing 43.4% in the East), while the sister parties of the CDU—the CSU and DSU—added another 7.1% to this total. The SPD party, on the other hand, only managed to secure 33.5% of the vote, with less than 25% of votes cast in the East going to the party. The electorate was clearly seeking a party that could respond positively to the challenges posed by the unification of the two Germanies.

As congratulatory telegrams arrived in the Chancellor's office recording 'an historic year for Germany and Europe' (François Mitterrand), 'an historic step in Germany's increasing importance in the future of Europe' (President Bush), Kohl articulated the challenges that faced his government and emphasised the need to push on with economic, monetary and social union at EC level, to bring the East German economy up to that in West Germany, to reform Germany's asylum policy and to put right the damage inflicted upon the environment by previous SED policies (*Frankfurter Allgemeine*, 4 December 1990).

Outside the country, unification awakened old concerns among Germany's neighbours about the underlying intentions of Germany in Europe. A survey carried out by *The Economist* (27 January 1990) revealed some of the feelings held on this issue. These are shown in Table 4.1. While the question of territorial expansion (Polish fears) was resolved by the *Einigungsvertrag* and the '2 + 4' agreement, the prospect of the united Germany becoming too strong economically (French and British fears) or the return of Fascism in some form were very much unknown factors.

GERMAN UNIFICATION: OPTIMISTIC ASSESSMENTS?

At the end of 1990 the euphoria surrounding German unification was quickly beginning to dissipate, as it became apparent that the magnitude of the upheaval facing the country had been seriously understated. The transformation of a centrally-planned economy to one based upon free-market principles was a huge experiment—politically, economically and socially; there was no theory on which to build. Germans, particularly in the East, did not want to hear that times would be difficult, preferring the sweeteners that no one would be worse off from unification and that taxes would not have to be raised to pay for it. Moreover, the CDU government appeared unprepared to tell West Germans that the economic strength and prosperity built up over 40 years in West Germany was not an end in itself

Table 4.1 *Results of a survey on German unification conducted in the UK, France, Poland and the USA (%)*

Do you favour German unification?	UK	France	Poland	USA
Favour	45	61	41	61
Oppose	30	15	44	13
Neither	19	19	14	9
Don't know	6	5	1	17
Would you be worried by a united Germany becoming Europe's dominant power?				
Yes, would be worried	50	50	69	29
No, would not be worried	37	43	25	62
Won't happen	10	4	6	1
Don't know	3	3	0	8
What is the cause of your worry?				
Might try to expand territory	28	15	54	26
Economy too strong	41	55	39	26
Return of Fascism	53	38	53	37
Other	4	3	3	2
Don't know	3	4	2	8

Source: *The Economist*, 27 January 1990 (total sample = 2677 respondents).

but rather should be used to overcome the division of Germany and indeed of Europe.

Optimism that existed at government level was based upon several factors:

(i)   There was complete faith in the role of the market to put things right.
(ii) The transfer of public funds and private investment from the West (and from non-German sources) would regenerate the East German economy.
(iii) The West German economy was regarded as sufficiently sound to cope with the new demands from the East and increased consumption in the East would also serve to stimulate the West German economy.
(iv) Growth in East Germany would lead to a fall in the number of East Germans seeking homes and jobs in the West.
(v)   The East German labour force was young and skilled.
(vi) East Germans would have no major difficulty in adapting to Western ways and values.

In 1991 with the West German balance of trade surplus wiped out, taxes raised, industrial output in the East down by over 50%, one million jobs lost and a further two million East Germans working short time, the gap between election statements and harsh reality was all too obvious. The following chapters examine the geographical nature of the united Germany and look at the ways in which the new *Länder* have been modernised since 1990, the problems encountered and the economic and social costs involved.

SUGGESTED FURTHER READING

Grosser, D. (ed.) (1992) *German Unification. The Unexpected Challenge.* Berg, Oxford.

Keithly, D.M. (1992) *The Collapse of East German Communism. The Year the Wall Came Down 1989.* Praeger, London.

Osmond, J. (1992) *German Reunification: a Reference Guide and Commentary.* Longman, Harlow.

Szabo, S.F. (1992) *The Diplomacy of German Unification.* St Martin's Press, New York.

Turner, H.A. (1992) *Germany from Partition to Reunification.* Yale University Press, New Haven.

Wallach, H.G.P. and Francisco, R.A. (1990) *United Germany.* Praeger, New York.

5 The new Germany: a human geography

INTRODUCTION

There is no doubt that unification has fashioned a new human geography of Germany. This chapter focuses in particular upon the socio-economic contrasts between the old and the new *Länder* at the time of German unification. Several themes are highlighted, including population issues, economic profiles, infrastructure changes, environmental questions and spatial patterns of regional inequality. Collectively they demonstrate the formidable challenges that confront policy makers in uniting two Germanies, whose geography has been moulded by substantially different social, economic and political processes.

TERRITORY AND POPULATION

The united Germany covers an area of 357 000 sq. kilometres and lies in the heart of Europe. The new Germany now has nine neighbours: Denmark to the north, the Netherlands, Luxembourg and France to the west, Switzerland and Austria to the south and the Czech Republic and Poland to the east. Unification has therefore served to re-emphasise Germany's geographical situation in, and responsibility towards, the European continent.

Despite being smaller in area than either France or Spain, some 79.1 million people live in the new Germany, making it the most populated country in Europe after Russia. Politically the new Germany is divided into sixteen *Länder* including Berlin. Table 5.1 shows the size of the *Länder* in terms of area and population. Less than one-quarter (18.5 million) of Germany's population lives in the new *Länder* with the united Berlin (3.4 million) accounting for just under one-fifth of the total. Most of the new *Länder* have a smaller population than the old *Länder* (excluding city states such as Bremen and Hamburg), although there are some exceptions: for example both Saarland and Schleswig-Holstein in the west are smaller in population size than most of the new *Länder*, while the *Land* of Sachsen (the most populated new *Land* with almost five million inhabitants) is larger than the western *Land* of Rheinland-Pfalz.

Table 5.1   *The new political division of Germany. Länder populations and area*

	Area (km²)	%	Population (thousands)	%
Berlin	883	0.2	3348	4.3
Bayerna	70 554	19.8	11 049	14.1
Niedersachsen	47 344	13.3	7185	9.2
Baden-Württemberg	35 751	10.0	9433	12.1
Nordrhein-Westfalen	34 070	9.5	16 874	21.6
Hessen	21 114	6.7	5569	2.5
Rheinland-Pfalz	19 849	5.6	3653	4.7
Schleswig-Holstein	15 729	4.4	2565	3.3
Saarland	2570	0.7	1054	1.3
Hamburg	755	0.2	1603	2.1
Bremen	404	0.1	662	0.8
Brandenberg	29 059	8.1	2641	3.4
Mecklenburg-Vorpommern	23 828	6.7	1964	2.5
Sachsen-Anhalt	20 445	5.7	2965	3.8
Sachsen	18 337	5.1	4901	6.3
Thüringen	16 251	4.6	2684	3.4
	356 954		78 149	

Source: Raumordnungsbericht, 1991.

The political unification of Germany in October 1990 led to the reconstitution of the former *Länder* in what had been East Germany. Five *Länder* were established. There was considerable pressure exerted, especially from those responsible for economic planning, against this decision. Several possibilities for a new territorial division were mooted (Rutz *et al.*, 1993).

Six months before political unification, a Ministry for Regional and Local Affairs was set up in East Germany whose brief included the future territorial division of the country. Although political pressures were moving towards the reconstitution of the former *Länder*, this was by no means a simple task since there were many communities in small administrative areas (*Kreise*) which between 1945 and 1952 had been part of *Länder* different from those proposed under the new territorial arrangements. Thirty-two *Kreise* containing over two million East Germans were affected in this way. It was decided that local people should vote on their territorial preferences. For example, the *Kreis* of Hoyerswerda, formerly in the *Bezirk* of Cottbus (one of the *Bezirke* proposed for inclusion in the *Land* of Brandenburg), had been in the *Land* of Sachsen between 1945 and 1952. Over 57% of the 80 000 inhabitants of the *Kreis* voted on the issue. Some 12% voted for Brandenburg while 88% voted in favour of Sachsen. Elsewhere some of the results were much closer. Citizens of the *Kreis* Altenburg were forced to choose between the *Länder* of Thüringen and Sachsen with the outcome being 46% in favour of the former and 54% in favour of the latter.

These figures have been used to support the argument for fewer *Länder* in the former East Germany. In particular, there are certain constitutional problems associated with the proposed territorial division, especially in relation to the number of representatives in the upper house of the German parliament (Bundesrat). Rutz (1991), in a stinging criticism of the five-*Länder* division of East Germany, provides comprehensive arguments based upon historical trading links, contemporary economic geography and financial common sense. The drawing of the *Land* boundary (between Sachsen and Sachsen-Anhalt) which cuts in two the Halle–Leipzig industrial complex is singled out for particular censure. A four-*Länder* proposal (Mecklenburg-Vorpommern, Brandenburg, Sachsen and Thüringen) and a more radical three-*Länder* solution with Sachsen and Thüringen merged are both offered in preference to the current situation.

In December 1992 leaders of the Berlin senate and Brandenburg parliament announced that Berlin and Brandenburg would merge to form one Federal *Land* by the end of the 1990s (*Suddeutsche Zeitung*, 7 December 1992). Between 1993 and 1999, Berlin and Brandenburg authorities will collaborate to draw up regional development plans. The economic planning and development of Brandenburg and Berlin are to be interwoven (*Verflechtungsraum*). Action programmes are expected to focus upon improving economic cooperation, waste disposal, transport, the construction of new airports to serve Berlin and new out of town hypermarkets.

The choice of capital not only for the new Germany but also for each of the new *Länder* was also a contentious issue. In Mecklenburg-Vorpommern, Schwerin (population 130 000) was chosen in preference to the Hanseatic port of Rostock (population 250 000) causing much local political backlash in August 1990 (Weiland *et al.*, 1991). Similarly, Magdeburg (288 000) was chosen over Halle (321 000) as the capital of Sachsen-Anhalt.

The unification of the two Germanies has fundamentally affected spatial patterns of population distribution and composition. Nine key points are outlined below:

A new population distribution

The German population is distributed very unevenly across the 16 *Länder*. Greater Berlin, with a population of over 3.4 million is the largest city in the new Germany and is expected to grow in size especially as a result of its designation as capital and seat of government for the new Germany (see Chapter 7). Elsewhere in the new Germany, regional concentrations of population are to be found in the Rhein–Ruhr region (some 5 million people) and the Rhein–Main and Rhein–Neckar regions, focused upon the cities of Frankfurt, Wiesbaden, Mainz, Mannheim and Ludwigshafen (see Figure 5.1). In addition, there are the regional capitals of Stuttgart and München, the city states of Bremen and Hamburg and in the new *Länder* the major industrial cities of Leipzig and Dresden. These urban concentrations contrast greatly with the thinly populated areas of the North German plain, the Eifel mountains, the Hunsrück, the *Bayerischer Wald* and large tracts of Brandenburg and Mecklenburg-Vorpommern.

A lower population density in the new *Länder*

Population density varies markedly between the old and new *Länder*. In the east there are only 171 people per sq. kilometre while in the west the figure is 244 people per sq. kilometre. Several of the new *Länder*, in particular Mecklenburg-Vorpommern and Brandenburg, have population densities lower than those recorded in the western *Länder*. Mecklenburg-Vorpommern in fact, while larger in area than Hessen and Schleswig-Holstein, has the lowest population density in the new Germany. Excluding the united Berlin only Thüringen and Sachsen have population densities higher than certain of the western *Länder* (see Figure 5.2).

A higher proportion of East Germans live in rural areas

In the new *Länder* there is a recognisable south–north gradient in terms of population density, with the north sparsely populated and mainly agriculture-based and the south densely populated and heavily industrialised. For example, over 55% of the population of Mecklenburg-Vorpommern live in rural *Kreise* compared to only 18% in Sachsen. A comparison of the two Germanies shows that 32% of the West German population live in towns and cities (c.f. 27% in the new *Länder*—many of whom are living in the *Gross Siedlungen* (see chapter 2)) while a further 19% are living in densely populated areas (c.f. 6% in the new *Länder*). In addition, while only 17% of West Germans live in rural areas, some 34% of East Germans are rural based. Unification has magnified the difference between densely populated and thinly-settled areas of the country.

A new pattern of central places

Contrasting economic and political systems in the two Germanies have promoted very different settlement patterns. The basic feature of the settlement pattern in the old *Länder* is a uniform distribution of central places of medium and large size, each well connected by a dense network of road and rail links. Their development as central places can be explained by

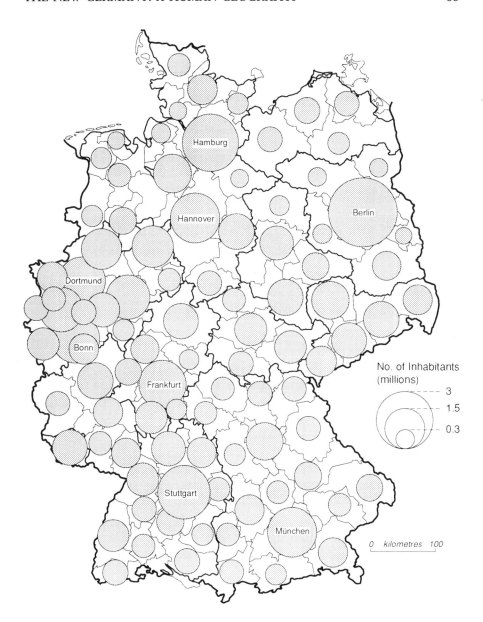

Figure 5.1 *The new Germany: population* (*Source*: Raumordnungsbericht, 1991)

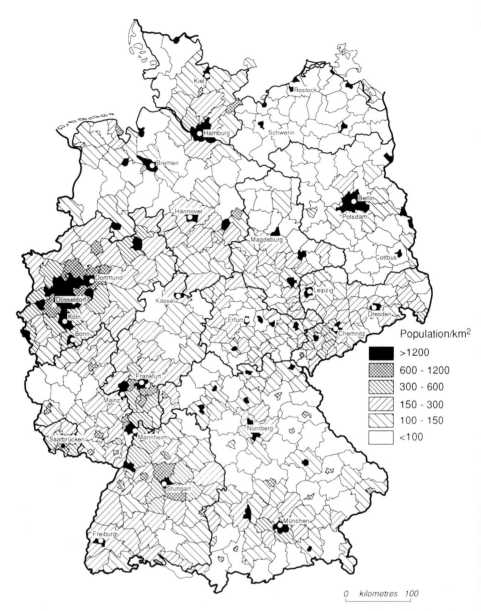

Figure 5.2 *The new Germany: population density* (*Source*: Raumordnungsbericht, 1991)

Table 5.2   *Population of largest cities in the new Germany*

Old Länder		New Länder	
West Berlin	2 068 313		
Hamburg	1 603 070		
		Ost Berlin	1 260 921
München	1 211 617		
Köln	937 482		
Frankfurt a.m.	625 258		
Essen	620 594		
Dortmund	587 328		
Düsseldorf	569 641		
Stuttgart	562 658		
		Leipzig	549 230
Bremen	535 058		
Duisburg	527 447		
		Dresden	521 205
Hannover	498 495		
Nürnberg	480 078		
Bochum	389 087		
Wüppertal	371 283		
		Chemnitz	313 238
Bielefeld	311 946		

Source: Raumordungsbericht, 1991.

the long tradition of independence accorded to small and medium-sized states historically in Germany and upon which the federal principles of West Germany have been based. In the new *Länder*, on the other hand, the settlement pattern has been considerably modified by the operation of the centrally planned economy, exemplified by the regional specialisation of economic activities, state housing policy and socialist methods of agricultural organisation. Consequently, a network of efficient central places has been poorly developed, towns and cities have become densely populated while rural regions are thinly settled. The suburbanisation process, a main feature of the old *Länder*, has been much less pronounced in the east, thus rendering the difference between urban and rural areas much more distinct. For example, 51% of the *Gemeinden* in Mecklenburg-Vorpommern have fewer than 500 inhabitants; these *Gemeinden* account for only 9.4% of the total population. However, the two cities of Rostock (population *c.* 250 000) and Schwerin (*c.* 127 000) account for almost 20% of the population of the *Land*.

Table 5.2 shows that compared to the old *Länder* the new *Länder* (with the exception of Ost Berlin) have very few large central places. Excluding Ost Berlin, only three cities in the new *Länder* are included in the top 20 largest in the new Germany. Leipzig, the most populated city in the east after

Table 5.3   *Population size classes: new Germany*

	Number of cities	
	Länder	
	Old	New
Population		
> one million	3	1
750 000–one million	1	0
500 000–750 000	7	2
250 000–500 000	12	2
100 000–250 000	45	10

Source: Raumordungsbericht, 1991.

Ost Berlin, is only half the size of München and almost three times smaller than Hamburg. Table 5.3 shows that in the city size range 250 000–500 000 the new *Länder* have only two cities compared with 12 in the old *Länder*, while for cities between 100 000–250 000 some 45 are recorded in the west compared to only 10 in the east.

Younger East Germans—ageing West Germans

The age/sex pyramid (see Figure 5.3) for the new Germany reveals the outcome of common historical events, particularly the two world wars, greater life expectancy for both West and East Germans and the impact of specific policies designed to affect the population size. The age pyramid for the old *Länder* shows that one in five West Germans is over 60 years old while only 18% of the East German population are in this particular age group. Moreover, there are differences between the old and the new *Länder* at the bottom of the age pyramid, where one in four East Germans is under 20 years old compared with one in five West Germans. It is, however, important to note that the migration of many thousands of younger East Germans away from the new *Länder* since 1990 will no doubt have altered this particular situation.

The age structure of the German population also varies regionally (see Figures 5.4 and 5.5). The percentage of young people—i.e. under 20 years in the population—varies greatly between the old and the new *Länder*. Low percentages are found in those most densely populated regions of the old *Länder*: for example, München, Düsseldorf, Bochum. High percentages, on the other hand, are found almost exclusively in the new *Länder*. The proportion of employable people, namely aged between 20 and 65, also varies across the regions of the new Germany. Regions with a high percentage of employable people coincide with those which, in the past, experienced high in-migration rates: for example, Stuttgart, Köln, Bonn and

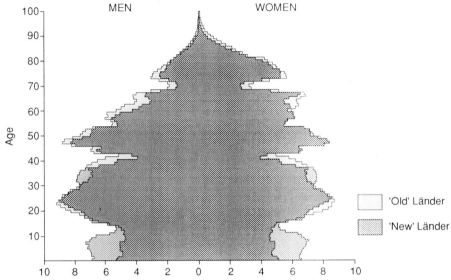

Figure 5.3 *The new Germany: population pyramid* (*Source*: Raumordnungsbericht, 1991)

München. Regions recording low percentages are generally those experiencing out-migration. In the new *Länder*, the industrialised southern area of Sachsen and the sparsely populated regions in Mecklenburg-Vorpommern are significant in this respect. Areas with a high proportion of elderly people—i.e. those over 65—include the middle Neckar and southern Bayern in the old *Länder* and parts of Sachsen, Thüringen and Brandenburg in the new *Länder*.

A higher birth rate among East Germans

Birth rates also vary between the new and the old *Länder*. While the birth rate between 1949 and 1974 was broadly comparable between the two Germanies, from the late 1970s, following measures introduced by the East German authorities to encourage women to have two or preferably more children, the East German crude birth rate reached over 14 per 1000 by the early 1980s compared with 10 births per 1000 in West Germany. Currently, the new *Länder* record a slightly higher crude birth rate (12 births/1000) than the old *Länder* (11 births/1000). Birth rates are regionally differentiated in the new Germany. Generally speaking, lower rates are recorded in urbanised regions in both the old and the new *Länder*: for example, in Rhein-Main and Sachsen. Conversely, the highest birth rates, especially in

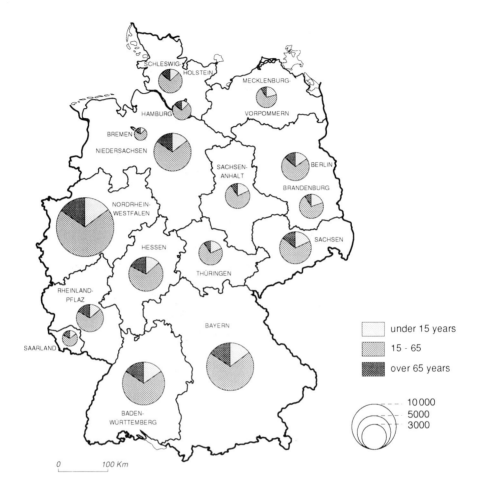

Figure 5.4 *The new Germany: population age structure*
(*Source*: Raumordnungsbericht, 1991)

the new *Länder*, are recorded in the more peripheral agricultural regions,
notably in Mecklenburg-Vorpommern where the crude birth rate exceeds
13.5/1000 (see Figure 5.6).

Death rates—highest in West and East German industrial regions

Death rates also vary between the new and the old *Länder*. Life expectancy
for those living in West Germany is higher for both men and women. West
German men can expect to live some 2.3 more years while women can

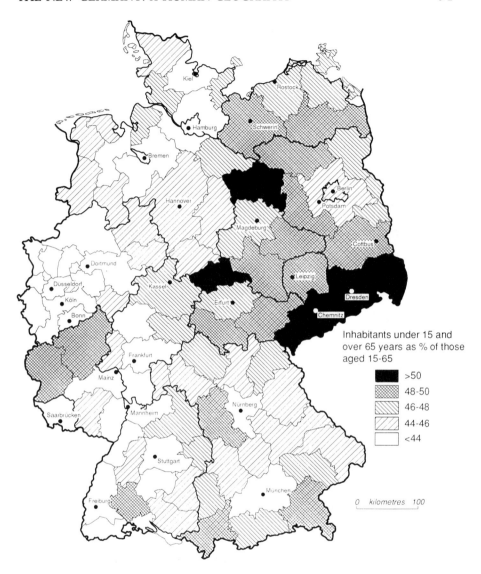

Figure 5.5   *The new Germany: age structure (dependency ratios)*
(*Source*: Raumordnungsbericht, 1991)

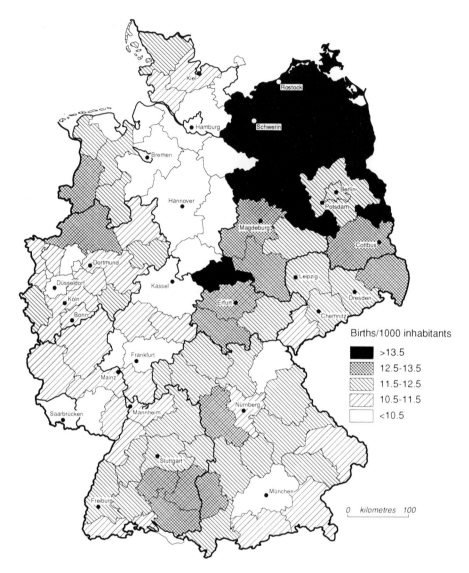

Figure 5.6   *The new Germany: crude birth rates* (*Source*: Raumordnungsbericht, 1991)

expect to live some 2.8 years longer than their East German fellow citizens. The regional pattern of death rates in the new Germany is not easy to interpret (see Figure 5.7). In the old *Länder* the highest death rates are recorded in certain heavily industrialised areas: for example, the Ruhr and in certain agricultural areas such as OstHolstein in Schleswig-Holstein. In both regions crude death rates vary between 12.5 to 13.5/1000. In the new *Länder* lowest rates are found in the north notably in Mecklenburg-Vorpommern, while the highest recorded rates are to be found in the heavy industrialised regions of Sachsen where crude death rates exceed 13.5/1000.

New journey-to-work patterns for east Germans

Migration represents the other component of population change in the new Germany. Since unification migration between the new and old *Länder* is regarded as an internal issue, and precise statistics on flows are not easy to obtain. There is no doubt, however, that German unification and the economic transformation of the new *Länder* has created new migration flows. For example, it is estimated that over 500 000 East Germans are currently commuting between the new and the old *Länder*. Figure 5.8 shows the regional net migration picture, though based upon data for 1990. Areas of strong positive net migration include Greater Berlin, southern Baden-Württemberg and southern Bayern. Areas of migration loss in the old *Länder* include the peripheral upland (for example, the Hunsrück in Rheinland-Pfalz) and coastal areas (such as Emsland and western Schleswig-Holstein), while in the new *Länder* large tracts of territory are experiencing population out-migration. For example, Meincke (1993) estimates that in 1990–1 Mecklenburg-Vorpommern experienced a net migration loss of 50 000 people.

A lower proportion of foreign workers and their families in east Germany

German unification presented two very different situations with regard to immigrant populations (*Ausländer*). In West Germany in 1990 there were 5.4 million *Ausländer* accounting for 8.2% of the total West German population. About 60% of them had been living in West Germany for 10 years or more and some 1.03 million are children and juveniles of whom approximately two-thirds were born in Germany. As discussed in Chapter 3, the foreign population in West Germany is very heavily concentrated regionally. In some *Länder* such as Baden-Württemberg the percentage of foreigners in the total resident population is significantly above the federal average. In some cities in Hessen such as Frankfurt-am-Main and Offenbach foreigners comprise over 20% of the total population.

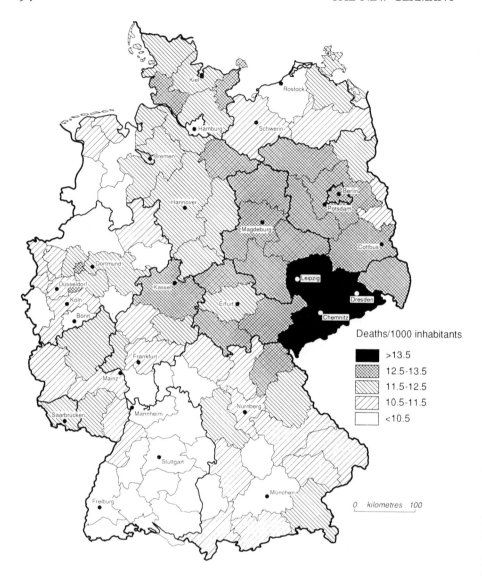

Figure 5.7 *The new Germany: crude death rates* (*Source*: Raumordnungsbericht, 1991)

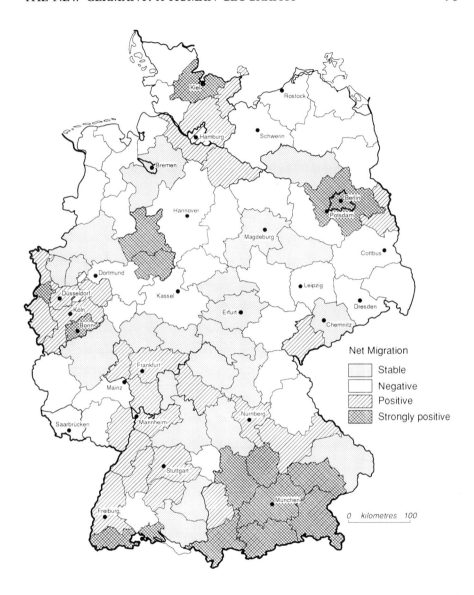

Figure 5.8 *The new Germany: net migration* (*Source*: Raumordnungsbericht, 1991)

In east Germany at the beginning of 1990 there were 191 200 *Ausländer*, of whom 81.4% were from one of five countries: Vietnam, Mozambique, Poland, Hungary and the former USSR. Unlike in west Germany, *Ausländer* accounted for only 1.2% of the total East German population. Some 90 600 *Ausländer* had come to East Germany on the basis of labour agreements (*Vertragsarbeitnehmer*) signed between the GDR authorities and various third countries (Hungary 1967 and 1973, Algeria 1974, Cuba 1978, Mozambique 1979, Vietnam 1980, Angola 1984 and China 1986). The Vietnamese, totalling over 60 000, were the largest group of foreign workers in East Germany in 1990. The majority of all foreign workers were men, with women representing less than 30% of the foreign population in the country. Moves towards German unification in 1990 resulted in the formal termination of the labour agreements between the GDR and Angola, Mozambique and Vietnam, while China and Cuba had ordered their workers home soon after the breaching of the Berlin Wall in 1989 (Herrmann, 1992). However, foreign workers were allowed a general right to stay for the contract period initially agreed upon by the GDR authorities. Funds (approximately DM3000/person) were also available from the German authorities to support the return home of those *Ausländer* in East Germany. By the end of 1990 many Angolans and Vietnamese workers had chosen to return home. Others, particularly Vietnamese, had sought political asylum in the old *Länder*. By the middle of 1991, therefore, only 6670 *Ausländer* from the former labour agreement countries were registered as employed in the new *Länder*. This figure comprised 4000 Vietnamese, 962 people from Mozambique, 50 Angolans, 552 Poles (non-commuters) and 1106 Poles (commuters).

ECONOMIC PROFILE OF THE NEW GERMANY

Calculations of the regional Gross Domestic Product (GDP) per capita show the extent of the economic disparities in the new Germany. Even within the territory of the former GDR in 1990, per capita GDP ranged from 78% in Mecklenburg-Vorpommern to 135% in Sachsen-Anhalt (average = 100%). However, it is not the extent of the differences in wealth between areas of the new *Länder*, significant as they are, but the magnitude of the economic gap between the old and the new *Länder* which is most disturbing. At the time of unification in 1990 differences in regional income levels between the old and new *Länder* were estimated to be more acute than those between northern and southern Italy (Selke, 1991). The total GDP for the new *Länder* in 1990 was 353000 million Ostmarks compared with DM2 110 940 million for the old *Länder*. Using an exchange rate of 1 Ostmark = 1DM, GDP per capita in the old *Länder* exceeds that in the new *Länder* by 1.6 times; for an exchange rate of 2:1, by 3.2 times and with a rate of 3:1, by 4.8 times. In all scenarios the new *Länder* have a GDP per

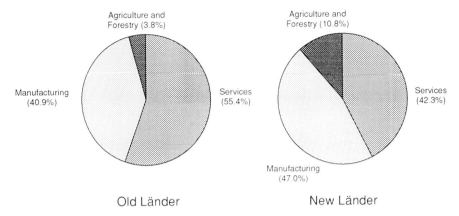

Figure 5.9   *Employment breakdown by economic sector in the old and new Länder*
(*Source*: Raumordnungsbericht, 1991)

capita less than 75% of the average for the EC, thereby joining the ranks of the Mezzogiorno, Greece and most of Iberia as the Community's poorest areas. Most significant is the fact that the new Germany now houses some of the Community's richest and poorest regions.

A comparison of the structure of the labour force between the old and new *Länder* shows a number of key differences—the proportion of the working population employed in the agriculture and forestry sector is almost three times higher in the new than in the old *Länder*; a greater proportion of workers is employed in the manufacturing sector in the new *Länder*; there is a smaller tertiary sector in the new *Länder*, with a significantly lower proportion of total employment accounted for by the financial sector and public and consumer-oriented services (see Figure 5.9).

The regional economic structure of the new Germany is characterised by extremely problematic sector concentrations, especially in the new *Länder* (see Figures 5.10 and 5.11). The key task of the modernisation of the new *Länder* is the diversification of a monolithic economy dominated over-whelmingly by heavy industry. Almost 85% of total industrial production in the new *Länder* in 1990 was accounted for by seven industrial sectors:

- mechanical engineering and motor car manufacture;
- electronics, precision engineering and optical goods;
- chemicals;
- steel and non-ferrous metals;
- textiles;
- foodstuffs;
- construction materials.

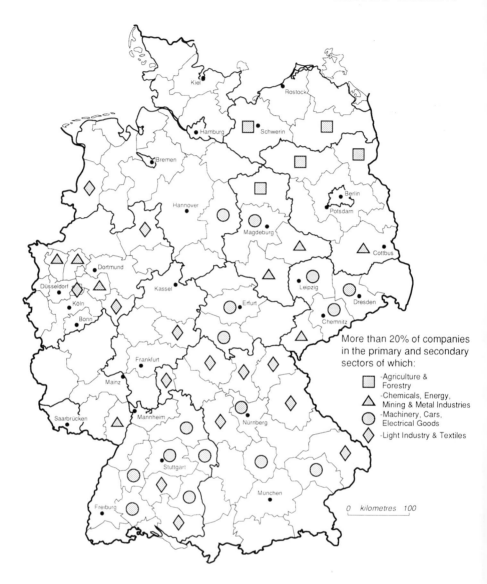

Figure 5.10 *The new Germany: regional economic specialisation*
(Source: Raumordnungsbericht, 1991)

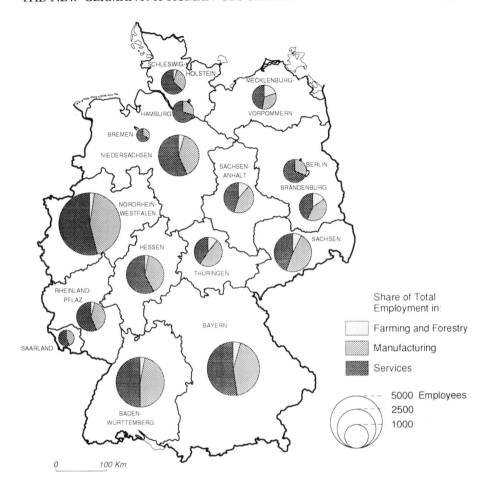

Figure 5.11 *The new Germany: regional economic structure*
(*Source*: Raumordnungsbericht, 1991)

The mechanical engineering, chemicals, and steel industries alone accounted for roughly half of all industrial production in the new *Länder* in 1990. A closer look at some of these seven key sectors reveals major differences between the old and the new *Länder* particularly in terms of productivity and technology.

The chemicals industry in the new *Länder*, which employed 140 000 workers in 1990, is in large part based upon outdated production processes. Alongside modern petrochemical plants there are many factories (especially for the production of synthetic fibres) which date back to the pre-war era.

The majority of chemical products manufactured in the new *Länder* in 1990 required little processing. Where processing did occur it was mainly of a basic nature: for example, brown coal to chemical raw materials. There were very few plants involved in the production of high-value-added chemical products. For example, plastic production accounted for only 12% of chemical products in the East in 1990 compared to 26% in the West. Productivity per worker in the sector as a whole in 1990 was little more than 50% of that in the old *Länder*. Moreover, the chemicals industry in the East due to its over use of brown coal and environmentally unfriendly technological processes is regarded as one of the major sources of pollution. The transition to a more efficient raw materials structure and the closing down of technically obsolete plant are deemed to be essential for the sector's future in the new *Länder*. The large Leuna plant near Leipzig demonstrates particularly well the economic situation of the chemicals industry in the new *Länder*. The 11-sq.-kilometre site employed over 27 000 workers in the late 1980s. However, years of under investment have made much of its manufacturing equipment rusty and obsolete. The plants are linked up by 700 kilometres of pipework, all of which by Leuna's own calculations needs replacing. The plant emits some 17 tonnes of sulphur dioxide into the air every hour as a result of its heavy use of brown coal as fuel. This figure is equivalent to 4% of SO_2 emissions from *all sources* in the old *Länder*.

The textiles sector also demonstrates the relatively low productivity levels of industry in the new compared to the old *Länder*. Per capita output of textiles in the East in 1990 was only 55% of the figure for the West. Textiles production in the East in 1990 was geared towards mass-produced goods from factories built during the 1920s and 1930s. The expectation is that many jobs will be lost in this particular industrial sector in the coming years.

The steel industry in the new *Länder* in 1990 was also characterised by outmoded production processes and productivity levels well below those in the West. Less than 40% of steel plants in the East are capable of using high-technology methods of production. In contrast, the low-cost continuous casting technology used in the West accounts for some 90% of all steel produced. Some 40% of steel produced in the East is manufactured by the open-hearth process—a process that has not been used in the West since the early 1980s. Unlike West German steel companies which have concentrated production on higher-grade steel products, the East German steel industry lacked the finishing capacities to produce other than simple steel products. While the carefully planned development of the steel industry in the old *Länder* has taken place in an EC context of surplus capacity, this was not a consideration in the East where employment in the sector increased considerably throughout the 1980s. However, production levels of steel per worker in the new *Länder* in 1990 were less than 45% of the West German figure.

One of the legacies of the centrally-planned economy is the existence of regions dependent upon single industries. For example, in Spremberg in the *Land* of Brandenburg, 62% (28 000 workers) of the workforce in 1990 were employed in the energy (brown coal) sector; 52% (52 000 workers) of the workforce in Merseburg (Sachsen-Anhalt) were employed in the chemicals industry and a further 42% (33 000 workers) of Bitterfeld's (also Sachsen-Anhalt) workforce were employed in the same industrial sector. In the state of Sachsen, 28% (15 000 workers) of the workforce in Chemnitz and 35% (10 000 workers) of that in Hohenstadt-Ernsthal were employed in the textiles industry in 1990. This rigidity in the labour market is especially problematic for the economic restructuring process.

At the time of unification there were also major differences between the old and new *Länder* with regard to farming. Numbers employed in agriculture, the contribution of farming and forestry to the GDP, the nature and level of agricultural production and the organisational structure of the industry all varied greatly. In 1989, after many decades of economic contraction, farming and forestry employed only 3.8% of the workforce and accounted for 1.8% of the GDP in the old *Länder*. In the new *Länder*, on the other hand, some 10.8% of East Germans were employed in the agricultural sector, which accounted for 9.2% of the GDP. Figure 5.12 shows the regional breakdown of agricultural employment in the new Germany. In most regions of the old *Länder* the proportion of the workforce employed in farming is low and only in a limited number of areas does it exceed 8% (central and southern Bayern, the Hunsrück in Rheinland-Pfalz, Emsland in Niedersachsen and northern and western areas of Schleswig-Holstein). Only in three *Kreise* in the old *Länder* (all in Bayern) is farm employment higher than 14%. This situation contrasts markedly with that in the new *Länder*. In 1989 the majority of *Kreise* in Mecklenburg-Vorpommern and many in Brandenburg had over 26% of their workforce engaged in agriculture. Even in some of the more industrially-based new *Länder* such as Sachsen and Sachsen-Anhalt farming provided a livelihood for over 20% of the workforce (see Figure 5.12).

Approximately 6.2 million hectares of land were used for agricultural purposes in the new *Länder* in 1989: i.e. some 58% of its total territory. By comparison, the figure for the old *Länder* was 12 million hectares: i.e. 48% of its territory. Unlike the old *Länder* the majority of agricultural land in the new *Länder* is under arable crops (76% compared to only 61% in the West). However, the new *Länder* are endowed with large areas of relatively poorer quality soils (see Figure 5.13). Land with a yield classification of below 35 (all German agricultural land is graded according to yields on a scale from 0 (poorest) to 100 (richest)) occupies much of Mecklenburg-Vorpommern and Brandenburg, while the best quality land is restricted to an area lying between Magdeburg–Leipzig–Erfurt. There, soils are graded over

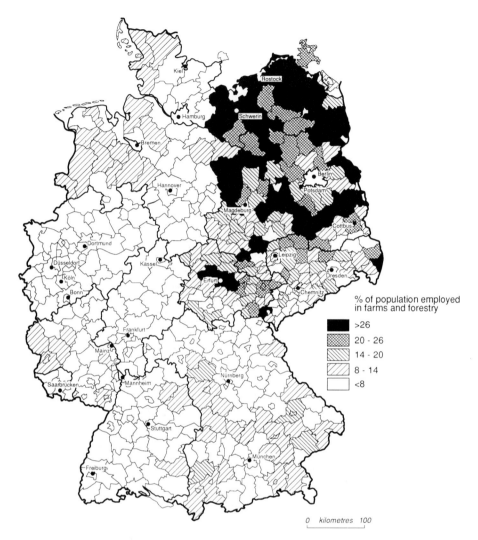

% of population employed
in farms and forestry

■ >26
▨ 20 - 26
▧ 14 - 20
▱ 8 - 14
□ <8

0   kilometres   100

Figure 5.12   *The new Germany: employment in farming and forestry*
(*Source*: Raumordnungsbericht, 1991)

60 on the index and compare with the most fertile lands west of the Rhein
in the old *Länder*. The soil index provides only a partial explanation of the
differences in agricultural productivity between the western and eastern
Länder. In 1989, for example, cereal yields in the eastern *Länder* were only
78% of those in the West. Similarly potato yields were only 70%, sugar beet
62% and milk yields 80% of western values. Poor productivity in farming in

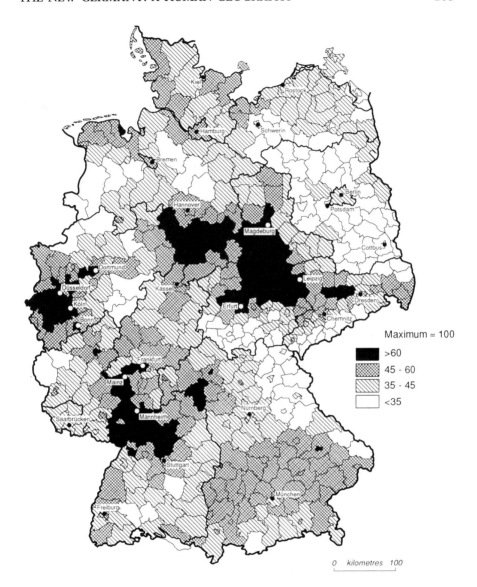

Figure 5.13 *The new Germany: agricultural yield index*
(*Source*: Raumordnungsbericht, 1991)

the new *Länder* is largely blamed on several factors—the lack of technology in the farm sector, work interruptions due to mechanical failure, statutory working hours not adjusted to the work process, lack of motivation in the workforce and high absenteeism rates.

The organisational structure of farming in terms of ownership, employment and the size of holdings also varies greatly between the old and new *Länder*. Some 95% of agricultural land in the East in 1989 was managed by state-owned estates (VEG) and agricultural production cooperatives (LPG), while only 5% was in private hands. This contrasts completely with the situation in the West. While there were 649 000 holdings (i.e. greater than 1 hectare) in the old *Länder* in 1989, there were only 4400 agricultural units in the new *Länder*. However, while the average farm size in the West was 18.2 hectares, the LPGs had an average size of over 4500 hectares. Over two-thirds of agricultural land in the new *Länder* in 1989 was managed by LPGs of between 3000 and 6000 hectares in size. Despite large-scale methods of production, the LPG and VEG units were extremely labour-intensive. It is estimated that labour input in agriculture was 60% higher in the East compared with the West. For example, even if one considers the larger holdings, that is, those over 50 hectares in the old *Länder* where 3.2 workers per 100 hectares were employed, labour input in the eastern farming sector was over four times greater (12.9 workers per 100 hectares). If one includes those working in the LPGs on duties such as machinery repair, construction or administration the figure increases to 14.2 workers per 100 hectares. The reform of the farm sector in the new *Länder* is therefore confronted with very difficult problems relating to agricultural organisation, land ownership and employment impacts.

The energy sector also reveals clear differences between the old and new *Länder* in respect to consumption and supply structures. In the old *Länder* great efforts to develop and apply energy-saving technologies have meant that primary energy consumption in 1989 was at the same level as in the early 1970s. The old *Länder* have also experienced a changing pattern of energy use away from oil and coal to nuclear energy sources. For example, oil accounted for 53% of energy consumption in the old *Länder* in 1970, yet by 1990 the figure had fallen to 40%. Similarly, brown and hard coal accounted for roughly 38% of West German energy consumption in 1970, although by 1990 this had also fallen to 27%. The increasing use of natural gas and nuclear energy sources to supply energy needs has been the most important aspect of the changing energy picture in the old *Länder*. For example, natural gas supplied only 5.5% of West German energy requirements in 1970, yet by 1990 this figure had dramatically increased to 17.7%. Likewise, nuclear energy sources provided less than 1% of energy consumption in 1970, but by 1990 this too had risen sharply to 12.2%.

The development trend and structure of primary energy consumption in the new *Länder* differ fundamentally from the West German picture. Unlike the situation in the old *Länder*, brown coal dominates the energy-supply industry. Since the 1970s this energy source constantly provided between two-thirds and three-quarters of East German energy consumption. Hard coal supplied over 10% of needs in 1970 although mining was stopped in the late 1970s because of exhaustion of deposits. The importing of hard coal from the COMECON countries, albeit on a relatively modest scale (hard coal accounted for 4% of total energy consumption in the new *Länder* in 1989) has replaced domestic sources of supply. Most of the demand for mineral oil and natural gas in 1989 was supplied by the USSR. East Germany's production of oil is insignificant although domestic natural gas production was able to satisfy one-third of consumption requirements in the late 1980s. Nuclear energy sources accounted for a much smaller proportion (2%) of total energy consumption in the new compared to the old *Länder* in 1990.

One of the principal problems in the energy sector in the new *Länder* is that the absence of energy cost-consciousness and obsolete plant have led to some of the highest energy consumption levels in the world. In 1989 per capita energy consumption rates in the new *Länder* were the third highest globally after the USA and Canada. Within the new Germany, therefore, per capita energy consumption of the new *Länder* was 26% above that of the old *Länder* in 1989. High energy consumption levels in the new *Länder* have been compounded by the inadequate heat insulation of East German homes, the inefficient heating systems with which some homes are supplied: for example, the regulation of heat in homes and buildings can often only be achieved by opening windows, and the State policy of providing massive subsidies for energy prices has deterred energy-saving measures.

The task of developing an energy policy for the new Germany is therefore likely to be a difficult one considering the differences in energy supply, consumption and the environmental situation between the old and new *Länder*.

INFRASTRUCTURE IN THE NEW GERMANY

Variations in technical (transport and communications, water supply, waste disposal) and non-technical (cultural, educational and health and welfare provisions) infrastructure provide further evidence of the economic and social contrasts in the new Germany. Improving the quality of technical infrastructure in particular is a major task in the modernisation and economic restructuring of the new *Länder*.

Unification has created a curious picture in the housing market in the new

Table 5.4 *Age of dwellings in the Old and New Länder*

New Länder

Period of Construction	<1918	1919–45	1946–70	1971–90
Multi-family units (%)	29	14	20	37
One- and two-family units (%)	48	30	12	10
(%) of all dwellings	37	13	19	31

Old Länder

	<1918	1919–48	1949–68	1969–87
Multi-family units (%)	16	11	43	30
One- and two-family units (%)	19	14	35	32
(%) of all dwellings	18	12	39	31

Source: Raumordnungsbericht, 1991.

Germany. Substantial differences in housing stock, type and quality as well as ownership levels now exist between the old and the new *Länder*. In the old *Länder* there were over 28.2 million dwellings in the late 1980s, an increase of more than one-third on the 1968 figure. Almost half of all housing is located in buildings with only one or two dwellings, though this figure varies greatly between suburban and central city locations as one might expect. In the new *Länder* 7 million dwellings were recorded at the end of 1991. Of this total, 4.8 million dwellings are multi-family units, normally apartment blocks, and the remainder one-family or two-family houses of which well over one-third are located in rural areas. While only one-third of all dwellings in the old *Länder* were built before 1945, one-half of dwellings in the new *Länder* are of that period, with a large proportion of these being one- or two-family houses. This contrasts greatly with the old *Länder* where over two-thirds of one and two-family houses were built after 1945.

There are great differences between the old and the new *Länder* in terms of the average size of dwellings. The average size of dwelling in the old *Länder* increased from 71 sq. metres in 1968 to 86 sq. metres in 1987. Almost 55% of all dwellings in the old *Länder* are over 80 sq. metres, with a further 36% between 50 and 80 sq. metres. Less than 9% of dwellings are under 50 sq. metres in size. Figures for the new *Länder* starkly contrast with those above. The average dwelling size in the new *Länder* in 1990 was 64 sq. metres, that is, less than the figure recorded for West Germany in 1968. Less than 30% of dwellings are over 80 sq. metres, roughly 50% are between 50 and 80 sq. metres and 20% are under 50 sq. metres in size (over twice the figure for the old *Länder*). Floor space/person also varies between the old and the new *Länder*, with West Germans having on average 10.8 sq. metres more living space than East Germans. For one-person households the difference is as much as 14 sq. metres (see Figure 5.14).

While most Germans living in the old *Länder* would take for granted having a central-heating system, WC and bath in their home (less than one-quarter of dwellings in the old *Länder* do not have central heating), those living in the new *Länder* would regard such basic necessities as luxury comforts. Less than half of all East Germans have centrally heated homes (although the heating systems of those homes do not bear comparison with those in the west). While 86% of homes in the city state of Bremen are centrally heated, only 38% of homes in Sachsen have this facility. Only in Ost Berlin, where 62% of homes have central heating, does the figure broadly compare with the old *Länder*. An inside toilet in the home is also, as Figure 5.15 shows, a basic facility that many East Germans do not possess. Fewer than two-thirds of homes in Sachsen, for example, are provided with this facility.

The ownership structure of housing also reflects the different social and economic policies that prevailed up to 1989. Almost 80% of dwellings in the West are privately owned compared with only 40% in the east. In the old *Länder*, only in the cities of Hamburg and the western part of Berlin, where community housing arrangements exist on a large scale (roughly 30% of all dwellings) is the private ownership pattern significantly broken. State ownership of housing is not a principal feature of the housing market in the old *Länder*, although, by contrast, 41% of dwellings in the new *Länder* are state owned. There is a regional pattern to the level of State ownership of housing in the East, corresponding to periods of State-sponsored construction of dwellings, especially in the 1980s. For example, the highest percentage of state-owned housing is to be found in Ost Berlin (almost 60% of housing there is state owned) which is not surprising given the degree to which the city became the focus for rapid housing construction (principally multi-storey apartment blocks) between 1985 and 1989.

The State policy of renting out apartments and homes at highly subsidised rent levels was largely to blame for the poor condition of a great deal of property in the new *Länder*. While only 9% of all dwellings are classified as being in good order, 40% are in a poor condition, 40% in a serious state of dilapidation and 11% classified as uninhabitable. The modernisation of urban areas of the new *Länder* is therefore a priority for the German authorities, although monetary union between the Ost- and D-Mark has compounded the situation with manifold rent increases.

The transport network in the new *Länder* while dense is characterised by poor quality standards compared to the old *Länder*. In addition the division of Germany after 1945 critically influenced the pattern of transport links within each of the German states. In both states west–east connections were

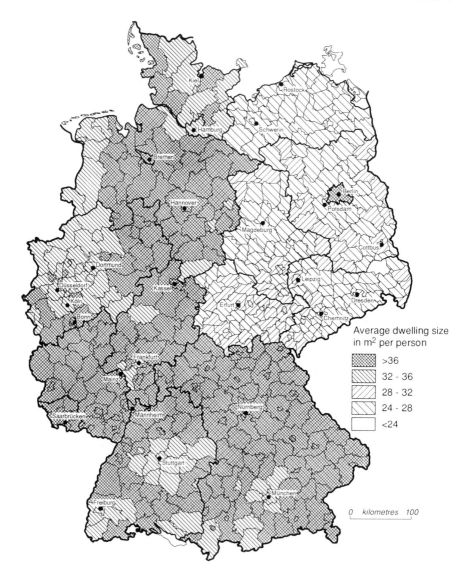

Figure 5.14 *The new Germany: size of dwellings* (*Source*: Raumordnungsbericht, 1991)

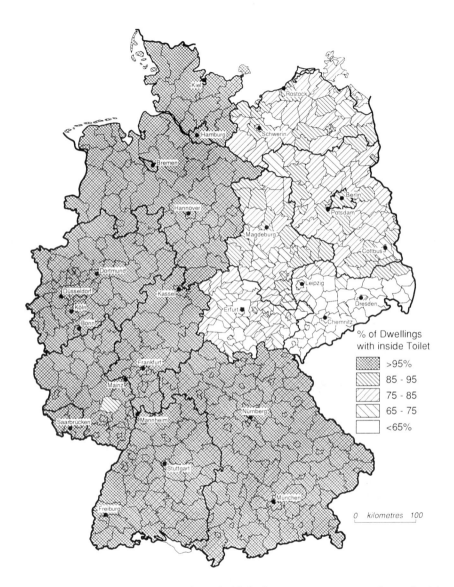

Figure 5.15   *The new Germany: household facilities* (*Source*: Raumordnungsbericht, 1991)

less well developed than those between north and south. For all transport modes there are considerable differences between the old and new *Länder* in terms of age of equipment, transport investment and state of repair. For example, the state of repair of the road system in the new *Länder* is visibly worse than in the old *Länder*. Some 21% of all roads in the new *Länder* are defined as being in a poor or very poor condition, while in rural areas the percentage is as high as 40%. The age of construction, for example of road bridges, also reflects the neglect given to maintaining an efficient transport system. Over 30% of all road bridges in the new *Länder* are over 70 years old, while 17% of them were built in the late-19th century.

The rail system in the new *Länder*, despite the high percentage of goods and raw material transported by rail compared to West Germany, also clearly shows the low level of investment devoted by the GDR authorities. Almost one-fifth of all track can only be used by locomotives travelling at reduced speeds making journeys more time-consuming, even over relatively short distances. Track speed limits in the new *Länder* are some 20–30% below those in the West.

The inland waterways and air transport systems do not reveal a better picture. For example, some 12% of the locks on the Elbe waterway in the new *Länder* are not functioning, making navigated passage difficult. Limited passenger use and poor airport facilities characterise the air transport system in the new *Länder*. While the 12 main airports in the old *Länder* handled some 80 million passengers in 1990, only 2.4 million passengers passed through the four GDR airports (Berlin Schonefeld, Leipzig, Dresden and Erfurt) in the same year.

In 1989 there were approximately 50 telephone subscribers per hundred inhabitants in West Germany, while in East Germany there were roughly 10. Some nine in every 10 households in the West had a telephone connection, whereas only every sixth household in the East had one. The pattern of telephone ownership was also regionally differentiated. In the former GDR capital, Ost Berlin, every second household had a telephone; in Rostock or Dresden, on the other hand, only every ninth household was connected to the telephone system. In addition, approximately 2000 of the more remote rural districts of the new *Länder* were not connected by telephone.

Water supply and waste disposal methods also reveal significant differences between the old and the new *Länder*. Of particular concern is the relatively high percentage of households in the new *Länder* (up to 25% in some regions) which are not connected to the public water supply and sewerage systems and the poor quality of drinking water in heavily-industrialised areas in the south, especially Leipzig-Halle, Chemnitz, Cottbus and Erfurt.

Table 5.5   *Health care in the New Germany (per 10 000 inhabitants)*

	Old *Länder*	New *Länder*
Doctors	29	24
Dentists	6	7
Pharmacists	6	2
Hospital beds	110	98

Source: Raumordnungsbericht, 1991.

It is generally regarded that the health and social welfare provisions of the GDR were adequate, though facilities offered could not hope to compare with those in the West in terms of quality. For example, there were 29 doctors per 10 000 inhabitants in the old *Länder* in 1990 compared to 24 per 10 000 inhabitants in the new *Länder*, although these figures fail to show the conditions under which doctors were working in the new *Länder*, and the limited availability of specialist medical practitioners compared to West Germany.

Shortage of labour in the GDR led the authorities to place a high priority on the extensive provision of child care facilities and generous maternity benefits with the dual aims of keeping women at work and to produce more (potential) workers. Even by the early 1980s differences between West and East Germany in terms of maternity leave provision were marked. While both East and West German women were given six weeks' leave before the birth of the child, only eight weeks' leave on full maternity pay were granted after the birth in the West compared to 20 weeks in the East. By the time of German unification, East Germany had developed the most generous maternity provisions to be found in any country, with East German women entitled to a full year's leave on full pay after having a baby. The GDR authorities had also placed a great deal of emphasis on child care facilities after mothers had returned to work. By 1989 therefore, around 790 crèches had been set up with over 353 000 places for children under three years. Some 56% of East German children of this age were cared for by crèche provisions. In West Germany, crèche provision was privately operated and compared to the situation in East Germany was poorly developed with only a little more than 1000 crèches across the country with places for only 28 300 children. Only 1.6% of West German children under three years were cared for by crèche provisions, reflecting the lower proportion of West German women in the labour market. Kindergarten provision for three- to six-year olds was also well developed in the East. Almost one million Kindergarten places were on offer in East Germany in 1989, and some 94% of children of this age were cared for.

Despite these State provisions encouraging women to have children and also to work, there were considerable pressures upon them in coping with the demands of both, as well as the added toil of daily existence in the GDR: for example, cramped housing conditions and endless struggles and queues to obtain goods of limited choice. These factors help to explain a high divorce rate that ended two marriages in every three in 1989—twice the West German figure.

While provisions were made for the care of the elderly in East Germany, pensioners did not receive the same degree of State support as that devoted to encouraging women to have children and to work. Average net monthly pension per worker in East Germany was barely half an average worker's income. In West Germany, on the other hand, elderly people generally had a wider variety of income sources in addition to their various pensions. Consequently the gap in income per person in the two Germanies in 1989 was greater than that measured simply by the difference in pensions alone.

Education policy in the two Germanies up to 1990 showed both similarities and key differences. In East Germany the whole education system was based upon the Socialist Education Act of 1965, within which school subjects and curricula were fashioned according to socialist principles and set out in a general programme that was binding. Political indoctrination began in the early years of a child's schooling and continued throughout the 10 years of compulsory attendance at the general secondary schools (Allgemein-bildende Polytechnische Oberschüle (POS)). Lessons on Marxist–Leninist interpretations of history and anti-Fascist struggles were supported by visits and short work placements at local factories and state farms where school children could experience socialist doctrine in practice. The 10 years at POS were followed at least for some (roughly 10% of school children) by two years' preparation for university entrance.

As in West Germany, vocational training was also given a high priority in East Germany with apprenticeships controlled and awarded according to the specific requirements of the planned economy. Some 720 vocational training centres were in existence in the new *Länder* in 1990 with over 120 000 young people enrolled on training courses.

The higher-educational sector in the new *Länder* comprises three types of institutions: universities and technical universities, technical colleges and engineering colleges. In total there are 55 higher-education institutions in the new *Länder* with over 40% of them in the state of Sachsen. Despite the larger number of higher-education colleges and universities in the old *Länder* (244 in total including 69 universities), pressure upon student places is equally intense. Whereas in 1969 only 8% of West Germans between 18 and 24 years went on to higher education, in 1991 one in every three members of this age group sought a university place. Increased demand has in part been controlled by tightening selection procedures, restricting sources of funding for students and by expanding existing universities in the old *Länder* particularly through the employment of more teaching staff. For such subjects as engineering, student numbers have been allowed to increase in both the old and new *Länder* since 1980 (172% increase in the old *Länder* between 1980 and 1989, 110% increase in the new *Länder* over the same period). Engineering students now account for over half of the total student body in the new Germany.

ENVIRONMENTAL SITUATION IN THE NEW GERMANY

Arguably one of the most significant distinctions between the old and the new *Länder* in Germany is with regard to the state of the environment. In West Germany the growth in environmental consciousness since the 1970s has had a major impact upon public policy priorities. This process is reflected in the reduction of emission levels of most pollutants in West Germany over the last few decades. For example, dust levels stood at 1.8 million tonnes in 1966, increased to 3.2 million tonnes in 1980 but had dropped to 0.55 million tonnes by the late 1980s. Similarly, SO_2 emissions fell from 3.4 million tonnes in 1966 to 2.2 million tonnes by 1988. Figure 5.16 shows the geographical distribution of sources of SO_2 emissions in the new Germany. In West Germany, although the Ruhr and the Rhein–Main regions remain the regional focuses of air pollution, considerable efforts have been made and success achieved in reducing pollution levels in both regions. For example, the dust fall-out in the Ruhr cities decreased by 63% between 1964 and 1988. In addition, tremendous efforts have been made to clean up the region's rivers including the Ruhr itself. Since the 1960s some 14 dams have been constructed along the upper reaches of the Ruhr, and 53 water collection works and 144 sewage plants, including the largest sewage plant in Europe at the mouth of the river Emscher, have also been built. The Ruhr has, in the space of 25 years, become the cleanest 'industrial' river in Germany. Environmental conservation in the Ruhr has been broadly based. For example in the 1980s well over 1400 hectares of slag heaps, 2000 hectares of wasteland and some 150 hectares of waste dumps were systematically regreened and reafforested.

The environmental situation in the new *Länder* contrasts greatly with that of the West. Air, water and soil have become heavily polluted and endanger general health and the natural environment. While, as shown above, emission levels fell consistently in the West over the last 25 years, in the East, they increased. For example, SO_2 emission densities in the new *Länder* increased from 39.4 tonnes/sq. kilometre in 1980 to 48.1 tonnes/sq. kilometre in 1988. Air pollution is concentrated in the Leipzig/Halle/Bitterfeld and Cottbus areas. Its high level is attributed to the energy policy pursued by

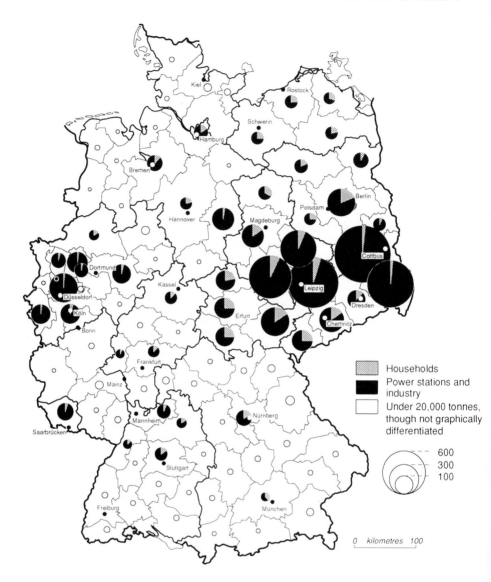

Figure 5.16 *The new Germany: SO$_2$ emissions* (*Source*: Raumordnungsbericht, 1991)

East Germany since the 1950s, in particular the dependence upon brown coal (70% of the energy sources used), outmoded and inefficient energy conversion technologies (50% of steam generators and 36% of steam turbines are over 20 years old), high levels of primary energy consumption (220 Gjoules/person is 25% higher than in West Germany) and a high percentage of energy-intensive production (such as aluminium products).

While in West Germany water quality measures have been in existence since the early 1970s, in East Germany there has been catastrophic disregard for water quality protection. Water quality levels therefore differ greatly between the old and new *Länder*. With an annual rainfall level of only 662 millimetres (West Germany, 877 millimetres) and the prolonged absence of effective environmental legislation, the new *Länder* have serious water quality problems. The main causes of water pollution in the new *Länder* have been inadequate control of effluent from industrial concerns, the lack of, or inadequate treatment capacity for, industrial and domestic water waste; the uncontrolled dumping of domestic and special waste; the discharge of various pollutants; and the discharge of organic waste products from farming. As a result almost half of East German water is unusable for drinking and only usable in part for industrial purposes, while a further 38% is only suitable for use as drinking water after complex treatment procedures. Brown-coal mining has also created serious difficulties for the water supply as a result of the lowering of the water table in areas of extensive coal extraction. In Sachsen for example, the ground water level has fallen by 80 metres in certain brown-coal mining areas.

CONCLUSIONS

This chapter has shown clearly that building on the common basis prior to 1945 the political and economic systems in the old and new *Länder* have created contrasting economic profiles, settlement patterns, labour markets, transport and communication links and environmental situations. The tasks of German unification are to create a modern capitalist economy in the new *Länder*, raise living standards, reduce economic disparities between the old and new *Länder*, clean up the environment and to link western and eastern Germany through infrastructure projects. The scale of these tasks *and* the degree to which they are being achieved are addressed in the following chapter.

SUGGESTED FURTHER READING

Dickinson, R.E. (1953) *Germany: A General and Regional Geography*. Methuen, London.
Mellor, R.E.H. (1978) *The Two Germanies. A Modern Geography*. Harper and Row, London.

Merkl, P. (ed.) (1989) *The Federal Republic at Forty*. New York University Press, New York.

Moreton, E. (ed.) (1987) *Germany between East and West*. Cambridge University Press, Cambridge.

Thomaneck, J.K. and Mellis, J. (1989) *Politics, Society and Government in the GDR. Basic Documents*. Berg, Oxford.

Wilkins, H. (1981) *The Two German Economies*. Gower, Aldershot.

6 Modernisation of East Germany since 1990

This chapter examines the priorities and mechanisms for the modernisation of the new *Länder*, the financial costs involved and assesses the progress made. It highlights the huge scale of the task of transforming a command economy to one that is market-led and emphasises the economic and social costs of the process.

REFORM PROCESS: PRIORITIES

Given the differences in wealth between western and eastern Germany, special financial arrangements and programmes have been introduced in an attempt to reduce income disparities. Following unification, the financial relationship between the Federal government and the *Länder* was modified to accommodate the new *Länder*. This was especially so with the proceeds of the sales tax which were normally divided in the ratio 65% to the Federal government and 35% to the *Länder*. Provisions were made for the new *Länder* to receive a greater share of proceeds over the period 1990–4. The financial equalisation law (*Finanzausgleichgesetz*), which had ensured the transfer of funds from richer to poorer West German *Länder* under the Basic Law, was also affected by unification, with the Federal government announcing a *Sonderstatus* (special situation) between the Federation (*Bund*) and the West German *Länder* up until January 1995 in order to grant preferential treatment to the new *Länder*. The transfer of monies to the new *Länder* was to be achieved through the creation of a German Unity Fund (*Fonds Deutsche Einheit*), to which DM115 billion were allocated for the five-year period 1990–4. Some 83% (DM95 billion) of this amount was to be obtained through borrowing on the international money markets. These measures, it was hoped, would significantly increase the relative prosperity of the new *Länder* in a short period.

The privatisation of East German industry and farming, labour-market measures (in particular retraining schemes), environmental clean-up, urban improvements and infrastructure projects were the priorities for Federal government expenditure in the new *Länder*. While some of these goals have been financed from the Unity Fund, it is impossible to be precise about the true financial costs to West Germany of unification. For example, borrowing by the Treuhandanstalt for privatisation and restructuring of East German companies is not part of the Unity Fund allocations. Consequently, in March 1992 the Bundesbank reported that net transfers from West to East Germany in the previous year had totalled over DM139 billion: i.e. equivalent to over 5% of West Germany's national product (Jeffries, 1992) and, staggeringly, some DM24 billion greater than the entire five-year budgetary allocation of the Unity Fund.

The retraining of the East German workforce is seen as an important element in the economic transformation of the new *Länder*. Since October 1990 the West German Employment Promotion Law (*Arbeitsförderungsgesetz*) has been extended to the new *Länder*. In 1991 more than DM25 billion were spent on labour-market measures in the new *Länder*. Short-time work payments (*Kurzarbeitergeld*), training and retraining grants (*Ausbildungsförderung*), and programmes to facilitate employment acquisition (*Arbeitsbeschäffungsmassnahmen*) have been the main elements of budgetary expenditure (Bundesministerium für Wirtschaft, 1992, 'Wirtschaftliche Förderung in den neuen Bundesländer'). By the end of 1991 some 550 000 East German workers were enrolled on training schemes. The Federal Ministry of Labour and Social Affairs has also offered early retirement schemes, and by early 1992 over 450 000 East Germans had taken up the offer.

Improving transport links between the old and new *Länder* is also regarded as a high priority. The poor transport infrastructure is viewed as a major obstacle to the privatisation and restructuring of the East German economy. As a result, a specific transport plan for uniting the two Germanies was announced in 1992 which involves a projected DM56 billion of investment in new and existing road, rail and canal links.

The critical environmental situation in the new *Länder* also required immediate Federal action. Emergency measures to deal with the most serious environmental problems were introduced soon after unification. In total, 462 emergency projects were funded with clean-up costs estimated at DM310 million. These included projects to improve the quality of drinking water, the prevention of soil contamination, the improvement of sewerage systems and the conversion of some power stations from brown coal to oil and gas use.

The transformation of the agricultural sector, in particular the break-up of the collective farms, and the improvement of living conditions in East Germany's rural areas were also deemed as essential. Similarly, towns and cities were in urgent need of modernisation, with housing often in a serious state of disrepair.

These priorities were outlined in a special programme for boosting the East German economy (*Gemeinschaftswerk Aufschwung Ost*) which was

Table 6.1   *Programme to boost the east German economy (Gemeinschaftswerk Aufschwung Ost): expenditure categories (DM bn.)*

	1991	1992
Local authority programmes (schools, hospitals etc.)	5.0	0
Job creation measures	2.5	3.0
Transport	1.4	4.2
Housing and urban redevelopment	1.1	1.1
Measures to attract private investors	0.4	0.6
Special programme—regional economic promotion	0.6	0.6
Aid to shipyards	0.1	0.4
Emergency environmental measures	0.4	0.4
Higher education institutes	0.2	0.2
Restoration of government buildings	0.2	0.05
Other	0	1.4
Total	12.0	12.0

Source: Raumordnungsbericht, 1991.

announced in March 1991 and to which DM24 billion were to be allocated between 1991 and 1993 (Table 6.1). The overall aim of the programme is to promote investment and to create jobs in the new *Länder*. The main emphases are upon local authority investment, job creation measures, support for private investment, regional economic promotion, aid to shipyards, environmental protection, housing and urban redevelopment, transport improvements and educational facilities (Raumordungsbericht, 1991).

Between 1990 and the announcement of the *Gemeinschaftswerk Aufschwung Ost* programme, considerable amounts of public funds were poured into East Germany in an effort to improve the fabric of urban and rural areas. In 1990 alone over DM1 billion were used to preserve historic areas in several East German towns including Chemnitz (Sachsen) and Wittenberg (Sachsen-Anhalt). Buildings of historic importance were selected for major renovation work. In the latter part of 1990 several towns were chosen as 'model towns' for renovation–preservation projects. Cottbus (Brandenburg), Gorlitz (Sachsen) and Jena (Thüringen) were among those towns chosen. In total some DM100 million were allocated for preservation measures in these and five other towns in the new *Länder*. Financial assistance was also given to local authorities in rural areas to improve facilities, village organisation and rural communications.

Some DM2.2 billion have been allocated to urban renovation and housing improvements under the *Gemeinschaftswerk Aufschwung Ost* programme for the period 1991–2. The provision by the East German authorities of low-quality rental housing, especially apartment blocks with rents fixed at

1936 levels, meant that many housing areas were in urgent need of attention at the time of German unification. Urban development was, therefore, of crucial importance in the modernisation of the new *Länder*. The Federal government has introduced several measures for the modernisation of housing and to encourage the private ownership of property. A subsidy of 20% of the purchase price (maximum DM7000) is offered to those wishing to purchase property previously rented from the State.

In August 1990 the West German programme to improve regional economic structure (*Verbesserung der regionalen Wirtschaftsstruktur*) was extended to the new *Länder* and Ost Berlin. At the same time it was decided that the former western frontier region between the two Germanies (Zonenrandgebiet) would no longer qualify for special Federal assistance after 1994. West Berlin was also to lose its privileged status for Federal subsidies.

In addition, as well as qualifying for Federal and *Länder* monies, the new *Länder* were to be eligible for European Community assistance (see Chapter 7). The European Community will jointly fund projects which aim to reduce long-term unemployment, improve economic infrastructure and which improve living and working conditions in rural regions.

INDUSTRIAL CHANGE, PRIVATISATION AND THE ROLE OF THE TREUHANDANSTALT

This section examines the role of the Treuhandanstalt (THA) in the modernisation of the economy of the new *Länder*. With German unification in October 1990, the Federal government took on the task of transforming the centralised command economy of the former GDR and integrating it into the social market economy of West Germany. The THA was given the unenviable task of carrying out the privatisation of both the industrial and agricultural sectors of the former GDR. As was shown in Chapter 2, over 90% of economic activity in the GDR in 1989 was in the form of State-controlled enterprises (*Kombinats*), operated from the central State ministries on the basis of detailed production targets and particular arrangements for subsidies and foreign-trade dealings. The 126 *Kombinats*, employing on average 20 000 workers, were to be broken up and transferred to private ownership, and if buyers could not be found, were to be closed.

Article 25 of the *Einigungsvertrag* (Unification Treaty) set out the precise task of the THA: 'the THA shall be charged with restructuring and privatising the former publicly owned enterprises to bring them into line with the requirements of a competitive economy'. The THA was therefore faced with the difficult task of privatising an economy that was characterised by over-specialisation on industrial production, obsolete capital equipment and product ranges, inefficient production techniques and the suppression of all forms of entrepreneurship. The first task of the THA was to break up the *Kombinats* into some 8 000 enterprises in order to facilitate purchase by West or East Germans or indeed foreign investors. Privatisation of former State enterprises took the form of conversion into limited liability or stock companies, both based upon the West German model. There are, however, certain properties in East Germany that do not fall within the privatisation remit of the THA. These include enterprises controlled by the municipalities and the former *Bezirke* as well as accompanying land. These have acquired trustee ownership by the Federal government. In addition the post and telecommunications (Deutsche Post) and rail (Deutsche Reichsbahn) industries of the former GDR are excluded from THA responsibilities.

The THA is based in Ost Berlin and has regional offices in each of the new *Länder*. The executive board of the THA includes representatives from the Federal ministries of finance and economy, the five new *Länder* and worker organisations. The THA is organised into eight administrative divisions: industrial sectors 1–6 (sector 3 includes agriculture and the food industry) and two other sectors dealing with personnel and finance. Most of the key posts in the THA are occupied by West German professionals brought in on account of their business experience.

There are *three* priorities for the THA:

- to privatise wherever possible;
- to restructure companies with a view to later privatisation;
- to close companies that have no competitive possibility.

The privatisation of former State-owned enterprises by the THA involves widespread advertising in an effort to attract as many potential buyers as possible. This enables the THA to gain a realistic assessment of the company's value (THA, 1991). No restrictions are placed upon domestic or foreign enterprises investing in the new *Länder* as long as they comply with European Community competition policies. Investors are able to acquire a 100% holding in East German companies. However, the THA pays particular attention to three issues when considering applications for company purchase:

- the retention of jobs;
- the continued operation and modernisation of the company by the purchaser and the investment required to ensure this;
- the implications for the suppliers and subcontractors in the new *Länder*.

In addition to the bidding price in assessing applications, the THA also takes account of the prospective buyer's participation in plans for environmental improvement. Where substantial environmental damage exists, the purchaser has to apply for exemption from bearing the full clean-up costs under the German Environmental Act (*Umweltrahmengesetz*). The purchaser must, however, assume some liability for the accumulated environmental damage caused before 1 July 1990, and this is reflected in a fixed basic sum payable as part of the purchase price. The THA is particularly sensitive to the burden that such liability places upon purchasers, especially small and medium-sized businesses (SMEs).

The restructuring of enterprises by the THA with a view to their sale involves a range of difficult decisions with particular regional and social implications. While the THA maintains in its publicity booklet *Treuhandanstalt: working for rapid privatisation, resolute restructuring, careful closure* (Bundesministerium der Finanzen, 1991) that 'while decisions must take account of labour and social policy requirements, they must be framed essentially on business principles' (p.18), in practice this is more difficult. In March 1991 new guidelines were drawn up for cooperation between the Federal government, the new *Länder* and the THA over issues relating to regional and structural policy. *Länder* representatives on the board of the THA scrutinise carefully all decisions of the THA for compatibility with their own regional and structural policy objectives. The THA recognises that in some sectors 'exposure to international competition has clearly identified regional trouble spots showing the effects of over 40 years of mismanagement' (op. cit., p.20). The brown coal (Brandenburg, Sachsen-Anhalt, Sachsen), chemicals (Sachsen-Anhalt), steel (Brandenberg, Sachsen), shipbuilding (Mecklenburg-Vorpommern), textiles (Thüringen, Sachsen) and optical/electronics industries (Thüringen, Brandenberg, Sachsen) are believed to be the most vulnerable sectors in the new *Länder*.

Restructuring, as interpreted by the THA, is the development of *potentially* viable firms into competitive enterprises with new product lines, markets and strategies. Management–worker consultations lead to business plans being drawn up by the company and subsidies for restructuring (essentially of a short-term nature) granted by the THA. These are normally in the form of loan extensions or by releasing the company from some of its financial liabilities. The latter may include existing or inherited debts. Many companies are in debt to the banking system of the former GDR as a result of loans taken out before monetary union on 1 July 1990. The THA is able to write off some of this debt as part of the restructuring process. Companies selected for restructuring are not, of course, able to prevent cuts in their work force, and emphasis has been placed by the Federal government on training and retraining measures for those workers made redundant as a result of privatisation, restructuring or company closure.

As regards closures, the THA claims to be 'making every effort to carry out with all due care the closure of enterprises that cannot be made viable' (op. cit., p.21). It sees the problems faced by individual enterprises and regions in the new *Länder* as not being

> attributable to the THA but to those responsible for a socialist planned economy. . . that proved to be incapable of creating sustainable employment for the working population of the acceding territory. . . any attempt to mitigate the responsibility of the failed regime is both inappropriate and inadmissible (op. cit., p.21).

The THA was faced in 1990 with a situation of having to privatise or restructure some 8000 large enterprises (i.e. those with over 250 employees) comprising over 40 000 plants employing well over four million people. The high number of enterprises has been the result of the splitting up of the former *Kombinats* for sale or restructuring. This process has continued since 1990 which explains why at times there have been more enterprises on the books of the THA than there were at the start (by the end of October 1991, 16 months after currency union, the 8000 enterprises had grown to over 10 000, while by the end of 1992 there were 11 850). This situation, therefore, makes long-term assessment of the THA's activities rather difficult (Jeffries, 1992).

The privatisation of the *Kombinats* progressed slowly in the first year after German unification. There were several reasons for this, not least the poor infrastructure conditions for investment, environmental pollution, and perhaps of most importance, the issue of property ownership. Many potential investors were deterred by the uncertain political situation concerning property ownership. There were thousands of people making claims on property that had been seized either by the Nazis between 1933 and 1945 or by the socialist authorities after 1945. The situation was partly resolved by new laws which favour investors over property claimants (*Investionsvorrangentscheidung*). If investors present to the THA a feasible business plan which guarantees the protection and creation of new jobs and the provision of investment, this is given priority over the claims of the former owners of the property if they are not prepared to undertake investment. The former owners consequently receive compensation from the Federal government for their loss. Each of the new *Länder* has set up offices to deal with asset and property disputes (Ämter zur Regelung offener Vermögensfragen), and they work closely with the THA.

The THA reported in January 1993 that over 9000 companies and parts of companies had been privatised, with over DM173 billion in new investment coming into the new *Länder*. Over 1.4 million jobs had been maintained or created as a result. The pattern of privatisation is differentiated across industrial branches (Carlin and Mayer, 1992). The industries with the lowest rates of privatisation are machinery, chemicals,

Photograph 8   *Success and failure in the modernisation of East German industry.*
The break-up of the former State-controlled industries and the search
for private investors has had a mixed success in the new Lander.
Even within particular industrial sectors, such as the machinery
industry in Leipzig, some plants have been closed while for others
buyers have been found

Table 6.2 *Progress with privatisation in the new Länder
(as of 1 February 1993)*

Number of THA firms	11 850
Firms sold by THA of which:	
sold to private sector	5528
returned to previous owner	1213
transferred to local authority	327
Firms in process of closure or closed	2340
Firms still in need of purchasers	2442

Source: Treuhandanstalt, 1993.

electrical and electronic products and light industry—all industries with previously high dependency on export markets in COMECON (especially the USSR).

As well as the privatisation of the larger concerns, the THA has tried to create a *Mittelstand* (middle group) of small businesses. As of 1 June 1992, 25 000 retail outlets, 1700 pharmacies, 550 book stores, 600 cinemas and more than 300 hotels and restaurants had been sold (THA, 1992).

The THA has adopted a cautious approach in referring enterprises to its closures department (*Abwicklung*). The reluctance to avoid closures has resulted in the THA having to inject substantial amounts of capital to assist ailing businesses. There has been a great deal of criticism from some quarters about the THA adopting a 'social cushioning' role with regard to its privatisation activities. Failure on the part of the THA to close down unprofitable companies runs the risk of endowing East Germany with a fossilised industrial sector with intrinsically obsolete modes of production. The reluctance to close down enterprises has left the THA with more than 2400 enterprises still in search of purchasers as of early 1993 (see Table 6.2). For example, in the highly industrialised state of Sachsen, well over 500 enterprises remain unsold. Companies which the THA has not been able to sell off include heavy engineering and industrial plants: for example, Takraf the Leipzig-based crane builder and SKET engineering in Magdeburg. In both cases West German engineering companies have shown little interest in acquiring additional capacity in the new *Länder*, considering the world recession in the industry. Carlin and Mayer (1992) suggest that there is a close relationship between branches where the rate of privatisation is low and the scale of closures. Enterprises in the chemicals, mining, heavy engineering and textiles sectors have been the most difficult for the THA to sell and have consequently experienced the highest closure rate since 1990.

To avoid closures the THA has been borrowing heavily to keep companies

Table 6.3   *Foreign investment in the new Länder, 1990–2*

Origin of investment	Investment (DM bn.)	No. of companies purchased	Employment
United Kingdom	1.5	66	13 975
Switzerland	0.6	64	13 755
France	2.2	48	14 743
Austria	0.4	36	7954
Netherlands	0.8	27	5489
Sweden	0.08	19	3351
USA	1.5	19	4747
Italy	0.4	14	3089
Denmark	0.3	13	2393
Belgium	0.08	9	2804
Others	2.6	32	26 977
Total	10.83	347	99 277

Source: Treuhandanstalt, Berlin, March 1992.

afloat. For example, the THA's takeover of Zeissoptik Jena, the largest East German producer of lenses, resulted in heavy financial losses, with the company only surviving through an injection of a credit guarantee by the THA of DM3.5 billion. Since 1990, therefore, the THA has had to increase its borrowing in order to carry out its tasks in the new *Länder*. In 1990, for example, the THA was in debt by DM4 billion while a year later the figure had increased to DM20 billion and had reached DM30 billion by the end of 1992. A further DM60 billion of debt is expected between 1992 and 1994. If we include the debts of the *Kombinats* that the THA inherited in 1990, then total debts of some DM250 billion have been accumulated by the THA in its efforts to privatise the new *Länder*. It is important to note that the THA debts are *in addition* to those financial transfers from West to East Germany for the modernisation of the new *Länder* that were discussed earlier.

The THA has also made tremendous efforts to secure foreign investment (i.e. non-German) in the new *Länder*. Table 6.3 reveals the number of privatised companies taken over by foreign investors up to March 1992. While investors from the United Kingdom have purchased the largest number of companies, it has been French investors who have made the highest amount of investment in the former GDR. There is a widely held view that the new *Länder* offer the key to France's future success in the European market (*Financial Times*, 28 July 1992, 'France sets sights across the Rhine'). French investors in the new *Länder* include the French oil company Elf Aquitaine, which is to run the former state-controlled petrol stations chain Minol and L'Air Liquide which has acquired 40% of the eastern market for industrial gases. Other examples of foreign investment in the new *Länder* include the Italian pharmaceutical company Menari Industrie Farmaceutiche Reunite which has bought Berlin Chemical AG and Spezialtechnik Dresden which has been purchased by American company General Atomics.

In an effort to increase the share of foreign investment in the new *Länder* (only 5% of privatised companies have been bought by non-German investors), the THA has embarked upon major advertising campaigns. Each week the THA advertises in major European and international newspapers those companies in the new *Länder* for whom buyers are sought. Each advertisement contains information on the company's turnover, products, management, personnel and real estate. Figure 6.1, for example, which appeared in the German paper *Die Welt* in August 1992, shows a typical advertisement placed by the THA which in this case seeks prospective buyers for a dairy in Hoyerswerda in north-eastern Sachsen. The dairy and its surrounding buildings, which were built between 1961 and 1968, produces fresh bottled milk, cream and butter and, we are told, has refrigeration and loading facilities. Emphasis is placed on the dairy's location in a fully industrialised region of the country and its proximity to the Polish and Czech borders. Prospective buyers are also informed that the region's workforce is highly qualified and ready to increase the company's output. The only condition is that the prospective buyer must guarantee employment for at least 50–70 workers.

While the THA has been able to attract interest from abroad in some of its companies, this has still not prevented major job loss. For example, the East German company Werk für Fernsehlektronik which manufactures television tubes has been sold to Samsung of Korea. While Samsung has promised to retain 800 of the present 1200 jobs, it is important to note that in 1989 the East German group employed almost 10 000 workers. Similarly, the former East German tyre monopoly Pneumant has been purchased by Iranian investors who will ensure job survival for 900 of the current 1800 workforce. In 1990 Pneumant had 6000 employees. These examples clearly illustrate the scale of the restructuring process already undertaken in the new *Länder* since 1990 and the very difficult circumstances in which the THA is forced to carry out its activities.

Company closures have made the THA very unpopular, especially in those localities where once dominant industries have been closed down. Public discontent with the way in which the THA was operating tragically fuelled the cause of the terrorist Red Army Faction who, in April 1991, assassinated Detlev Rohwedder, the chairman of the THA's executive board.

A long menu of investment allowances, grants, loans and tax incentives is offered to those businesses contemplating investment in the new *Länder*. Investment grants are offered by the Federal Ministry for the Economy

Ausschreibung

Im Rahmen der übertragenden Sanierung bieten das Direktorat Abwicklung und die Liegenschaftsgesellschaft der Treuhandanstalt mbH (TLG) die

Molkerei Hoyerswerda GmbH sowie den Betriebsteil Weißwasser

im Freistaat Sachsen zum Erwerb an.

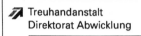 Treuhandanstalt
Direktorat Abwicklung

Liegenschaftsgesellschaft
der Treuhandanstalt mbH (TLG)

**Molkerei Hoyerswerda GmbH
Industriestraße B
O-7700 Hoyerswerda**

**Betriebsteil Weißwasser
Puschkinstraße 3
O-7580 Weißwasser**

Der Verkauf erfolgt nur bei Erhaltung oder Schaffung von mindestens 50 bis 70 Arbeitsplätzen.

Das Unternehmen
stellte als milchwirtschaftlicher Betrieb Frischmilch in Flaschen, Sauermilchgetränke, Butter und Speisequark her. Es verfügt über funktionstüchtige Kühlräume, einschließlich Umschlagtechnologie. Der Standort eignet sich sehr gut für die Ansiedlung kleiner und mittelständischer Unternehmen der Lebensmittelbranche und artverwandter Industrien.

Fläche und Bebauung:
15 005 m², davon 4 700 m² bebaut mit Produktions-, Verwaltungs- und Lagergebäuden (Bj. 1961 bis 1968, baulich guter Zustand, Skelettbauweise). Es bestehen günstige Umgestaltungsmöglichkeiten.

Lage:
Hoyerswerda liegt rund 30 km von der A 13 (Dresden–Berlin) entfernt, nahe der Grenze zu Polen und der CSFR. Das Unternehmen befindet sich in einem voll erschlossenen Industriegelände.

Fläche und Bebauung:
1 817 m² Grundstücksfläche, bebaut mit Wohn- und Geschäftshaus, Wirtschaftsgebäude, Garagen und Nebengebäuden (Bj. 1905). Das Grundstück verfügt über einen Wasser-, Gas- und Elektroenergieanschluß. Die Abwasserentsorgung ist gewährleistet.

Lage:
Weißwasser ist eine Kreisstadt im Nordosten von Sachsen, 40 km von Cottbus, 15 km von der A 15 (Cottbus–Berlin), 10 km von der polnischen Grenze entfernt.

Investieren Sie im Freistaat Sachsen.

Nutzen Sie durch den Erwerb dieser Unternehmen die Vorteile bereits erschlossener und bebauter Gewerbestandorte.

Qualifizierte Arbeitskräfte in der Region sind bereit, gemeinsam mit Ihnen leistungsfähige Unternehmen aufzubauen.

Besichtigungstermine vereinbaren Sie bitte mit **Herrn Peter, Telefon: Hoyerswerda/62 11 oder 23 75.**

Ausschreibungsbedingungen und weitere Informationen erhalten Sie bei der **Treuhandanstalt,** Direktorat U4 A, Leipziger Straße 5–7, O–1080 Berlin, **Telefax: 030/3154-1788.**

Abgabeschluß für alle Gebote: **21. September 1992, 12.00 Uhr,** Zimmer 3222 bei der

Treuhandanstalt
Direktorat U4 A

Leipziger Straße 5–7
O–1080 Berlin

Figure 6.1   *Treuhandanstalt advertisement*

(Wirtschaftsministerium) for industrial and commercial developments (excluding retail trade, warehousing and transport). Levels of grant aid vary according to the type of project. For example, construction projects can receive up to 23% of the investment costs though there are only limited funds available under this scheme and there is no legal entitlement to them. Potential investors in the new *Länder* are, on the other hand, legally entitled to investment allowances which amount to 12% of the individual company's manufacturing costs. They are tax free and are offered to those companies producing capital goods (except cars, planes and low-quality capital items). Other tax breaks include the non-levy of capital gains tax on company assets in the new *Länder* (up to 1993) and the possibility of offsetting initial start-up costs against taxation. The Federal government also offers grants towards the cost of consultancy, information and training for those starting up companies in the new *Länder*.

Since 1990 the private banks have played an increasing role in the development of the new *Länder*. A number of loan measures for investment in the new *Länder* are offered by them. However, they have been cautious not to over-commit themselves in the new *Länder*, often preferring to loan to those companies in the East which have strong links with West German firms or in other cases providing loans on condition that the bank is represented on the board of the East German company. The private banks have also offered their advisory services to those investing in and managing companies.

The economic development of the new *Länder* is envisaged not only by the sell-off of former State-controlled enterprises by the THA but also by new production plants being constructed by Western companies in the region. Some of the largest West German companies have sought to locate some of their operations in the new *Länder*. In July 1992, for example, Mercedes announced that they were to build a new production plant near Magdeburg in Sachsen-Anhalt at a cost of DM25 million. It is envisaged that the plant will employ over 200 workers and is expected to be opened in 1994 (*Magdeburger Volkstimme Zeitung*, 29 July 1992).

Since German unification, the THA has accomplished a great share of the tasks empowered to it—a high level of company sell-offs (79% of all THA companies) to national and foreign buyers, company restructuring and a relatively limited number of closures (20%), considering the acute economic difficulties encountered. The THA has had to negotiate a path through, on the one hand, the need for urgent privatisation, and, on the other, to carry out these duties with due regard for both workers and regional economies. In this light the THA could not hope to function optimally in either situation. Its activities must also be viewed in the wider context of the magnitude and immediacy of the economic collapse in the new *Länder*. For example in 1993, of the original 4.5 million people employed in THA companies in 1990, employment has only been secured for 1.4 million, less than one-third of the original workforce.

MODERNISATION OF THE ENERGY INDUSTRY

As Chapter 5 clearly demonstrated there are many problems associated with the modernisation of the energy industry in the new *Länder* and its integration into the energy network of the old *Länder*. The priorities for the modernisation of the former East German energy industry can be summarised as follows:

- to reduce dependence on brown coal and thereby reducing the environmental damage caused by the energy industry;
- to improve the safety situation of nuclear power stations in the new *Länder*;
- to ensure more efficient use of energy particularly in the domestic sector;
- to link the new *Länder* to the electricity, gas and oil grids of the old *Länder*.

Reducing dependence on brown coal as an energy source is a major task in the new *Länder*, although it is certain that even in the medium term brown coal will continue to play a key role, albeit reduced, in overall energy supply. Concern stems not only from the high level of emissions from out-dated brown-coal power stations (over half of all steam generators in such stations are more than 20 years old, while in the Halle region power stations dating from the 1920s are fully integrated into the energy supply network), but is also over the damage caused to the landscape by large-scale brown-coal extraction. By the end of 1991 some eight brown-coal power stations in the new *Länder* were closed down on the grounds of age and inefficiency.

Extensive open-cast mining requires careful landscape restoration after use in order to maintain the water table at an acceptable level and to prevent serious water supply and effluent disposal difficulties. In the Cottbus area (Brandenburg) where two-thirds of brown coal in the new *Länder* is mined, there are already many difficulties caused by decades of environmental neglect. The West German brown-coal company Rheinbraun, which has restored large areas of land in Nordrhein-Westfalen after mining operations have ended, has been involved in scientific and technical cooperation with authorities in Brandenburg in an effort to clean up areas of brown-coal extraction.

The former GDR authorities had planned for a substantial increase in nuclear power in the 1990s to meet the growth in energy demand. However, the failure of the GDR-built nuclear power stations to meet western safety standards resulted in their total shutdown by the end of 1990.

Improving energy efficiency in the new *Länder* will not only require substantial investment in new technology but also the incorporation of energy conservation policy in urban development and regeneration schemes. In addition, a revised energy-pricing policy should have some impact upon energy use.

The organisation of the former GDR's supplies of grid-based energy was arranged quite differently from that in West Germany. The absence of transmission lines from the old to the new *Länder*, and the ways in which the West and East German grids were integrated into different systems, has meant that there is only limited scope in the short term for supplying the new *Länder* with electricity from power stations in the West. The priority, therefore, will be to construct interconnection systems. In 1991 the first of these systems was built between Helmstedt (Niedersachsen) and Wolmirstedt (Sachsen-Anhalt), and three others were planned for completion in 1993.

Plans are also in progress to link up the natural gas grids in the new and old *Länder*. It is expected that Western European gas will increase its share of the German market at the expense of supplies from the former USSR. In December 1989 Ruhrgas AG and the GDR Schwarze Pumpe gas collective (responsible for gas supply throughout the former East Germany) signed agreements involving the connection of the gas pipeline systems between Bad Hersfeld (Hessen) and Jena (Thüringen). Since the end of 1992, natural gas has been supplied from West Germany to homes and factories in the new *Länder* of Sachsen and Thüringen. Other West German gas companies have also been involved in construction and supply deals for gas between the old and new *Länder* since 1990.

While some progress has been made in the modernisation of the energy industry in the new *Länder* since German unification, there remains a great deal more to be done before the new Germany has a completely integrated energy market.

MODERNISATION OF EAST GERMAN TOWNS AND CITIES SINCE UNIFICATION

The extent of urban decline in the GDR demanded urgent measures in the months following the breaching of the Berlin Wall in November 1989. Urban renewal in East Germany became one of the main priorities for both West German and GDR expenditure in the months preceding full economic and monetary union in July 1990. The aim of urban policy has, since 1989, been twofold: first, to improve general living conditions in urban areas in the new *Länder* and second, to preserve cultural and other historic buildings and monuments there. Many of East Germany's historic town centres (*Altstädte*) had been allowed to deteriorate considerably in the 40 years of socialist rule. In early 1990, therefore, the West German Federal Ministry for regional planning and city development in conjunction with the East German authorities agreed upon an emergency programme for improving urban areas. Some DM770 million were allocated to improving over 700 towns and villages in East Germany. As well as modernising those buildings which were in an obvious poor state of repair, specific schemes for protecting and renovating various historic and cultural sites were also implemented. For example, the historic centre of Wittenberg, the Theater Platz in Chemnitz

Photograph 9   *Urban decline in Leipzig-Plagwitz.* Run-down properties, buildings
stained by the East German economy's dependence upon brown coal
and a poor standard of facilities characterise most East German
towns and cities

and church houses in Demmin were all regarded as in need of urgent
attention.

In May 1990, a bolder scheme to improve urban areas in East Germany
was initiated which set out a framework for cooperation between municipalities, planners and East German citizens based, of course, upon West
German practices. The *Modellstadt* programme, as it was termed, resulted in
the selection of five towns (one in each state)—Stralsund (Mecklenburg-
Vorpommern), Brandenburg (Brandenburg), Weimar (Thüringen), Meissen
(Sachsen) and Halberstadt (Sachsen-Anhalt)—which would serve, as their
name implied, as models for development for other towns and cities in East
Germany. In June 1990, many smaller towns and villages were included in
the programme; these were selected on the basis of their role as central
places or as possible growth poles for regional development. The list
included Penzlin and Mollenhagen in Mecklenburg-Vorpommern, Wiesen-
berg in Brandenburg, Landsberg in Sachsen-Anhalt and Kandler in Sachsen.

A clearer picture of the great contrast in living conditions in urban areas
of West and East Germany emerged after German unification. Consequently,
the programme *Gemeinschaftswerk Aufschwung-Ost* devoted a sizeable
proportion of funds to urban improvements in the new *Länder*. Critics of
the earlier *Modellstadt* programme had argued that the towns selected could

offer little practical guidance to those urban centres experiencing great difficulties in adjusting to economic change or those wishing to undertake extensive city centre renewal as a means of improving their economic prospects. As a result, another six towns were designated as *Modellstädte*— Gustrow (Mecklenburg-Vorpommern), Cottbus (Brandenburg), Naumburg (Sachsen-Anhalt), Gorlitz (Sachsen), Jena (Thüringen) and Mulhausen (Thüringen).

Urban development companies from West Germany have, not surprisingly, taken a leading role in the modernisation of towns and cities in the new *Länder*. For example, the Kommunalentwicklung Baden-Württemberg GmbH, which is based in Stuttgart, is involved in the urban projects in Meissen and Jena, while in Weimar, Naumburg and Cottbus the German city development company (Deutsche Stadtentwicklungsgesellschaft GmbH) based in Frankfurt-am-Main is actively involved.

Brandenburg was one of the five towns in East Germany selected in 1990 to act as a *Modellstadt*. It provides a good example of the range of tasks being carried out under the programme. The three main aims of the *Modellstadt* programme in Brandenburg are:

- to improve shopping and office facilities in the town;
- to improve living conditions for the town's inhabitants;
- to protect the town's historic centre.

It is widely acknowledged that the number of retail outlets and office space in the town needs to be increased, while at the same time guarding against traffic congestion in the historic centre. It is therefore planned to turn the central area of the town into a pedestrianised zone with car-parking facilities built on the edge of the town. It is recognised too that the town will be placed under considerable development pressure as the expected growth of Berlin occurs (Birkholz, 1993). Particular worries focus upon possible housing shortages and the poor availability of hotels, guesthouses, restaurants etc. to cope with the expected increase in tourists to the town *en route* to or from Berlin.

The modernisation of the old quarter of Brandenburg, where currently 8000 people live, is regarded as a priority. Attention is to focus upon improving the condition of housing, in particular the installation of central heating and hot water systems based upon clean fuel sources in many of the older properties and the refurbishment of courtyards and entrance halls of the apartment blocks.

The conservation of the historic centre is to be achieved through a carefully managed traffic policy, grants for the maintenance of properties of special historic importance and control over the nature of building development in the area.

The town's authorities have surveyed local inhabitants in order to gauge public reaction to the schemes and to elucidate opinion on various planning issues. A survey conducted in 1991 of 60 households in Brandenburg showed that 98% of those interviewed felt that the availability of goods in the town had improved since unification, 33% thought that the improvement of the town had proceeded too slowly since unification, 78% felt that the transport system had deteriorated since 1990 and half of all respondents believed that the town had become dirtier. Some 43% of those interviewed cited transport improvement as the most important priority for the town in the coming years—an issue that comprised not only road and street improvements but also more pedestrianised areas, cycle paths and traffic calming measures. The second-most important priority as seen by those interviewed is the need to improve the condition of housing in the town. Other issues raised included the need for better quality shops rather than kiosks (many such establishments had sprung up all over East Germany since 1990); 92% of those interviewed thought that a main supermarket should be built as a priority and a further 78% a new department store. At the end of 1991 the town's mayor, eager to maintain public involvement in the town's planning, held a public meeting to discuss the *Modellstadt* programme which was attended by well over 300 residents, at which many of the above issues were discussed further.

Urban planning programmes have also been implemented at *Länder* level. Mecklenburg-Vorpommern was the first of the new *Länder* to announce an urban development programme in 1991. That programme and subsequent ones for 1992 and 1993 have been based upon funding from Federal, *Länder* and local authority sources. In 1993 some DM323 million were allocated to various urban development programmes in the *Land*. Of this amount DM116 million have been allocated for specific development projects, DM52 million for the preservation of historic monuments, DM26 million for *Modellstädte* (see above) and a further DM127 million from *Land* funds for a range of urban-renewal schemes. Regarding the latter individual local authorities (*Gemeinde*) have made applications to the *Land* for funding. Some 127 *Gemeinden* applied for funding for various urban renewal schemes in 1993. Some 19 towns and cities in Mecklenburg-Vorpommern are involved in the schemes for the preservation of historic monuments.

Since 1991 over 100 individual town development plans have been drawn up and implemented, well in excess of 1000 building improvement schemes have been achieved and some 5000 surveys for the modernisation of urban areas in Mecklenburg-Vorpommern have been undertaken. Despite these impressive statistics, urban redevelopment in the state is confronted by a range of difficulties. These include continued problems regarding rights of ownership and compensation claims, complicated legal situations, problems of speculation in the land market, steadily increasing construction costs, difficulties in persuading potential investors to invest and the banking sector adopting a guarded approach to lending. In addition the problems are compounded by poor quality or absence of cadastral surveys showing rights of ownership, the poor availability of experienced local architects and the inexperience of local authorities regarding urban development.

One major problem in Mecklenburg-Vorpommern as elsewhere in the new *Länder* concerns the large residential estates (*Gross Siedlungen*). These estates, of which there are 69 in the new *Länder* (19 are in the state of Brandenburg) were constructed to provide residents with all their assumed needs—schools, kindergartens, shops, leisure activities etc.

The modernisation of the *Gross Siedlungen* presents a major challenge to municipalities in the new *Länder*. Fifteen *Gross Siedlungen* were built in Mecklenburg-Vorpommern between 1950 and the mid-1980s with over half constructed in the 1970s. In the port of Rostock, five *Gross Siedlungen* were built in the north-west of the town in the 1970s, and by 1990 over half of the town's 250 000 inhabitants were living there. Over 37 000 people live on one of the Rostock estates, making it one of the largest of all the *Gross Siedlungen* in the new *Länder*.

The architectural, functional and social problems of the *Gross Siedlungen* are highlighted and aggravated by the economic impact of the modernisation process in the new *Länder*. There is a very real danger that the *Gross Siedlungen* could become centres of despair and discontent with serious political consequences. The Gross Klein estate in Rostock is fairly typical of the problems facing municipalities in the new *Länder* (Hohn and Hohn, 1993). The contraction of the shipbuilding and engineering industries in Rostock since 1990 have resulted in unemployment levels nearing 20%. Many of the residents of the estate have, therefore, lost their jobs since German unification. The neighbouring estate of Lichtenhagen has an unemployment level of 17%. The estates are blighted by rapidly increasing crime and vandalism, a deteriorating condition of most properties particularly stairwells and entrance lobbies to the apartment blocks, the lack of adequate green open space, poor shopping facilities and a general economic climate largely unattractive to potential investors. Residents of Gross Klein who were interviewed by Hohn and Hohn (1993) gave very negative comments about life on the estate. They complained about the poor quality of their flats, in particular the inefficient and out-moded central heating systems; the poor quality of windows, doors and baths; and the lack of security to their homes. In addition they complained about the lack of open space, the poor facilities for sport and leisure activities, the catastrophic parking situation and the negative image associated with the estate, described by one respondent as a '*Wohn silo*' (accommodation silo).

The town authorities of Rostock have begun to tackle some of the problems. A new shopping centre linked to the S-Bahn is planned for 1994 and a social club is also to be built in an effort to reduce the anonymity of life on the estate. Work on improving properties has already begun. In addition, community initiatives for improving the estate are also being encouraged: for example, neighbourhood groups. Although these efforts are welcomed, there is still much to be done to assist the *Gross Siedlungen* in the new *Länder*. The extent of dissatisfaction with events since 1990 among residents of these estates is to some extent reflected by the incident at the *Gross Siedlung* in Lichtenhagen in 1992 (see Chapter 7).

FARMING, RURAL AREAS AND THE FOOD INDUSTRY

In 1989 some 11% of the East German workforce were employed in the farm sector, with over 70% of these working in the *Landwirtschaftlichen Produktionsgenossenschaften* (LPGs) and another 28% in the *Volkseigenen Guter* (VEGs) (see Chapter 2). At the time of German unification 4530 LPGs and 580 VEGs were recorded in the new *Länder*. Support prices for agricultural production were set at relatively high levels, resulting in over 12% of the GDR budget allocated to subsidising the farm sector in that year. As Chapter 2 described, the food system was managed by the State monopolies who paid little attention to product quality, neglected investing in the industry and worked with incentives that were not linked to labour productivity.

As Chapter 4 demonstrated, economic and monetary union with West Germany led to a massive fall in demand for goods produced in East Germany, including foodstuffs. The transformation of the East German farming industry has involved the disbanding of the LPGs and their replacement by private farms run on either an individual or group basis. The food processing and distribution industries have been put under the control of the THA with a view to their privatisation, restructuring or closure. The entire farming industry in the new *Länder* is also now subject to the rules and procedures of the European Community's Common Agricultural Policy and at the same time eligible for grants from the Community's agricultural budget.

The *Landwirtschaftsanpassungsgesetz* (Agricultural Adaptation Act) of 1990 (and later changes to it on 3 July 1991) set out the terms for the restructuring of the east German agricultural sector and, in particular, the legal forms that would replace the LPGs and the VEGs. The Act came after many months of intense debate among German politicians, agricultural economists and farmers' groups which was frequently covered in the quality German press (see for example the German journal *Agrarwirtschaft* and, in particular, contributions from Henrichsmeyer (August 1990) and Kohne (September 1990), the *Frankfurter Allgemeine Zeitung* (22 January 1991 and 7 February 1991).

Table 6.4 *Restructuring of the agricultural sector in the new Länder since German unification*

Legal Status	April 1991 No.	%	August 1991 No.	%	% total farmland	Av. farm size (hectares)
Producer groups:						
LPG	2287	17.8	1424	9.0	40.1	1450
GPG	79	0.6	50	0.3	0.0	40
Other	62	0.5	22	0.1		
E.G	477	3.7	830	5.3	27.6	1710
AG + GmbH	459	3.6	744	4.7	14.9	1030
Partnerships (KG, OHG)	263	2.1	531	3.4	5.7	550
Indiv. farmers	6878	53.6	9918	62.6	11.3	60
full time			5722	36.2	10.0	90
others	2074	16.2	2188	14.0	0.2	4
Total	12 824	100	15 806	100	100	325 (average)

Source: Bundesministerium für Landwirtschaft, Bonn, 1992.

The LPGs were to be transformed into other legal forms by no later than 31 December 1991 or otherwise disbanded. Those livestock LPGs without land were to be compulsorily closed. The VEGs were to be placed in the hands of the THA with a view to land sale or leasing. The overall aims of the modernisation process were to convert East German agricultural production away from quantity to quality in line with CAP developments, reduce the number of people employed in the farm sector, render farming more environmentally friendly and to improve the marketing arrangements for agricultural production.

Table 6.4 shows the changing organisational situation of agriculture in the new *Länder* in 1991. By the end of that year only 34 LPGs had not adopted a new legal form as requested by law and were subsequently dissolved. The *Eingetragenen Genossenschaften (E.G)* is a cooperative structure with members contributing their own labour and capital, proceeds being divided among the membership. Some 830 E.Gs were established in the new *Länder* by August 1991 and are seen as a transitional stage between the former LPGs and other organisational forms. In Sachsen-Anhalt, 343 E.Gs had been set up by April 1992.

In 1989 850 000 East Germans were employed in the farm sector. By January 1992 only 250 000 remained in farming, with 175 000 having retired (90 000 of whom having taken early retirement), 105 000 on

Table 6.5   *Brandenburg: farm employment, 1989–92*

Year	Employment in farming	Full time	Workers/ '000 ha	of which full time
1989	179 300	c.160 000	12.6	11.0
1990	126 000	c.90 000	8.9	6.3
1991	61 500	c.50 000	4.9	3.9
1992	50 000	c.40 000	4.2	3.2

Source: Ministerium für Landwirtschaft, Land Brandenburg, Potsdam, 1992.

Table 6.6   *Brandenburg: breakdown of farm sector loss, 1989–92*

Beginning of year						End of year
	Employed in farming	Natural retired	Early retired	Unemployed	Training courses	Employed in farming
1989						179 300
1990	179 300	5200	16 700	16 600	15 800	126 000
1991	126 000	7500	19 000	22 000	26 500	61 500
1992	61 500					50 000(?)

Source: Ministerium für Landwirtschaft, Land Brandenburg, Potsdam, 1992.

retraining courses and 150 000 made redundant. Of those left in farming over half are on short working hours. The East German farm sector has, therefore, experienced in a most dramatic way the full effects of the transformation of a centrally-planned economy to one which is market-led.

The restructuring of East German agriculture has created a critical situation in some regions. In February 1992 the Federal Ministry of Agriculture announced that the farm sector in Mecklenburg-Vorpommern and Brandenburg had been the most severely affected since opportunities for non-farm employment there were most limited (Bundesministerium für Landwirtschaft, 1992).

Almost 180 000 people were employed in the farm sector in Brandenburg in 1989. Within one year over 50 000 had been forced out of the sector, and by early 1992 only 61 500 remained—a rate of transformation unparalled in the post-war agricultural history of Europe.

Elsewhere in the new *Länder* the decline in agricultural employment has also been rapid. For example, in Thüringen 128 000 people were employed full time in farming in 1989, a figure that was reduced to 34 000 by the end of 1992 and is expected to fall to around 20 000 by 1994. The restructuring of the East German farm sector since 1989, including the implementation of the EC's CAP, has had important effects upon production levels. For example, in Thüringen between 1989 and 1992, numbers of beef cattle fell by 29%, milk cattle by 30%, pigs by 56%, sheep by 54% and poultry by 57%.

Reductions in livestock numbers and contractions in labour supply have also affected the production of arable crops in the new *Länder*. For example, in Sachsen-Anhalt where dairy cattle numbers fell from 272 000 in December 1990 to 195 000 by January 1992, and pigs from 1.9 million to 900 000 over the same period, arable output (especially for fodder) has fallen significantly. The area under potatoes, for example, has fallen from 73 000 hectares in 1990 to 23 000 hectares in 1992. In addition, EC programmes, such as the five-year set-aside scheme for arable land (*Flächenstillegung*) (a special one-year scheme for the new *Länder* was also offered by the Federal government in 1991), cattle slaughter premiums, milk quotas, and extensification grants have also fashioned the modernisation of the farm sector in the new *Länder* (Jones, 1991; Jones *et al.* 1992). For example, the take up of set-aside grants has been considerable in the new *Länder*, not only because of the higher proportion of poorer quality arable land compared to West Germany but also because of the transitional situation regarding the break up of the LPGs, the creation of new organisational forms and the need to resolve land ownership questions. Over 600 000 hectares have been set aside in the new *Länder*, with some *Länder* such as Brandenburg having 20% of their arable land set aside (Ministerium für Landwirtschaft, 1992).

The privatisation of the food industry has proceeded at a rapid pace. Over half of the 810 food-processing and distribution companies had been privatised by early 1992 resulting in DM4.1 billion of investment and 20 300 jobs secured. Foreign investors have been particularly attracted to the East German food industry. Twenty investors have purchased 38 privatised companies. The French company, Gervais Danone, has bought the Milchwerke Hagenow GmbH in Mecklenburg-Vorpommern and also in the same state, Coca-Cola has purchased the soft drinks company Wismaria Getränke GmbH. Scandinavian investment has been particularly high, with two Swedish investors purchasing eight cereals and feedstuffs companies, and seven meat companies having been bought by three Danish investors (Bundesministerium für Landwirtschaft, 1992).

Privatisation of some branches (for example, sugar, starch and potato) has already been completed, while the sale of meat companies has been more difficult often because of the poor state of buildings and equipment or because of their location in city centres or residential areas. The THA expected to complete the privatisation of the food industry by the end of 1993. Those companies which prove impossible to sell will be closed (THA, 1991).

The THA is also responsible for administering agricultural and forestry land (VEG—'Volkseigene Guter') which had been expropriated during the

Third Reich and in the land reforms undertaken by the Soviet occupiers between 1945 and 1949. In total, 1.95 million hectares of agricultural land and 1.96 million hectares of forest previously farmed by individuals or the LPGs are under THA administration. The land will not be given back to the original owners (except in certain situations see (b) below), who will instead be eligible for compensation. The THA is therefore faced with having to sell or rent out the land and has drawn up a set of priorities for this task (Hagedorn *et al.*, 1992).

In principle, everybody is eligible to buy or rent land from the THA. However, it there is more than one person interested in the same land, then preference will be given to:

(a) East Germans who had previously farmed their land as part of an LPG and now wish to enlarge their holding by land purchase or lease;
(b) former landowners whose land had been expropriated during the period 1945–49, provided that they are prepared to move to the new *Länder*;
(c) companies originating from the reorganisation of the LPGs requiring land in order to fulfil the requirements of a modernisation and development plan;
(d) new entrants to the farming profession who will be resident in the new *Länder* and/or cooperating with local farmers.

The THA also applies upper limits to the amount of land that it is prepared to sell or lease out. The average size of full-time family farms is not to be smaller than 90 hectares (average farm size in West Germany is 17.6 hectares). The THA has also played a key role in easing the financial burden on privatised farms caused by debts accrued under the centrally-planned system. A debt relief scheme was introduced by the THA in 1991 and a balance sheet discharge scheme also set up.

Since 1989, the East German farm sector has clearly experienced a dramatic transformation—the number of people employed in farming has been halved, over 30% of beef livestock have been slaughtered, well in excess of half a million hectares of arable land have been taken out of production, all the LPGs have been converted into new legal forms and over three-quarters of the food industry has been privatised by the Treuhandanstalt. However, these changes do not mark the end of the process of agricultural restructuring in the new *Länder*. Farm employment levels are expected to continue to fall as the capital situation of farm businesses deteriorates, and the East German farm sector has to make further adjustments to radical decisions taken outside of Germany over the wider reform of European agriculture.

Since December 1991 the modernisation of rural East Germany has been assisted by the allocation of Federal and *Länder* monies under an extended programme for 'improving the structure of farming and coastal protection' (*Verbesserung der Agrarstruktur und des Küstenschutzes*). Some DM4.3 billion were allocated to the programme in 1992 for all of Germany, of which DM2.6 billion were from Federal funds. It is widely recognised that the break up of the LPGs has had far-reaching effects upon levels of employment, countryside functions and rural community life in the new *Länder*. Under the above programme all the new *Länder* have implemented schemes to modernise their rural regions. Such schemes have included village renewal (*Dorferneuerung*) through social projects (e.g. the construction of club houses, sports halls, kindergartens), infrastructure schemes (roads, sewerage etc.), the protection of cultural monuments of rural life and the conversion of former buildings belonging to the LPGs and VEGs to other economic uses.

The actual priorities for expenditure under this programme vary considerably among the new *Länder*. For example, of the DM438 million that were allocated under the programme in 1992 to the *Land* of Mecklenburg-Vorpommern, 40% was used for modernising farms in less-favoured regions, 30% for improving rural water supply, 14% for improving marketing facilities and a further 10% for improving rural roads (some 560 kilometres of roads within and between rural villages have been built in Mecklenburg-Vorpommern since 1991) and for village renewal schemes. In Sachsen, meanwhile, where village renewal is seen as a key priority of rural policy, nine model villages have been designated (three in the *Bezirk* of Chemnitz (Auerswalde, Borstendorf, Forchheim), four in Dresden (Gohrisch, Schonfeld, Wachau, Wittichenau) and two in Leipzig (Ruckmarsdorf, Thallwitz)). The model villages are intended to serve as an example of the way in which modernisation of the countryside can take place through effective planning. Also in Sachsen, efforts are underway to convert land where brown-coal mining has occurred back to agriculture and forestry purposes and in addition revitalise devastated villages. Similar projects are underway in the neighbouring *Länder* of Sachsen-Anhalt and Brandenburg.

Environmental conservation is also a new feature of rural policy in the new *Länder*. Since 1990, some 13 402 sq. kilometres of land has been designated as lying within newly established national or nature parks. Five national parks have been established in the new *Länder* covering an area of 4921 sq. kilometres. Three of the parks are in Mecklenburg-Vorpommern (Vorpommersche Boddenlandscaft, Jasmund auf Rugen, Muritz), one in Sachsen-Anhalt (Hochharz) and one in Sachsen (Sachsische Schweiz). The new Germany now has nine national parks with its two largest located in Mecklenburg-Vorpommern. Three new nature parks have also been created in the new *Länder* (Schaalsee in Mecklenburg-Vorpommern, Dromling in Sachsen-Anhalt and Markische Schweiz in Brandenburg) in which agricultural practices are strictly controlled. There are now 67 such parks in the new Germany. In addition to national and nature parks, six biosphere reserves (*Biosphärenreservate*) have been designated in the new *Länder* with the largest at Schorfheide-Chorin in Brandenburg covering over 1200 sq. kilometres.

TRANSPORT AND TELECOMMUNICATIONS

The nature of the transport systems in and between the two Germanies reflected their different political and economic paths over the previous 40 years. In West Germany, emphasis had been on linking the major metropolitan regions of northern and southern Germany through considerable investment in road and rail systems. By 1990 over 9000 kilometres of motorway linked West Germany's principal cities. In the East, however, less than 2000 kilometres of motorway had been built under the socialist regimes with an overall road network density of 0.44 kilometres/sq. kilometre, a figure substantially lower than that for West Germany (0.70 kilometres/ sq. kilometre). The poor physical condition of roads compared with those in the West reflected the lower priority given to maintaining a modern efficient road system in East Germany. Emphasis in East Germany had been placed upon the rail system; consequently at the time of unification the rail network density in East Germany was 0.13 kilometres/sq. kilometres, a figure that compared very favourably with that for West Germany (0.12 kilometres/ sq. kilometres). However, in 1990 less than one-fifth of all lines were electrified (Weiler *et al.*, 1990), and the stability and technical standard of most track was well below recommended safety standards as applied in West Germany (Raumordnungsbericht, 1991). In the 1980s while government expenditure on transport, post and telecommunication approached 5% of total government spending in West Germany, the figure averaged less than 2% in East Germany (West German Embassy, 1985). Consequently, German unification brought with it massive infrastructure demands.

In January 1992 the Federal transport minister announced a major transport programme under the banner of German unification for which DM56 billion was allocated (Bundesministerium für Verkehr, 1992) (see Figure 6.2). This programme has three main aims:

(1) to link important economic regions in West and East Germany;
(2) to improve communication links within the new *Länder*;
(3) to integrate the new *Länder* into the wider European transport network including that of Eastern Europe.

In total 17 transport projects have been agreed (nine rail, seven road and one canal scheme). All the projects are intended to meet the above aims. The

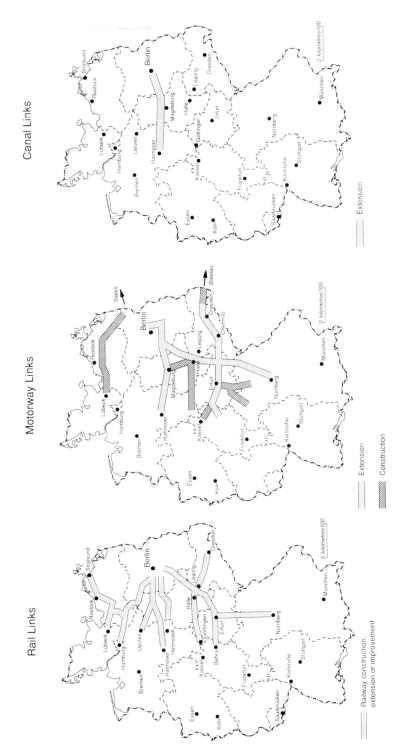

Figure 6.2 *The new Germany: transport project—German unity*

Photograph 10   *New high-speed express service Hannover–Berlin.* While substantial reductions in journey times have been achieved in the old *Länder* as a result of the introduction of the ICE express, there is still a great deal of track modernisation work to be done in the new *Länder* before similar achievements can be recorded there

rail schemes have been allocated over half of the total budget and comprise five corridor programmes:

Berlin–Hannover and then on to Dortmund, the Ruhr and Köln;
Berlin–North Sea ports (Hamburg, Lübeck, Rostock);
Berlin–Stuttgart/München;
Sachsen/Thüringen–Rhein/Ruhr;
Sachsen/Thüringen–Rhein/Main.

Each of the schemes involves track improvement and electrification which, it is hoped, will lead to considerable cuts in journey times. For example, the journey from Berlin to Hannover will be reduced from four to one and three-quarter hours and that from Frankfurt to Leipzig from five and a half to three hours. The most expensive rail project links Nürnberg with Berlin via Bamberg-Erfurt, Leipzig–Halle, thereby creating an important axis between the high-tech industries of southern Germany, the industrial regions of middle Germany and the capital Berlin.

Over DM23 billion have been allocated for road and motorway construction and improvements. In Mecklenburg-Vorpommern a four-lane road is planned to link the Baltic coast towns with Schleswig-Holstein and Hamburg, while in Sachsen-Anhalt a four-lane road linking Halle with Göttingen in Niedersachsen and with connections to the proposed new autobahn Hannover–Braunschweig–Magdeburg–Berlin is to be built. This autobahn together with another linking Nürnberg–Leipzig–Berlin will firmly establish Berlin as the hub of major links between West and East Germany.

One project to connect Berlin/Magdeburg with the North Sea ports of Hamburg and Bremen by improving navigation on the Elbe–Havel canal and the Mittelland canal is also planned, and will involve the construction of a canal crossing over the river Elbe at Magdeburg. It is hoped that this investment will lead to an increase in the volume of goods transported by inland waterways in the new *Länder*, where currently less than 5% of goods are freighted by this mode (cf. 25% in west Germany).

These projects are regarded by the Federal transport ministry as urgent for the economic and spatial integration of the new *Länder*. However, there is likely to be some debate where their implementation conflicts with both established planning processes and environmental legislation. In addition, plans are afoot to privatise the entire German railway system, with a proposal outlined in July 1992 to amalgamate the Bundesbahn in the western states and Reichsbahn in the east to create a new limited liability company (Deutsche Eisenbahn Aktiengesellschaft). Track, passenger and freight traffic are expected to be run as separate administrative and accountancy entities (German Embassy Press Release, 27 July 1992).

German unification also ended Allied control over air traffic to and from Berlin, allowing the German airline Lufthansa to resume flights to the city after an enforced break of 45 years. Since 1990, the division and control of air space above Berlin and East Germany has been reorganised. Previously airports in West Berlin could only be reached via three air corridors which could be used only by British, French and American airlines. Since unification Berlin and East German air space has been controlled by the Federal Air Traffic Control agency based in Frankfurt-am-Main. There has been a considerable increase in the number of scheduled flights between West and East German cities over the last two years. In 1989 Lufthansa operated only six weekly flights to East Germany (Leipzig), in 1990 65 flights and in 1991 183 flights carrying almost one million passengers a year. Pressure upon existing airports in East Germany is therefore increasing, and there are plans to construct a new international airport to the south of Berlin.

Improving telecommunications in the new *Länder* is also a main priority. In 1989 over 60% of telephone lines in East Germany were shared, the equipment itself was mostly between 30 to 60 years old and to have connected the 1.2 million households waiting for a telephone would have taken at least a further 20 years. The Federal government issued a statement soon after unification on the need to establish and implement as quickly as possible a coherent policy for telecommunications in the united Germany. The Deutsche Bundespost Telekom (DBT) was given the responsibility for modernising the telecommunications system in the new *Länder*, with some of its work contracted out to the large commercial firms of Bosch and Siemens. In the first year of their operation in East Germany, over 250 000 households and 150 000 East German businesses had telephones installed. The number of connecting lines between West and East Germany was increased to 31 000 in both directions in the space of six months, compared with fewer than 3000 in each direction at the time of German unification.

At a cost of some DM55 billion to be spread over the five years up to 1997, the DBT hopes to increase the number of telephones from 1.9 to 9 million, FAX connections from 5000 to 360 000, mobile radion links from 1000 to 300 000 and the number of public call-boxes from 25 000 to 68 000. In addition, a digital overlay network linking exchanges in all of the new *Länder* (Berlin, Rostock, Leipzig, Magdeburg, Dresden, Erfurt and Chemnitz) with those in the West, has been set up. It is hoped that the standard of telecommunications in the new *Länder* will reach that of West Germany within seven years.

The technological profile of postal services within East Germany was estimated to be 30 years behind that of West Germany. The DBT is intending to spend DM4 billion over the next five years to improve the system. Some important changes have been made, in particular postal charges in the East have been brought up to those in the West, thereby eradicating the former practice of some west German firms bulk-posting mail in the East; also, the postal code system has been changed in line with new automatic mail scanning.

THE ENVIRONMENT—THE BIGGEST CHALLENGE?

The severity of the environmental situation in the new *Länder* has been caused by energy and industrial policies dependent upon the intensive use of brown coal and other raw materials, high levels of energy consumption and outmoded production processes. The situation has also been aggravated by long-term neglect of environmental precautions, excessively low funding for environmental protection measures and an environmental technology industry which has been underresourced (EC, 1990).

Air pollution is one of the most serious issues facing the new *Länder*. In 1990 the new *Länder* had the highest emissions of sulphur dioxide (SO_2) in Europe, with approximately 49 tonnes/sq. kilometre, a situation largely attributed to East Germany's energy and chemicals industries. While West Germany reduced SO_2 emissions by more than half between 1980 and 1990, in East Germany levels increased by over 25% over the same period. Dust pollution (which had risen in some localities by 10% since 1980) and carbon monoxide levels in the new *Länder* were the highest in the world at the time of German unification. The effects upon the East German population have been catastrophic. Figures supplied to the EC in 1990 on the state of the East German environment (EC, 1990) revealed that the number of respiratory diseases among children had risen constantly since 1974, with one in every second child reported as afflicted. In addition, in those most highly polluted regions of East Germany one child in three was reported to be suffering from endogenous eczema. As well as the effects upon the East German population, high levels of air pollution have badly damaged the country's forests with over half of all trees affected (*SüddeutscheZeitung*, 28 February 1990).

Water pollution is a further major problem caused by the lack of treatment safeguards, the over use of pesticides in the agricultural sector, the uncontrolled dumping of domestic and toxic wastes and acid rain. In 1990, the European Commission estimated that about 20% of available water in East Germany was not suitable for drinking purposes because of high pollution levels. Nevertheless, over 1.2 million East Germans were supplied with water with nitrate contents well in excess of recommended safety levels. Some of the most polluted stretches of water are in the industrial regions of the new *Länder*. The Mulde and Saale rivers in Sachsen-Anhalt have been particularly affected by industrial and domestic pollution from the Halle–Bitterfeld–Leipzig (Sachsen) conurbation.

The Ministry of Environment in Sachsen-Anhalt published two detailed reports in 1990 and 1991 on the state of the environment and emission levels (Ministerium für Umwelt, 1990; 1991). The reports not only reveal the extent of environmental pollution in Sachsen-Anhalt but also provide valuable insights into the magnitude of environmental problems in the new *Länder* as a whole.

The concentration of major brown-coal, chemicals and cement industries in the Halle–Bitterfeld–Merseburg region in the south of the *Land* has resulted in Sachsen-Anhalt having the most serious level of air pollution in the united Germany. Figure 6.3, for example, shows the level of SO_2 emissions in the city of Halle compared to the Rhein–Ruhr area of West Germany. In 1985, SO_2 emission levels in Halle were six times those of the Ruhr. The overriding aim of the environmental programme announced by the environment ministry in Sachsen-Anhalt is to bring environmental quality standards up to West German levels by the end of the decade. Air-quality improvement is to be achieved by legal measures: i.e. setting of emission levels for industry, the conversion of energy demand away from brown-coal use, the application of new technology to industry to reduce its dependence upon primary materials and research into harmful substances and ways of

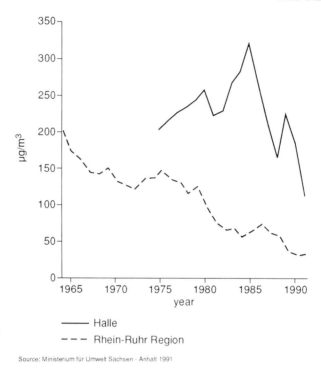

Source: Ministerium für Umwelt Sachsen · Anhalt 1991

Figure 6.3   *SO₂ emissions: Halle and Rhein–Ruhr regions*

reducing emission levels in major urban areas. The prevention of further water pollution is to be achieved through public-works programmes including purification and treatment plants and tighter inspection and monitoring of water quality levels. Soil pollution through the dumping of toxic wastes is also to be monitored carefully and controlled legally. Additional measures to improve the environment include plans for the creation by 1995 of national parks, nature parks and conservation areas with clearly defined environmental objectives.

In 1989, over 60% of Sachsen-Anhalt's energy requirements were met by brown-coal production and over 80% of electricity was generated by power stations run on brown coal. Reform of the *Land*'s energy sector was seen as essential in reducing levels of environmental pollution. In the autumn of 1991 the *Land* government announced a series of measures to reduce dependence on brown coal as the principal source of energy generation. It was intended that oil and natural gas would supply over 70% of the *Land*'s energy requirements by the year 2000, while brown coal would not exceed 19% of these requirements. To achieve these energy goals several investment

Table 6.7 *Sachsen-Anhalt: emission levels in major industrial sectors, 1989–91 (tonnes)*

	1989	90	91	1989	90	91
		Dust			SO^2	
Chemicals						
Buna AG	57.3	28.8	26.2	87.3	84.2	83.9
Chemie AG Bitterfeld	18.8	8.5	5.7	42.6	23.0	19.2
Leuna AG	22.0	13.5	12.4	173.8	109.5	98.5
Energy						
MEAG Halle	3.1	1.4	1.1	20.8	19.0	17.8
Kraftwerk Harbke	33.6	24.8	4.3	24.6	16.4	14.5
Braunkohlen AG Deuben	32.0	21.8	19.7	79.4	62.5	42.6
Cement						
Zementwerk Bernburg GmbH	31.2	15.0	11.2	0.4	0.5	0.4
Karsdorfer Zement GmbH	38.0	21.0	na	1.9	1.1	na

Source: Ministerium für Umwelt des Landes Sachsen-Anhalt, 1990.

projects have been announced since 1991 including closures of brown-coal stations, the reduction of emission levels of existing stations through modernisation programmes, investment in new oil- and gas-fired stations and improvements in the electricity supply grid. The brown-coal station Zschornewitz was closed on environmental grounds in 1992, the gas-fired station Zschornewitz is to be expanded by the year 2005, a hard-coal power station is to be built at Stendal in the north of the *Land*, while three modern brown-coal power stations are to be built on sites formerly part of the Buna AG and Leuna AG chemical companies.

The privatisation, restructuring and closure of former *Kombinats* by the Treuhandanstalt combined with new environmental legislation in Sachsen-Anhalt have had a significant effect upon the emission levels of harmful substances. For example, Kraftwerk Harbke, the brown-coal power station which in 1988 was responsible for 17% of industrial emissions in the *Bezirk* of Magdeburg, has, following the closure of three cooling towers, seen dust levels decrease from 33 678 to 4329 tonnes, and SO_2 emissions fall from 24 667 to 14 547 tonnes over the period 1988–91 (see Table 6.7).

Reducing levels of water pollution in Sachsen-Anhalt is another major task. Long stretches of waterway have been severely affected by industrial, agricultural and domestic pollution. For example, intensive agricultural practices in the north of the *Land* have led to high nitrate levels in drinking water. Even by the end of 1991, over 30 000 homes were still being supplied with drinking water with nitrate levels over 50 milligrams/litre.

With the river Elbe traversing the *Land* on its route from the Czech Republicto the North Sea, multi-national efforts to combat water pollution have also been initiated. In October 1990 an international commission for the protection of the Elbe was set up. An emergency action plan to clean up the Elbe was announced in Magdeburg in December 1991. Closer monitoring of industrial discharges into the Elbe as well as the construction of treatment and purification plants along its banks and those of its tributaries have been planned. In Sachsen-Anhalt four major plants are to be constructed—at Magdeburg, Halle, Wittenberg and Wolfen south of Dessau. They are in locations where water quality levels are at their lowest (see Figure 6.4). In Prague in May 1992, it was announced that measures to clean up the Elbe were to be intensified with additional funds to be provided by the European Community.

In 1990 the Federal government allocated DM1.4 billion for emergency environmental programmes in the new *Länder*. One year later, work on 462 projects was well advanced and DM0.3 billion of the budget already spent. Some DM58 million were spent in the *Land* of Mecklenburg-Vorpommern, where over half of the funds were used for the partial closure and modernisation of the nuclear reactor in the Baltic town of Greifswald.

Since 1989, pollution levels in the new *Länder* have fallen quite significantly. In 1991, total SO_2 emissions were 550 000 tonnes (a decrease of 10.5% since 1989) and total dust emissions 300 000 tonnes (a decrease of 13.5%). These achievements have not been without considerable cost to employment levels. The Federal Environment Ministry has estimated that 43% of the decrease can be accounted for by company closures, 55% by reductions in industrial output and only 2% by the application of new environmental technologies (Raumordungsbericht, 1991). The EC has also observed that to reduce pollution levels by half in some of the most polluting economic sectors such as the chemicals industry would require a minimum 25% decrease in capacity in the short term (EC, 1990). While the Federal government has estimated that the clean up of the East German environment will cost in the order of DM25 billion, this is widely regarded as being too optimistic. Several economic institutes have maintained the real costs to be between DM130–220 billion over the next decade (*Frankfurter Allgemeine Zeitung*, 30 March 1990).

REGIONAL PLANNING IN THE NEW *LÄNDER*

The economic transformation of the new *Länder*, in particular their transition from a command to a market-oriented economy, has fundamentally changed the demands upon Germany's regional development policy. Differences in regional income levels between the old and new *Länder* in Germany are more acute than between northern and southern Italy; Germany now has its own equivalent of the Mezzogiorno. German regional policy as noted in Chapter 3 dates back to 1965 with the

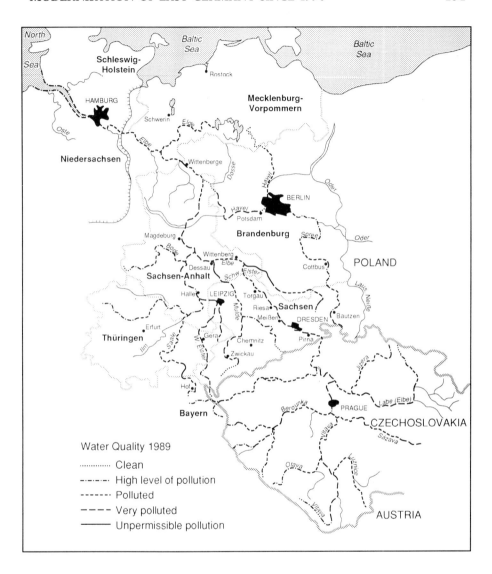

Figure 6.4 *Pollution of the River Elbe*

introduction of the Federal Regional Planning Act which outlines the tasks, objectives and principles of regional planning. Following German unification the Act was amended in order to accommodate the new *Länder*. The main aim of regional policy in the new Germany is to create equal standards of living for people in all parts of the country. However, raising living standards in the new *Länder* to those of West Germany is not expected to be achievable in the short term. Even the most optimistic forecasts predict comparable standards of living between West and East Germans to be achievable by no earlier than the year 2010, assuming that quite spectacular rates of economic growth are recorded in the new *Länder* over the coming years.

Regional policy for the new *Länder* as outlined by the Minister for Regional Planning in the summer of 1991 is to chart a middle way between growth-orientated development strategies and the equalisation of living standards. Regional policy is to be based upon the assumption that only regions with a strong economy can act as 'development motors' for the new *Länder* as a whole (Selke, 1991). On the basis of their economic structure and development potential, 12 regions in the new *Länder* were selected for this purpose:

(1) Berlin
(2) Halle-Leipzig
(3) Dresden
(4) Central Thüringen
(5) Magdeburg

These five regions are expected to have high development potential, although their distribution across the new *Länder* further marginalises the northern rural areas and the southern peripheral regions. As a result five towns were selected to serve as higher-order centres for surrounding regions:

(6) Rostock
(7) Schwerin
(8) Neubrandenburg
(9) Cottbus
(10) Chemnitz

In addition, the Polish–German border region is seen as having good potential for economic growth. Two centres are regarded as being in a favourable position to benefit from this:

(11) Stralsund/Greifswald
(12) Frankfurt an Oder

Following these broad Federal regional policy guidelines, each of the new *Länder* has drawn up a regional development plan or programme. For example, a draft of the first regional planning programme for Sachsen-Anhalt was presented to the *Land* parliament (Landtag) in early June 1992, while that for Mecklenburg-Vorpommern was presented a few weeks later. Each programme outlines the basic conceptions for desired spatial development which are then put into concrete form by the appropriate local planning institutions. Each plan normally contains information on the delimitation of planning regions, urban hierarchies and central place functions, development axes, as well as directional statements on the desired overall development of the *Land*. A closer look at the regional programme for Mecklenburg-Vorpommern shows the main features of regional planning.

The location of Mecklenburg-Vorpommern in relation to the old *Länder* (Schleswig-Holstein and Niedersachsen), the new *Länder* (Berlin and Brandenburg) and to other countries (Poland and the Scandinavian states) is regarded as a very favourable attribute for the *Land*'s future development as an industrial base, agricultural producer and tourist centre. However, the economic transformation of the new *Länder* since German unification has particularly hit the *Land*'s key economic sectors such as agriculture. In 1989 194 000 people were engaged in farming, a year later this had fallen to 140 000, and by the end of 1991 had dropped to 76 000. It is estimated that only 40 000 people are currently employed in farming in the *Land*: i.e. a dramatic reduction of 80% in farm employment in less than four years. Much of the industrial base of the region is linked to the processing of foodstuffs, and here too, despite some success in attracting domestic and overseas investment, the privatisation process has caused many redundancies. The other major industrial sector in the *Land*—shipbuilding and repair industries—has also been hard hit since 1990; the port of Rostock suffered particularly badly with one in five of the town's workforce now unemployed.

The future development of Mecklenburg-Vorpommern, as envisaged in the regional plan, is to be based upon the expansion of higher-order centres, the reorganisation and revitalisation of rural regions and special measures for those areas with structural weaknesses. Development axes, based upon major transport infrastructure improvements linking the *Land* to Berlin and other old and new *Länder*, are a principal feature of the plan (see Figure 6.5).

The growth of higher-order centres is one of the priorities of regional policy in Mecklenburg-Vorpommern. Five towns have been designated as high-order central places—Schwerin (the *Land* capital), Rostock, Neubrandenburg, Greifswald and Stralsund each serving catchment areas of a radius of 10–15 kilometres. A network of secondary-level centres has also been designated and this includes the smaller towns of Wismar and Gustrow. The urban network is to be connected by several interregional development axes: for example Rostock–Gustrow–Berlin and Lübeck (Schleswig-Holstein)–Wismar–Rostock–Stralsund–Greifswald–Stettin (Poland).

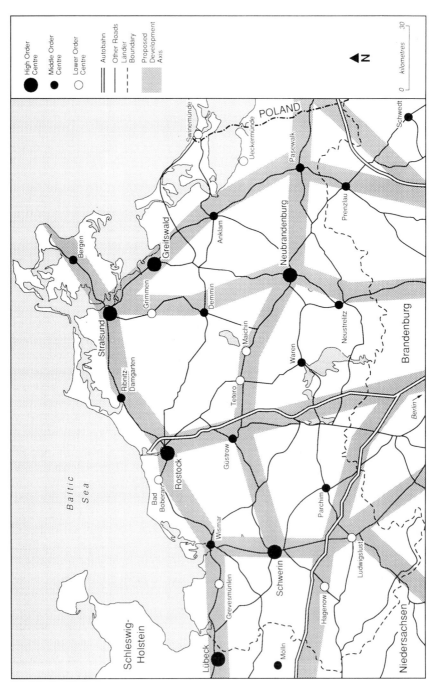

Figure 6.5 *Mecklenburg-Vorpommern: regional development programme*

Table 6.8   *Soviet troops in the new Länder, 1990*

	Number	%	per 1000 inhabitants
Berlin	4400	1	1
Brandenburg	137 800	32	52
Mecklenburg-Vorpommern	50 400	12	26
Sachsen	74 900	18	15
Sachsen-Anhalt	107 200	25	36
Thüringen	51 600	12	19
Total	425 900	100	23

Source: Zarth, 1992.

With over 1.5 million hectares of agricultural and forestry land and a thinly distributed largely rural-based population, it is not surprising that the regional plan devotes a great deal of attention to the future development of the *Land*'s rural regions. The privatisation of the farm sector and the disbanding of the collective farms (LPGs) have seriously altered the nature and organisation of farming as well as social relations in rural areas. Rural out-migration has become one of the most pressing issues in Mecklenburg-Vorpommern since German unification. Development efforts are therefore to be concentrated upon assisting the reorganisation of farming, particularly the means of private ownership, improving the layout, facilities and appearance of rural villages, financing improvements in rural transport, encouraging the diversification of rural employment through work and training programmes and protecting the rural environment. Many of these aims are to be supported by Federal, *Land* and EC monies.

Additional regional development problems stem from the planned withdrawal of Soviet troops from Mecklenburg-Vorpommern. Of notable significance is the fate of military-supply industries in particular areas and the uses to which former military sites and buildings can be put. Some 33 000 hectares of former military land exist in Mecklenburg-Vorpommern alone. This is a problem facing all the new *Länder*. In 1990, over 425 000 troops of the Soviet army were stationed on East German soil, with almost one-third garrisoned in the *Land* of Brandenburg (see Table 6.8). Over 260 military sites (barracks, tank depots, airfields, hospitals, munitions depots, chemical weapons stores etc.) were located in the *Land* (Prufer, 1992). The conversion of former military sites for industrial and urban development purposes, especially where environmental clean-up is required, can only be undertaken at great cost to Federal, *Land* and local governments. In the *kreis* of Neuruppin (Brandenburg) 5% of the land area was occupied by the Soviet military and was home to some 40 000 troops. The regional development plan for Brandenburg has placed great emphasis on the conversion of former military sites to civilian uses. The redevelopment of Neuruppin has become a pilot project for the rest of the *Land*, with an elaborate scheme to convert the former tank depot into a science and industrial park already well underway. The local authority has already commissioned soil and environmental surveys, built an information centre where potential investors can obtain details of the project's purposes and site availability and drawn up details of the residential developments that are intended.

MODERNISATION IN THE NEW *LÄNDER*: CASE STUDY OF SACHSEN

Sachsen is a densely populated and major industrial region of the new Germany. Beginning in the early 19th century, industrial development based on local resources of coal and iron ore led to a level of economic growth unparalleled elsewhere in Germany except by the Ruhr region. By 1900, Sachsen and the Ruhr had become the industrial heartlands of Germany. By 1936, Sachsen had surpassed the Ruhr as Germany's leading industrial area and had also achieved the position of the most highly industrialised region in the world (Munziger-Archiv, 1991). After 1945 the Sachsen region became integral to the economic development of East Germany and by 1989 was responsible for over 30% of the GDR's industrial output (see Figure 6.6).

As part of East Germany, Sachsen was broken up into three *Bezirke* (Karl-Marx-Stadt (Chemnitz), Dresden and Leipzig) within which chemicals, machinery, cars and textile industries were the focus of development, sustained by exports to the Eastern Bloc, especially to the USSR. Sachsen became a highly specialised economic region of the GDR. For example in 1989, one year before German unification, the region's textile industry employed over 150 000 workers and accounted for over three-quarters of total East German textiles production. In some localities, for example in Karl-Marx-Stadt (Chemnitz), the textile industry accounted for over one-fifth of the city's industrial production. Similarly, in the heavy industry, machinery and car sectors, Sachsen accounted for over 40% of the GDR's output in 1989. The town of Riesa on the river Elbe was the centre of the region's steel industry, Leipzig and Plauen the focus for textile and printing machinery, Gorlitz on the region's eastern border with Poland specialised in carriage work and Zwickau in the west was a principal car manufacturing centre, exporting over 100 000 Trabant models to the USSR each year from 1950. Between Leipzig–Borna–Altenburg were located Sachsen's major deposits of brown coal. Elsewhere in the region, pharmaceuticals, photographic and electronic industries were also well established. In 1989,

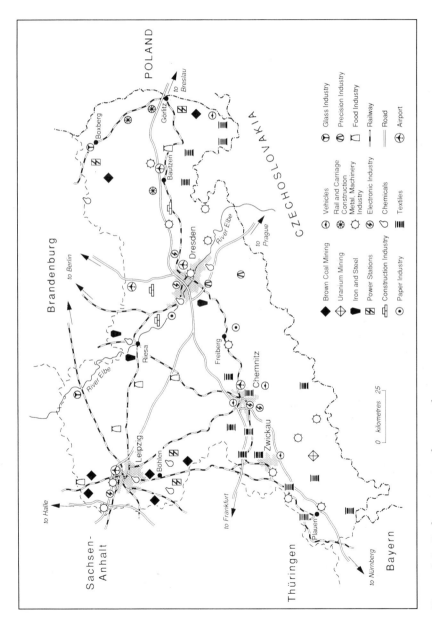

Figure 6.6 *Sachsen—regional geography*

for example, Sachsen produced approximately one-third of the GDR's electronic goods.

In 1989, over 35% of all East German industrial workers were employed in companies in Sachsen. Some 44% of the region's workforce were employed in the industrial sector, 19.5% in services and only 7.2% in agriculture (contrast Mecklenburg-Vorpommern in the north with its high agricultural dependence). Some 678 000 workers were employed in the brown-coal and uranium-mining sectors, a further 360 000 in machinery and car industries and over 80 000 in the electronics industry (Harder, 1991).

Sachsen's high level of industrialisation rendered it potentially the most vulnerable region of the former GDR after German unification. Since 1991 employment in the manufacturing sector in Sachsen has fallen by half from over 650 000 to a little over 300 000. Some sectors have been particularly hard hit. The textile industry, for example, now employs fewer than 22 000 workers (cf. 150 000 in 1989) and the mining industry fewer than 320 000 workers (cf. 678 000 in 1989) with 20 000 mining jobs being lost between March–April 1992 alone (Sachsisches Staatsministerium für Wirtschaft und Arbeit, 1992).

As of September 1992 some 302 000 people were registered as unemployed in Sachsen, and over 68% of this total were women. Currently 13% of the workforce in Sachsen are unemployed (18.5% of the female workforce are now unemployed) representing 27% of all people unemployed in the five new *Länder*. In addition, some 94 000 workers in Sachsen are on short working time (38% of the total for the five new *Länder*). Despite the magnitude of these figures Sachsen, together with Ost Berlin, has the lowest unemployment rate in the new *Länder*. There are several reasons for this. Although there are many companies in the *Land* that the THA has been unable to sell, its success rate has nevertheless been remarkably high. Second, the unemployment figures do not include those individuals on training programmes (117 000) or those who have taken early retirement (171 883); third, a further 70 800 workers have left Sachsen since 1991 to seek permanent work in West Germany. Indeed, Sachsen heads the table of those leaving the new *Länder* in search of employment in the West (29% of the total). Some 10% of all movements from East to West are currently between Sachsen and Bayern, and a further 8% between Sachsen and Baden-Württemberg.

In 1991 the THA took control of 3764 former State businesses in Sachsen. By April 1992, a total of 2352 enterprises (62%) had been transferred to private ownership. This privatisation has meant employment assurances for over 332 000 workers and led to DM43 billion of investment in the region. Currently, one-third of all private investment in the new *Länder* is going to Sachsen. Some DM2 billion of private investment in Sachsen has been by non-German investors.

Rather differentiated progress has been achieved in regard to the privatisation of Sachsen's manufacturing sector. Some industrial branches have witnessed fairly rapid privatisation (e.g. the building industry where 69% of companies have been privatised), while others such as the textile and clothing industry (17.4%) and the leather and shoe industry (10.4%) have seen privatisation efforts proceed at a much slower rate. Mechanical and electrical engineering—two important elements of the regional economy in Sachsen have also seen disappointing progress with only 31% and 33% of companies having been privatised.

Of the 4284 Treuhand companies in the new *Länder* still not privatised by the summer of 1992, 1412 (33%) were located in Sachsen and are in the *Land*'s traditional industrial sectors such as mechanical engineering (226 companies), textile and clothing (151), food industry (80) and electrical engineering/electronics (62). In this latter sector 109 000 jobs are at stake.

Productivity has been increased following company privatisation. For example, the textile industry in Sachsen has increased its productivity by 185% since 1991. However, despite low starting levels, productivity rates even in those most successful industrial branches in Sachsen are well below those for comparable West German firms. For example, productivity in the printing trade is less than 60% of that of West German firms, the food industry records less than 48%, the mining industry 47% and the steel industry only 39%.

Sachsen has been particularly affected by the sharp fall in demand from Russia and the other CIS states. However, the Eastern bloc remains Sachsen's principal trading partner. In 1992 the former USSR provided over 21% of Sachsen's imports and took some 42% of its exports. The former Czechoslovakia provided a further 10% of Sachsen's imports. Trade with Eastern Europe has been maintained (although not at pre-1990 levels) through the Federal government's programme of providing credit guarantees to the Eastern European countries, particularly to those in the former USSR. A report in *Die Welt* (24 August 1992) on the export dependence of the new *Länder* upon Eastern Europe showed that in one sector alone—machinery— export dependence on the former USSR had increased from 53% to 68% between 1988 and 1991, yet the value of these exports had fallen from DM14.9 to 4.4 billion.

Environmental degradation as a result of industrial development under socialism has been a major problem facing planners and potential investors in Sachsen. The use of brown coal both for domestic and industrial purposes in the former GDR has created some of the worst environmental conditions in Europe (Honsch, 1992). The industrial regions of Leipzig and Halle (in neighbouring Sachsen-Anhalt) record the highest levels of SO_2 emissions in the new *Länder*, with both cities commonly regarded as Germany's dirtiest and most polluted (Harder, 1991); this has prompted their designation as environmental crisis regions (Ministerium für Umwelt des Landes Sachsen-Anhalt, 1990).

Since German unification, the brown-coal-mining area south of Leipzig with its briquette works and power stations has undergone some important changes. In August 1990, it was announced that the brown-coal coking plants of Bohlen and Espenhain and their briquette works and power station would close. In addition, it was declared that of the total of 14 briquette works in the Leipzig region only two or three would continue after 1994. For the brown-coal-mining area plans are afoot to convert large tracts of it into a 'European Energy and Environmental Park' and efforts are also being made to diversify the economic base of the region, in particular through the development of service industries. In 1991 the chambers of trade and industry in Leipzig set up a 'Development Company for the South Leipzig region' (ESG—Entwicklungsgesellschaft Südraum) with the aim of promoting economic development, tourism and leisure activities as well as attracting inward investment. The Kommunalverband Ruhrgebiet (KVRG), based in Essen in Nordrhein-Westfalen, an organisation that has built up a reputation in work of this kind, has provided the ESG with useful advice and information (Honsch, 1992).

One of the largest investment projects for environmental improvement is based at Lauta near Hoyerswerda in north-east Sachsen, where one of Europe's largest recycling centres has been constructed on the site of the former Lauta aluminium works. The recycling plant, which is owned by a Bayern-based company, is expected, when fully operational, to recycle over 50 000 Trabant cars each year.

At the time of German unification, Sachsen had the densest transport network in the whole of the former GDR. However, roads, railways and the region's two airports (Leipzig-Schkeuditz, Dresden-Klotzsche) were urgently in need of repair. Improving the transport infrastructure in Sachsen, as elsewhere in East Germany, was one of the priorities outlined by the Federal government in 1990.

The programme comprises 17 projects, some of which are designed to improve transport links between cities in Sachsen and others to increase the region's accessibility to other areas of the country, particularly to the West and Berlin. In addition, some projects aim to develop further Sachsen's links with Prague and with the Polish industrial belt.

Improving the rail link between Nürnberg (Bayern) and Berlin, thereby connecting southern Germany with the Sachsen industrial belt and the capital, is the boldest and most costly of all the projects. Some DM12 billion (21% of the total budget) have been allocated to track improvement and new constructions to accommodate express trains travelling at speeds of up to 250 kilometres/hour. It is expected that Halle (Sachsen-Anhalt) and Leipzig will serve as important nodal centres in the future transport system.

This is confirmed by the allocation of a further DM2.6 billion for improvements to the rail link between the conurbations of Leipzig and Dresden in Sachsen.

There are several motorway projects designed to improve links between Sachsen and the rest of Germany. Over DM4.7 billion have been allocated to improving the A9 autobahn link between Nürnberg and Berlin via Halle-Leipzig. This will connect with the new autobahn, the A14, to be built between Magdeburg and Halle in Sachsen-Anhalt, with links to Leipzig and other cities in Sachsen. Sachsen's links with the Ruhr region are to be improved through expenditure (DM1.6 billion) on the main road link between Göttingen (Niedersachsen)—Nordhausen (Thüringen) and Halle-Leipzig. The second-most costly project (DM7 billion, i.e. 12.5% of the total budget) is that designed to improve the road links between Kassel (Hessen), Erfurt (Thüringen) and Chemnitz; Dresden and Gorlitz in Sachsen. This project is intended not only to improve links between Sachsen and middle Germany but also as a key element in the transport network linking Western and Eastern Europe.

COSTS AND EFFECTS—FINANCIAL, SOCIAL AND ECONOMIC

The financial costs of uniting the two Germanies have spiralled since 1990. In 1992 they accounted for 23% of the national budget. In total the new *Länder* received DM155 billion of financial assistance in 1992 from West Germany while income from the new *Länder* was only DM27 billion. With only 13% of total VAT and 4% of total income tax revenue coming from the new *Länder*, West Germany has borne the brunt of the costs of German unification. However, less than one-quarter of these transfers have been directly used for investment purposes. Most are for pensions, health care, welfare or unemployment benefits for East Germans. Such payments have created a dependency culture in the East and have led to greater resentment among West Germans about unification. The demand by East Germans for greater economic parity with West Germans has, in practice, meant further sacrifices on the part of those in the West. This has involved West Germans paying a 7.5% surcharge on income tax and higher duties on petrol, cigarettes and insurance premiums in order to fund the costs of unification. The Chancellor's earlier promises that no one would be worse off through unification have, therefore, a very hollow ring.

Chancellor Kohl, addressing the CDU conference in Düsseldorf in October 1992, warned of possible tax increases and the need for realistic pay settlements as necessary measures to pay for the growing costs of unification. Kohl called upon all Germans to make a 'mighty effort' to prevent the entire country falling into economic crisis. His government is faced with an acute dilemma: sharply declining revenues from the West and sharply rising

Table 6.9 *Financial transfers to the new Länder, 1990–3 (DM bn.)*

	1990	91	92	93
German Unity Fund	22	35	31.5	23.5
Federal transfers	18.5	43	55	69
Gemeinschaftswerk Aufschwung Ost		12	12	
Social security transfers	2.5	25.5	37	41
of which:				
unemployment benefits	2	25.5	32	33
pensions	1		5	8
Total	45	130.5	155	166.5

Source: Bundesministerium der Finanzen, Bonn, 1993.

demands on expenditure from the East, where some DM140 billion were spent in the first 10 months of 1992 (see Table 6.9). Forecasts of economic growth in West and East Germany were all revised downwards at the end of 1992 as the German economy was expected to face severe difficulty in the next few years.

Former SPD leader Bjorn Engholm in a speech in Sachsen-Anhalt in the summer of 1992 told his audience that they should not be under any illusions over the length of time necessary to bring living conditions in the East up to those in the West, suggesting that 10 years may not in itself be long enough (*Die Welt*, 14 August 1992).

It is now widely agreed that the costs of German unification will continue to rise in the foreseeable future. Difficult decisions were taken in 1993 when the main political parties in Germany agreed on a 'solidarity pact' over the future financing of the development of the new *Länder*. It is now estimated that around DM150 billion/year will need to be transferred to the new *Länder* for the indefinite future if income levels in the new *Länder* are to reach 80% of those in West Germany by the end of the 1990s. The 'pact' sets out how the financing of the new *Länder* will take place after 1995 and the priorities for investment—in particular the need to stabilise and modernise the industrial sector of the new *Länder*, to clean up environmental damage, to improve existing and build new housing in the East, to carry out an active employment policy and promote the sale of products manufactured in the East. Revenue is to be raised by the introduction of an income tax surcharge, increasing tax levels on private wealth, redistributing income from the old to the new *Länder* and by cutting public expenditure in the West. The Treuhandanstalt's costs are also expected to rise despite the fact that the agency had previously expected to complete the bulk of its privatisation activities by the end of 1994. Resistance in the old *Länder* to subsidising further the new *Länder* is almost certain to grow.

The transformation of the command economy of the former East Germany into one based upon free-market principles has had a colossal structural impact. Since the Berlin Wall was breached, the Gross Domestic Product of the new *Länder* has fallen by almost 50% from DM142 billion in 1989 to a little over DM77 billion by 1992. The integration of the new *Länder* into the market economy of West Germany has had a critical impact upon the labour market in the East. Since mid-1989 the number of people employed in the new *Länder* has fallen from 9.9 million to 6.3 million. Of these, some 650 000 jobs are being maintained through specific labour-market policy measures—in particular—short-time working and job-creation measures. Without these measures, it is estimated that only just over half the 1989 workforce would be in employment. In 1993, the total number of unemployed people in the new *Länder* had risen to 1.2 million (from a level of 0.6 million in the second half of 1990). The figure would be much greater if it were not for several factors: the 600 000 East Germans who have moved to West Germany since 1989, the 550 000 East Germans who live in the East but commute daily to jobs in the west (of whom 60 000 commute daily between Sachsen-Anhalt and Niedersachsen (*Die Welt*, 21 August 1992)); the 800 000 East Germans who have taken early retirement since 1989, the 400 000 East Germans on vocational training schemes and, of course, those 650 000 people referred to above who are supported by job-creation schemes. Despite the reluctance of the THA to close down unviable plants in the new *Länder*, the privatisation of the East German economy has caused the unemployment rate in the East to soar rapidly from a level of 1.6% in 1990, to 11.8% in 1991, and to 15.8% in 1993. Manufacturing output in the new *Länder* is less than two-fifths of the 1990 level (*Magdeburger Volkstimme Zeitung*, 29 July 1992). Since 1989, over 2 million of the sector's 3.6 million workers have been made redundant, as East German manufacturing industry has been unable to maintain any degree of competitiveness. In addition, major job losses have also occurred in the agricultural sector where some 70% of all farm jobs have been lost since 1989.

Women have been most affected by the contraction in the labour market in the new *Länder* and the difficulties of securing alternative employment either locally or in other regions (western) of Germany. Although in the former GDR there were as many working women as men in the labour force, there are now disproportionately more unemployed women than men. They now represent about 63% of all unemployed workers in the East and at 20%, their unemployment rate is nearly double that of men.

The new *Länder* now account for less than 8% of the GDP of the new Germany yet have almost one-fifth of its workforce. In other words, productivity in the East is barely one-third of that in the West.

Despite the heavy financial, economic and social costs incurred in the

Table 6.10   *Relative wealth of German Länder*
(income per capita), 1992 (DM)

Hamburg	67 290
Bremen	50 730
Hessen	46 600
Baden-Württemberg	43 430
Bayern	41 740
N-R Westfalen	38 190
Saarland	35 010
Rheinland-Pfalz	34 990
Berlin	34 910
Schleswig-Holstein	34 770
Niedersachsen	34 170
Brandenburg	11 940
Sachsen-Anhalt	11 530
Sachsen	11 050
Mecklenburg-VP	10 750
Thüringen	10 110

Source: Bundesministerium der Finanzen, Bonn, 1993.

process of German unification, figures released in late 1992 on the relative prosperity of the German *Länder* starkly revealed the extent of the differences in wealth between the old and the new states of the new Germany. Inhabitants of the city state of Hamburg have an average income six times greater than those from Thüringen—Germany's poorest state. Perhaps more significant is the fact that per capita income in West Germany's poorest state—Niedersachsen—is almost three times higher than in East Germany's richest state—Brandenburg (see Table 6.10).

In August 1992, the influential magazine *Der Spiegel* summed up the prevailing social and economic climate in what was increasingly being seen as the *dis*united Germany. 'German against German' was the headline as an overweight beery-faced West German with a malicious glint in his eye stands back to back with a gaunt, despondent-looking East German in a threadbare jacket. They are bound together with metres of black, red and gold rope. Some explanations are given to understand what is described as deep economic depression in the East and indifference (*gleichgultigkeit*) in the West.

Unification, far from being an integrative experience, is proving a divisive one for Germans. The psychological gap is as wide as the economic chasm that divides the two Germanies. There have been many reasons for this. Expectations on the part of both West and East Germans were too high in 1990, with political leaders making unification seem such that neither side considered that they would be worse off. Impatience soon grew in the new

Länder as people demanded the same living standards as their fellow west Germans. Visits by East Germans to West Germany merely served to increase this impatience. The handling of unification and the activities of the THA in selling off some of the best East German companies to West Germans, whose concern in maintaining jobs seemed to be suspect in many East German eyes, also fuelled resentment. With high levels of unemployment, lower wage rates for East Germans and prospects of sustained growth in the economy of the new *Länder* diminished, it is perhaps not surprising that many citizens in the East have become disillusioned with German unification.

Many West Germans hold the view that the East Germans were unrealistic in their demands, failing to realise that West German success had not occurred over-night. Growing financial transfers to the new *Länder* were beginning to be felt more acutely by West Germans, who were also increasingly dissatisfied with the political leadership and the apparent lack of gratitude on the part of East Germans for the sacrifices that the West was having to make. West Germany also has its own economic problems— declining competitiveness brought about by ever shorter working hours, rising wage costs, and even longer holidays; growing regional disequilibria; and demographic difficulties. It is important to recognise that these economic problems are structural problems of the old Federal Republic. As Chancellor Kohl announced in late 1993: 'We would have to solve them even if German unification had not happened' (*Financial Times*, 25 October 1993). While German unification may present an 'opportunity for new thinking' (op. cit.), for many Germans in both West and East, it is proving to be a very painful experience.

SUGGESTED FURTHER READING

Carlin, W. (1992) 'Privatisation in East Germany 1990–1992', *German History*, **10** (3), 335–51.

Hall, D. (1990) 'Planning for a united Germany', *Town Planning Review*, **58**, 19–28.

Jeffries, I (1992) 'The impact of reunification on the East German economy' in J. Osmond, *German Reunification: A Reference Guide and Commentary*. Longman, Harlow. 152–9.

Mellor, R.E.H. (1992) 'Railways and German unification', *Geography*, **77** (3), 261–4.

Schmidt, I. (1990) 'Former GDR communities in radical change', *International Journal of Urban and Regional Research*, **14** (4), 667–75.

Schonfeld, R. (1992) 'Germany: Privatising the East', *The World Today*, **48** (8), 152–5.

Wild, T. (1992) 'From division to unification: regional dimensions of economic change in Germany', *Geography*, **77** (3), 244–60.

7 The new Germany in the new Europe

The unification of Germany created a new country with a larger area and total population and new eastern borders. German unification led many people outside of Germany to fear a revival of 1930s-style German territorial aims and ambitions, an economy that would dominate the rest of Europe and an enlarged country occupied by a people who, on the basis of past experience, could not be trusted. The need to anchor the new Germany to Western European political and institutional structures was therefore of the greatest importance. However, the new Germany has its own priorities and responsibilities. It is, as we have seen, engaged in the costly transformation of its eastern *Länder*. Furthermore, it has inherited the responsibilities of the new *Länder* with regard to Eastern Europe, and now once again occupies a central territorial position linking western and eastern parts of the continent. It is, therefore, in a strong position to further its ties with the east and to expand its interests there. This chapter examines the incorporation of East Germany into the European Community, looks at how the new Germany compares in socio-economic terms with other Community countries, investigates the changing relationship between the new Germany, Eastern Europe and the former USSR and, through a discussion of the Bonn–Berlin capital city debate, demonstrates how Germany is facing up to its past and actively planning for its future.

INCORPORATING THE NEW GERMANY INTO THE EUROPEAN COMMUNITY

This section reviews how the institutions of the EC responded to German unification and, in particular, considers the terms upon which the new *Länder* were integrated into the Community in the space of three months at the end of 1990. The unification of Germany took place at a time when the EC was preoccupied with negotiations regarding the completion of the single market programme and closer economic, monetary and political union. The European Commission had already given its opinion on enlargement of the Community in response to Austria's application (July 1989) for full membership of the EC. The Commission's view was that enlargement questions would not be addressed until after the single market had been completed, that is, 1993 at the earliest. Deepening the Community was therefore given precedence over its widening. German unification thus occurred at a most inconvenient time for the EC.

The prospect of German unification set off alarm bells among many Community countries, particularly France and the United Kingdom, about the role an expanded Germany—both economically and politically—might perform in the Community. The new Germany would not only be the largest country in the EC in terms of population size (almost one-third bigger than France, the UK and Italy) but also in economic terms would account for over a quarter of the EC's agricultural and industrial output. In addition, German would become the most widely spoken language in the Community. For the French, German unification would strengthen European integration only if it took other countries' interests into account and was placed in the framework of broader European developments (Spence, 1991a). In the UK deep-rooted suspicions about the German 'character' and dislike of the prospect of a federal Europe as a means of harnessing the new Germany to the Community coloured British opinion on the unification question. For the European Commission and several states of the Community, German unification could serve as a vital catalyst in attempts to speed up the process of European integration. Full EC economic, monetary and political union could bind the new Germany to Western European political and economic institutional structures, thereby preventing the expanded Germany from playing an independent role in Europe.

The legal mechanisms by which the former German Democratic Republic could be incorporated into the Community was the first question that had to be addressed at EC level. Of primary concern was whether the EC would need to draw up an accession agreement for what would be a new member, or could East German membership of the Community be achieved simply by the expansion of the territory of an existing member state, that is, the Federal Republic of Germany. The prospect of the GDR becoming the 13th member of the Community and the resulting political, legal and institutional problems persuaded many, including the West German government, that the best course of action would be to treat the GDR as part of the territory of an existing state. As it transpired, the unification process in Germany resulted in this becoming the only route by which the new *Länder* could become part of the Community (see Chapter 4).

The incorporation of the new Germany into the EC raised three major immediate questions:

(i) Would the EC institutions need to be reformed to accommodate an expanded Germany?

(ii) Would the new Germany inherit the rights and obligations of the former GDR, particularly with regard to trade with the USSR and Eastern Europe?

(iii) Would specific economic arrangements (known in Community language as 'transitional measures') need to be made for the new *Länder* in order for them to participate in the EC market?

The institutional structure of the EC has been developed with due regard for the delicate balance of power between the smaller and larger member states. The decision-making structure of the Community has been designed so that the smaller countries are not over-shadowed by the larger members— France, Italy, the UK and West Germany. These four countries have themselves been granted an equal number of European Commissioners, MEPs and voting rights in the Community's institutions as a result of their broadly comparable population size. Unification led to a 30% increase in the population total of the new Germany, thereby giving grounds for additional voting powers for Germany in the Community's institutions. In practice this would mean another European Commissioner being appointed by Germany and a further 18 MEPs representing the new *Länder* (Jones and Budd, 1994). This would have upset the institutional balance of the Community, and thankfully for the EC, the German government did not press the issue. More recently, the European Community has agreed to an increase in the number of MEPs from the new Germany.

The GDR's trading links with the COMECON countries also created a problem for the Community. The main issue centred upon whether the GDR's treaties with COMECON should become void on German unification or whether they should be respected by the EC. The Community took the decision to respect the GDR's treaties with the USSR and the countries of Eastern Europe and there were three reasons for this. First, since the democratic reforms in Eastern Europe in 1989, the EC has increased its support for the political and economic transformation of Eastern Europe. Various aid and trade packages have been concluded by the EC with several East European states including Hungary, Poland and the Czech Republic. The Community felt that increasing tariffs on East European exports to the former GDR would be contrary to the spirit of cooperation that the EC was hoping to build up with these countries. Furthermore, the imposition of tariffs would also retard the process of economic reform in Eastern Europe. Third, the EC was eager not to accelerate the collapse of the economy of East Germany after unification by jeopardising East German markets in the COMECON countries. However, the terms of German monetary union critically affected the East German–COMECON trading relationship.

The application of all EC rules and regulations (known in Community language as 'Acquis Communautaire') to the territory of the former GDR would obviously not be possible immediately. Consequently, the European

Commission was responsible for investigating the entire range of Community legislation and assessing the extent to which it could be applied in the new *Länder*. Detailed transitional arrangements were to be drawn up for those economic sectors in the new *Länder* where problems would result from the full application of EC legislation.

The speed of political events in Germany in 1990 gave the EC little time in which to investigate comprehensively the possible consequences of the GDR joining the Community. Although hampered by unreliable economic data, and a rapidly changing political picture in Germany, the EC's institutions were nevertheless able to take decisive measures regarding East German membership of the Community. The Community was able to pride itself on being able to take decisions quickly when it mattered. The Commission's main concern was that German unification should not be allowed to take place to the detriment of European integration and, in particular, that it should not jeopardise the completion of the single market programme. In addition, the trade benefits of East German membership of the Community to the EC's member states were to be emphasised (Spence, 1991b). Throughout 1990, therefore, the Commission presented a very optimistic scenario of the opportunities for the EC of having the former GDR as part of the Community club.

The challenges and difficulties for the EC of German unification were spelt out in a Commission report (see *Bulletin of the European Communities 4/ 90*, 1990, Brussels). This provided detailed coverage of the impact of German unification upon all policy areas covered by the EC treaties. With German economic and monetary union in July 1990, and political union three months later, a great deal of West German legislation was applied directly to the new *Länder*. Much of this was already Community-wide legislation, for example competition policy, the free movement of people and capital, and therefore caused little contention for the EC.

Several policy sectors, however, did present varying degrees of difficulty for the EC in accommodating the new *Länder*. With regard to the single market programme, goods manufactured in the new *Länder* which did not comply with EC Directives would not be able to move freely within the single market. Transitional measures were set up for the following sectors: the food industry, pharmaceuticals, chemicals, veterinary and plant health, animal nutrition, mechanical and electrical engineering, textiles, packaging, tobacco and mobile telephones. This last sector was problematic in that the Soviet military in East Germany were using wavelengths reserved for mobile phones by a Community regulation on standards. State aids to industry, in particular for shipbuilding and steel, were allowed to continue, though the EC insisted that regional aid to West Berlin and the frontier zone between the two Germanies (*Zonenrandgebiet*) had to be phased out.

In the transport sector transitional measures were introduced to cover such issues as the validity in the EC of GDR driving licences, the use of the tachograph and the application of Community law on railways. None of these issues was greatly contentious for the member states of the EC. Similarly in the energy sector few problems presented themselves. The West German government had in 1990 instructed the East German authorities to close down their nuclear power plants on the grounds of safety; consequently this was not an issue for the Community in its assessment of the impact of German unification on the energy sector.

The greatest difficulties for the EC in incorporating the new *Länder* into the Community were to be found in the following four policy areas—external trade relations, agriculture, environment and budgetary issues. External trade relations proved to be a particularly thorny issue. With around 60% of the GDR's total foreign trade in 1989 being with the COMECON countries and 40% of this being with the USSR alone, there were major problems for the new *Länder* in adopting the EC's customs tariff for industrial and agricultural goods. The contractual trade obligations of the GDR with the COMECON group presented real headaches for the EC. In 1990, the European Commission estimated that over 3000 contractual agreements existed between the GDR and COMECON. These included investment agreements, medium-term trade accords and sectoral investment and trade packages. For example, the GDR had signed comprehensive trade agreements with the USSR for the period 1991–5, which involved the supply of 17 kilotonnes of oil, 8 billion cubic metres of gas and 4.5 million tonnes of coal in exchange for GDR exports of machinery, equipment, chemicals and consumer goods. In addition, the GDR had agreed to participate in major investment programmes in the USSR: for example, the supply of machinery and equipment for the construction of the natural gas pipeline from Yamburg to the western border of the USSR. Under considerable pressure from the USSR and the other COMECON countries, the EC agreed to suspend customs duties on goods imported into the new *Länder* from Eastern Europe for a limited period (to the end of 1992). Both agricultural and industrial goods from the COMECON group were to be included in the transitional measures.

The application of the EC's most elaborate set of rules and regulations—the Common Agricultural Policy (CAP) to the new *Länder* was also problematic. The reform of the farm sector in the East required not only the disbanding of the State collective farms but also the introduction of new pricing structures. GDR agricultural policy was based upon achieving maximum levels of self-sufficiency through high levels of State support for what was a highly inefficient farm sector. This goal was to be achieved at the expense of the environment. Applying the CAP to the new *Länder*, therefore, would require substantial cuts in agricultural production and labour and a shift to more quality-based output and more environmentally-friendly farming practices. On the production side, the application of the CAP in the new *Länder* required a contraction in cereals and milk output—the two most serious items in terms of over-production in the EC market. As regards cereals, the application of a set-aside policy (see Jones *et al.*, 1993) led to over 600 000 hectares of arable land being taken out of production in 1990–1, while the slaughter of dairy herds in order to meet EC milk quota requirements led to 120 of the 264 dairies in the new *Länder* being shut down in the space of a few months in 1990–1.

Studies by the EC in 1990 revealed the extremely serious pollution of soil, air and water in parts of the GDR as well as uncontrolled waste disposal and poorly maintained and dangerous nuclear installations. The Commission's belief was that even a relatively long transitional period (up to the end of 1995) would be insufficient to remedy the catastrophic environmental situation in the GDR. The German government, however, took the view that environmental standards could be met within this time period, although extensions might be required at a later date. The worry for the European Commission was that by allowing transitional measures for environmental policy in the GDR, member countries within the Community might relax their own environmental standards. In addition, the Commission was concerned that transitional measures for a period of five years could be used by producers in the new *Länder* to guarantee market shares. To combat, in part, this problem the Commission would require detailed environmental improvement statements from those companies operating in the new *Länder*.

The budgetary arrangements for the new *Länder* in respect of EC membership also proved to be a contentious issue, as member countries strove to limit their EC budget contributions and preserve the level of payments they received from Community coffers. The poorer member states of the Community—Spain, Portugal, Greece and Ireland were most concerned that their aid from the EC would be cut as a result of East German membership of the Community. The eventual agreement reached was that the EC would allocate ECU3 billion for the new *Länder* for the period 1991–3 and at the same time honour its budgetary commitments to all member states. The ways in which these EC funds were to be spent in the new *Länder* are discussed below.

THE NEW GERMANY IN THE EUROPEAN COMMUNITY

German unification not only created a new economic and social geography within the country but also changed the nature of Germany as one of the EC's member states. German unification resulted in the creation of a new Germany, a Germany with different economic and political circumstances to the former Federal Republic. This section looks at how the new Germany

Table 7.1 *Rank positions of the former West Germany and the new Germany in the EC for selected economic and social indicators*

	Rank in EC (12 members)	
	Former West Germany	New Germany
Territory	5	3
Population total	1	1
Population density	3	4
Birth rate	11	5
Death rate	3	1
% Population <15 years	12	12
% Population >65 years	1	4
% Workforce in agriculture	8	6
% Workforce in industry	1	1
% Workforce in services	9	10
Agricultural area	5	4
Hard-coal output	2	2
Crude-iron output	1	1
Crude-steel output	1	1
Car production	1	1
Ships launched	2	1
Telephone ownership	2	8
Car ownership	2	8

Source: Based upon figures from Eurostat 1989; and the *Overseas Statistical Yearbook*, Federal Statistics Office, Wiesbaden, 1989.

compares with the other member states of the Community according to a range of economic, demographic and social indicators and investigates the role the new Germany plays in the EC.

Table 7.1 shows the rank position of West Germany and the new Germany in the EC for selected economic and social indicators. Even taking into account the changes that have occurred in the new *Länder* since 1990, the figures clearly demonstrate the ways in which unification has altered the face of Germany.

In terms of area, the new Germany is now the third largest country in the EC after France and Spain, while the new *Länder* are indeed larger in area than the Benelux countries together. Significantly, half of the EC's member states are smaller in area than the new *Länder*. The new Germany is the largest EC country in terms of population size, having well over one-third more inhabitants than the UK. It is larger than the combined populations of Spain, Greece, Portugal, Belgium, Denmark and Ireland. However, the less densely populated new *Länder* have resulted in the new Germany dropping from third to fourth place behind the Netherlands, Belgium and the UK in terms of population density (see Figure 7.2).

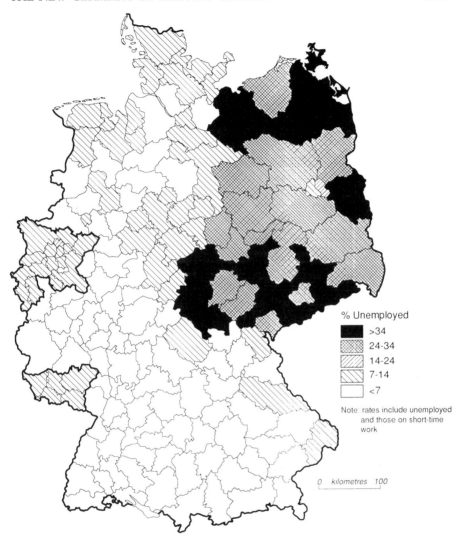

Figure 7.1 *The new Germany: regional unemployment rates, 1991 (Source:* Raumordnungsbericht, 1991)

Unification has fundamentally affected the demographic situation in the new *Länder*. This is no better highlighted than by birth and death rates. Before unification West Germany had the lowest birth rate in the EC apart from Italy, while now the new Germany has the fifth highest birth rate. Death rates show a more dramatic change, with the new Germany now occupying first rank with 11.4 deaths per 1000 people (EC average 9.9). The

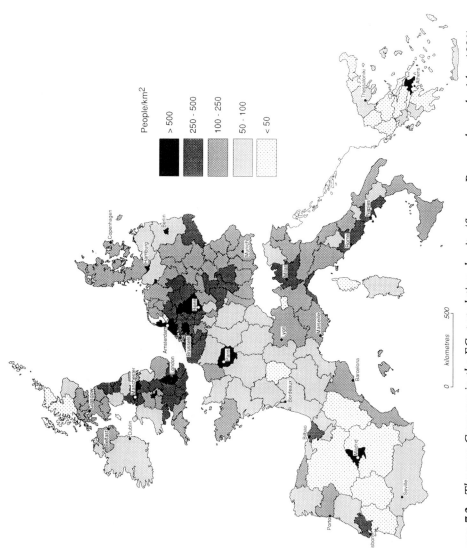

Figure 7.2 *The new Germany in the EC: population density (Source: Raumordnungsbericht, 1991)*

new Germany also has the lowest proportion of inhabitants under 15 years and has dropped from first to fourth place for proportion of people over 65. The UK and Denmark head the EC table.

Measured in terms of GDP per capita, West Germany was the richest country in the EC in 1989–90 after Luxembourg. Conversely, per capita GDP in East Germany in that year was only 56% of the EC average. The former GDR is, therefore, poorer than all EC member states except Greece and Portugal. The economic nature of Germany has been fundamentally altered by unification. For example, in 1990 West Germany was ranked eighth in the EC in terms of the percentage of its workforce employed in farming; after German unification it was ranked sixth. Consequently, the new Germany has a *higher* proportion of its workforce in farming than its neighbour, France but only almost the same area of productive agricultural land as the UK. Unification has also served to emphasise the leading industrial position occupied by Germany in the EC in terms of hard coal, crude iron and steel, paper and car production.

While West Germany held the position of one of the EC's most prosperous states, especially if one were to consider the quantity and variety of goods and services available and consumer durable ownership, the new Germany, on the other hand, presents a less affluent picture. For example, West Germany had the highest level of car ownership in the Community after Luxembourg, while the new Germany has dropped to eighth position with only the poorer Mediterranean members and Ireland having fewer cars per thousand inhabitants.

Figures show the unemployment levels and GDP per capita for the new *Länder* and the other regions of the EC in 1990. While the economic situation of the new *Länder* has deteriorated further since 1990, the figures are able to demonstrate the relative poverty of the former GDR compared with other EC regions. With a per capita GDP less than 75% of the EC average, the new *Länder*, along with Greece, Ireland, much of Iberia and southern Italy represent the Community's poorest regions. For this reason they have been designated by the EC as eligible for assistance from EC structural funds. Under EC Council Regulation 3575/90 some ECU3 billion were allocated to the new *Länder* from the Community's structural funds for the period 1991–3. This aid was to be coordinated in the context of a Community Support Framework (CSF) and was to be allocated according to the different development priorities, between *Länder* and between the different Community funds (ERDF, ESF etc.) (EC, 1991).

All of the territory of the new *Länder* was designated by the European Commission as an Objective 1 region, i.e. where Gross Domestic Product (GDP) per capita was less than 75% of the EC average. Eastern Germany was thus viewed by Brussels as being in the same economic league as most of the Community's Mediterranean regions (see Figure 7.3). The new

176

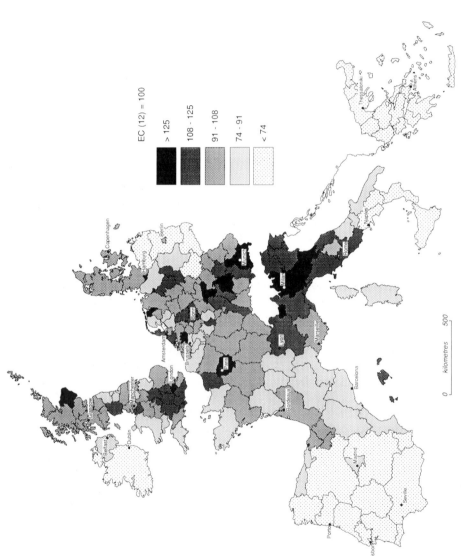

Figure 7.3 *The new Germany in the EC: regional GDP per capita (Source: Raumordnungsbericht, 1991)*

Germany is home, therefore, not only to many of the EC's richest regions (Oberbayern, Darmstadt, Köln) but also to some of its poorest.

Nine development priorities were drawn up by the EC in consultation with the Federal and *Länder* governments. The priorities and proportion of total EC funds allocated to them are shown below:

Priority
1. Promotion of infrastructure related to economic activities (22%);
2. Support for productive investment (23%);
3. Development of human resources (16%);
4. Combating long-term unemployment (3%);
5. Facilitating youth employment (8%);
6. Development of agriculture, forestry and fisheries (12%);
7. Improvement of the living and working conditions in rural areas (13% for priority 7 + 8);
8. Improvement of the agricultural, forestry and rural environment (see 7);
9. Technical assistance (3%)

Much of EC aid to the new *Länder* was to be used to support projects and schemes which had been earmarked for national expenditures. Priority 1 schemes envisage the modernisation and extension of industry-related infrastructure investments such as the development of new industrial sites and the redevelopment of old sites, the improvement of local transport links to industrial areas, energy and water supply, sewage disposal and assistance for the creation of small and medium-sized enterprises.

Priority 2 schemes support aims to accelerate the diversification of the industrial sector, in particular through the creation of producer–service industries. The creation of high-quality jobs associated with the innovative capacity of companies, technology transfer and funds for the dissemination and application of new research are intended.

The success of Priority 1 and 2 schemes is regarded as being dependent upon improvements in manpower development and training (Priority 3). Vocational and occupational mobility schemes are targeted at those sectors where economic restructuring will result in substantial changes to the labour–capital mix. Support is given especially to vocational training schemes organised in 'off-firm' centres.

As Chapter 6 clearly demonstrated, the economic transformation of the new *Länder* has given rise to high levels of unemployment particularly among the female workforce. Priority 4 schemes therefore focus upon training opportunities for the long-term unemployed and recognise the weaker situation of women in local labour markets.

The impact of economic restructuring upon youth employment is the focus for Priority 5 schemes. Greatest concern lies with the effect that company closures will have upon apprenticeships. Consequently, work placements, the promotion of self-employment and recruitment subsidies are encapsulated in this scheme.

Priorities 6, 7 and 8 focus exclusively upon rural areas in the new *Länder*. Under Priority 6 schemes attention is focused upon aid for family farms for investment purposes, assistance to those farmers in more marginal farming regions of the new *Länder* and aid for improvements in the processing and marketing of agricultural produce in order to meet EC sanitary and hygiene standards. Priority 7 schemes are designed to assist the improvement of working and living conditions in rural areas. Assistance is provided not only for production-related infrastructure investment but also for productive investment outside the agricultural sector. EC funds are therefore used to finance the construction of roads, farm tracks and sewers, the installation of water supply and drainage pipelines, the modernisation of farm buildings and the promotion of rural tourism. Priority 8 schemes enable EC funds to be used for the protection of the natural environment. This includes nature conservation programmes and, in conjunction, developing the recreational potential of the countryside.

Technical assistance (Priority 9) includes preparatory studies, advice and consultancy on the identification of appropriate projects and their implementation and the monitoring, evaluation and exchange of experience. These measures will cover all the Priority schemes, 1–8. Particular attention within each scheme is to be given to the gathering of accurate statistical information on social and economic trends within the new *Länder*, an issue that dogged the EC in its preparatory investigation of the new *Länder* before their membership of the Community.

The allocation of EC funds among the new *Länder* (five *Länder* plus Ost Berlin) was determined by using population totals, since the EC did not have the necessary statistical information normally required for expenditure allocations. Consequently, as Table 7.2 shows, the highest proportion of EC funds was allocated to Sachsen (24%) followed by Sachsen-Anhalt (17%). While Mecklenburg-Vorpommern has the lowest total allocation (excluding Ost Berlin) with only 14%, it accounts for over one-quarter of total expenditure of the European Agricultural Guidance and Guarantee Funds (EAGGF) in the new *Länder*, reflecting the dominance of agriculture in the regional production structure.

The transformation of the new *Länder* is already well underway, though at considerable financial cost. Germany's preoccupation with its domestic economic problems has therefore seriously affected its role in the EC over the last few years. As noted in Chapter 3, the political development of the EC has been dependent upon a close relationship between France and Germany. At the time of German unification both countries spoke of German union within European union. This belief focused upon the new

Table 7.2 *EC expenditure in the new Länder under the CSF programme (ECU million)*

	Total	ERDF	ESF	EAGGF
Mecklenburg-Vorpommern	409.2	177.3	80.1	151.8
Brandenburg	475.8	239.9	103.7	132.2
Sachsen-Anhalt	505.4	268.2	114.9	122.3
Sachsen	732.7	444.0	182.8	105.9
Thüringen	432.7	244.4	102.3	86.0
Ost Berlin	164.2	116.2	46.2	1.8
Non-regional	225.0	–	225.0	–
Technical assistance	55.0	10.0	45.0	–
	3000	1500	900	600

Source: EC, 1991.

Germany being contained within a French-dominated EC. Consequently, the 'full steam ahead' to ratify the Treaty of Maastricht for closer economic, monetary and political union in the EC was based upon the view that only by substituting an EC currency (the Ecu) for the Deutschmark could Germany's economic power and inherent political power be contained. Attention throughout the EC has been more than usually focused upon Germany since unification. Spence (1991b) suggests that the most important lesson for the EC has been the short-term failure of German unification, arguing that since German economic and monetary union in July 1990 the new *Länder* have been in almost permanent crisis. The ballooning costs of propping up the new *Länder* have heightened German worries over inflation and caused tighter monetary policies to be adopted. The implications of this decision have not been limited to the new Germany. The Community's member states are, through their membership of the EC's monetary system, tied to the fortunes of the German economy. German unification has thus come to determine the speed and success of EC integration.

High German interest rates have created major strains within the EC's monetary system since 1990. The crumbling in 1993 of the Exchange Rate Mechanism (ERM), one of the pillars of EC monetary policy contained in the Maastricht treaty, has severely retarded the pace of EC integration. It remains to be seen how the Community will soldier on from this major set-back.

German unification created not only a new EC state but also a new European actor. The new Germany occupies a key geographical position in the new Europe. The historical links of the new *Länder* with the COMECON countries serve to re-emphasise Germany's commitment and responsibility towards Eastern Europe. Since 1990 the German government has actively promoted the idea of a widening of the EC to encompass the new democracies of Central and Eastern Europe. The new Germany has an obvious policy interest in maintaining the stability and increasing the prosperity of its East European neighbours be it to prevent large flows of migrants into Germany or to secure German investment and trade outlets there. The new Germany can therefore be expected to play a pivotal role in the EC's relations with Eastern Europe. This is discussed below.

THE NEW GERMANY IN THE NEW EUROPE

Following the breakup of the Communist bloc in Eastern Europe and the wish of the newly found democracies to seek closer political and economic links with Western Europe (particularly with the EC), the strategic position of the new Germany to prosper from these developments has become readily apparent both within and outside the country. However, at the same time, the enormous political changes in Eastern Europe are also seen by many Germans as a source of chaos, cash demands and refugees. Such is the position of the new Germany in the new Europe.

Speaking in 1990, the former West German Chancellor Helmut Schmidt announced:

> we Germans must not become too occupied with only the GDR; in bridging the gaps between West and East Germany we must, at the same time, avoid creating new economic and social gaps from the other European parts of Europe. Germany must participate in the joint financial effort in favour of Poland, Czechoslovakia, Hungary and others. If these states wish to be associated with the European Community they ought to be accepted. Full membership and participation may become goals for the end of the 1990s (Richard Dimbleby Lecture, 3 May).

The German foreign minister also echoed these views in the same year, calling for the creation of 'one Europe, a Europe that includes all European countries without exception' (Press Release, German Embassy, 24 October 1990). The new Germany has played a key role in shaping EC policies towards Eastern Europe and the former USSR and has acted as a driving force behind Community support for reformist countries in the region. The EC has focused upon short- and medium-term support for the reform processes and this has involved aid and technical assistance through participation in the Poland and Hungary Aid Relief Programme (PHARE), the signing of association agreements and trade concessions with several East European countries and the creation of a European Bank for Reconstruction and Development (EBRD) which grants loans for fostering the transition towards market-oriented economies and the promotion of private initiative. The PHARE programme has four main aims—to improve access to Western

Table 7.3   *German aid to the former USSR 1989–92*
            (DM bn.)

Item	
(1) Non-repayable grants	18.19
(2) Loan and export guarantees	41.65
(3) Transfer Rouble balance	17.10
(4) Financing of investment projects	2.90
Total	79.84

Source: German Embassy Press Release, 15 September 1992.

markets for East European products; to stabilise and improve food supply; to ensure environmental protection; to facilitate economic restructuring. In addition, the EC has set up educational cooperation programmes (known as TEMPUS) which aim to encourage the mobility of students and teachers between the EC and Eastern Europe.

The German financial contribution to these EC schemes exceeds that of individual Community members. German financial support to the former USSR is also considerably greater than that from any other Western country. Since the end of 1989 Germany has provided almost DM80 billion in aid to the former USSR (see Table 7.3). Private donations from individuals, churches and political parties have accounted for DM0.4 billion of this total. Non-repayable grants (item (1)) are largely to finance Soviet troop withdrawals from the new *Länder* including transport costs, retraining measures and a housing construction programme for returning military personnel. In addition, funds are also used for technical assistance and food aid under EC programmes for the former USSR. Indeed, Germany has contributed almost one-third of all funds for EC programmes in Eastern Europe and the former USSR. Item (2) allocations are credit guarantees for food and other goods, while item (3) constitutes in effect a German loan to the former USSR since it relates to trade conducted between the former GDR and COMECON in 1990 under a transferable-rouble basis. The item refers to claims arising from surpluses on exports to the USSR in that year from the new *Länder*. Item (4) costs refer to the financing of two projects in the former USSR, one a gas project at Yamburg, the other an ore project at Krivoi Rog.

Efforts to attract West German and foreign investment into the new German *Länder* have also emphasised the proximity of the East European market and the possibility for investors of using the former GDR as a springboard into the East. The German foreign minister, speaking in late 1990 declared: 'investment in Germany, in the five new federal states, is an appealing proposition not least because now is the time to gain a foothold in the development of the economies of Central and Eastern Europe. Thanks to its good contacts and expertise, East Germany can be a useful springboard for investment in any part of the Central and East European market' (Embassy Press Release, 24 October 1990). The European Commission (*Regional Development Studies*, 1992, p.88) also commented that 'many foreign companies perceive Central and Eastern Europe as an expanding new market and a production base for supplying Western Europe, with the advantage of cheap labour'. While reliable statistics on foreign investment are difficult to obtain, it is clear that the level of foreign investment in Eastern Europe has increased steadily as East European governments have eased restrictions on Western companies. Since 1989, the greatest level of foreign investment in Eastern Europe has been in Hungary, Poland and the former Yugoslavia. The tourism sector has, so far, been the principal recipient of foreign investment (EC 1992a). The car industry has also benefited from a high degree of foreign investment, with many car manufacturers investing heavily in joint ventures in Central and Eastern Europe. The German car giant, Volkswagen, was quick to realise the opportunities for expanding its operations eastwards, completing in 1990 a DM9.5 billion deal with Skoda in the former Czechoslovakia. This deal will not only result in the extension and modernisation of the Skoda plant and the construction of a new engine-making plant in Bohemia but will also lead to the integration of Skoda into Volkswagen's world-wide production system. Throughout the countries of Eastern Europe, German firms already occupy the leading position in terms of the number of joint ventures. For example, of the 4429 joint ventures established in Hungary by late 1990 over 1100 involved German investors; in 1993 a German Chamber of Commerce was opened in Hungary.

The Eastern market on the new Germany's doorstep is expected to lead to substantial trade flows in both directions. However, the level of German trade with Eastern Europe and the former USSR has fallen quite considerably since 1989. As Table 7.6 shows, the value of German imports from Eastern Europe and the former USSR fell from DM52 billion in 1989 to DM39 billion in 1991, while exports figures also showed a similar decline. However, this overall picture disguises key differences between the old and new *Länder* in their trade relations with Eastern Europe and the former USSR (Tables 7.4, 7.5, 7.6). The restructuring of the economy of the new *Länder* since 1990 has had a major impact upon its trade with its former partners in COMECON. The value of import and export trade has declined sharply. For example, exports from the new *Länder* to the former USSR (previously its largest trading partner in COMECON) have fallen from DM16.6 billion in 1988 to DM9 billion in 1991. However, it is important to recognise that although levels of trade between the new *Länder* and Eastern Europe and the former USSR have fallen since German

Table 7.4 *Trade flows between the new Länder (inc. Ost Berlin) and their principal trading partners in Eastern Europe and the former USSR, 1988–91 (DM bn.)*

	1988	1989	1990	1991
Imports from				
Former USSR	16.5	15.0	9.1	4.2
Poland	2.9	2.9	1.8	0.7
Former Czechoslovakia	3.3	3.1	1.7	0.7
Hungary	2.3	2.3	1.2	0.2
Exports to				
Former USSR	16.6	16.5	17.7	9.0
Poland	3.0	3.1	2.9	0.9
Former Czechoslovakia	3.9	3.8	3.4	0.6
Hungary	2.6	2.5	2.6	0.3

Source: *Statistisches Jahrbuch (Deutschland)*, Wiesbaden, 1992.

Table 7.5 *Trade flows between the old Länder and their principal trading partners in Eastern Europe and the former USSR, 1988–91 (DM bn.)*

	1988	1989	1990	1991
Imports from				
Former USSR	6.8	8.5	9.1	9.8
Poland	2.9	3.5	5.1	6.4
Former Czechoslovakia	2.1	2.4	2.7	4.3
Hungary	2.2	2.6	3.2	4.0
Exports to				
Former USSR	9.4	11.2	10.3	8.6
Poland	2.8	4.4	4.6	7.4
Former Czechoslovakia	2.4	2.7	3.0	4.3
Hungary	2.7	3.6	3.3	3.8

Source: *Statistisches Jahrbuch (Deutschland)*, Wiesbaden, 1992.

unification, these former COMECON countries still represent very important trading markets for East German firms. For example, in 1988 the former USSR was the source for 39% of imports into the new *Länder* and at the same time was the destination for 41% of the new *Länder*'s exports. In 1991, a similar situation existed with the former USSR still providing 39% of the new *Länder*'s imports and taking almost 52% of their exports.

Unlike the new *Länder*, the value of trade between West Germany and

Table 7.6 *Trade flows between the new Germany and Eastern Europe and the former USSR, 1989–91 (DM bn.)*

	1989	1990	1991
Imports from			
Former USSR	23.6	18.2	14.1
Bulgaria	1.5	0.9	0.5
Former Yugoslavia	7.1	7.6	7.7
Poland	6.5	6.9	7.2
Romania	2.8	1.5	1.2
Former Czechoslovakia	5.6	4.4	5.0
Hungary	5.0	4.4	4.2
Total	52.1	43.9	39.9
% New Germany's Imports	9.5	7.6	6.1
Exports to			
Former USSR	28.1	28.1	17.6
Bulgaria	2.8	2.2	0.7
Former Yugoslavia	7.9	8.4	6.9
Poland	7.5	7.6	8.4
Romania	2.0	2.6	1.2
Former Czechoslovakia	6.5	6.4	4.9
Hungary	6.2	6.0	4.2
Total	61.0	61.3	43.9
% New Germany's Exports	8.9	9.0	6.5

Source: *Statistisches Jahrbuch (Deutschland)*, Wiesbaden, 1992.

Eastern Europe and the former USSR has increased rapidly since 1988. It has been with countries other than the former USSR that the greatest increases in trade value have been recorded. For example, West German imports from Poland increased by 122%, from Czechoslovkia by 100% and from Hungary by 77% between 1988 and 1991. West German exports to these countries have also shown large increases over the same time period (Poland 158%, Czechoslovakia 77%, Hungary 39%). However, while these figures show the growing importance of the East European market for West German firms, the West European market (EC and EFTA) remains of greatest significance accounting for 70% of West Germany's exports and 67% of its imports in 1991.

The new Germany's trade relations with Eastern Europe and the former USSR therefore show a rather complicated situation: actual trade falling between the new *Länder* and the east yet the east remaining the largest foreign market of the new *Länder*; substantial increases in trade between

West Germany and Eastern Europe and the former USSR since German unification yet Western Europe remaining West Germany's principal market. The overall effect of this upon the new Germany's trade is that Eastern Europe and the former USSR provided 9.5% of the new Germany's imports in 1988 yet only 6.1% in 1991 and similarly took 8.9% of the new Germany's exports in 1988 yet only 6.5% in 1991. In the short term, therefore, there have not been major shifts in the trading pattern of the new Germany. However, in the medium and long term, a revitalised economy in the new *Länder* combined with Germany's historic ties with Eastern Europe could give the new Germany a leading role in the pattern of trade between Western and Eastern Europe. As Neuss (in Grosser, 1992) remarks, 'the new Germany will be much in demand as a partner for the newly reformed Eastern and Russian states and the CIS' (p.137). There is no doubt that securing this role will be a priority for the new Germany. Consequently, one should expect a series of German initiatives towards this end. The promotion of the German language in Eastern Europe can be regarded as part of this strategy.

In *Die Welt* on 24 August 1992 a small item entitled 'Sonderprogramm deutsche Sprache für den Osten' (Special programme for the German language in Eastern Europe) was included. The promotion of language and culture should not be underestimated in the process of economic growth and domination. Gruner (1992) suggests that 'on the basis of geography and its special European position Germany, deliberately but not arrogantly, must take on a constructive and creative responsibility for the growing together of Europe, though without presenting itself as the "master" of this process' (p.221). The Sonderprogramm is a clear attempt to augment Germany's economic and political ambitions and responsibilities towards Central and Eastern Europe.

In 1991 Germany spent DM49 million on promoting its language and culture across the world. The German government has announced that between 1993 and 1995 DM45 million will be spent each year on similar activities in Eastern Europe, where the previously compulsory teaching of Russian has been lifted and the popularity of German is increasing. German monies, directed through a network of institutions such as Goethe Institutes and the German Academic Exchange Service (DAAD), will be spent on the purchase of teaching materials, the construction of libraries and the organisation of various cultural events. Following the setting up of a main Goethe Institute in Moscow, further regional institutes were established in 1992 (in Riga, Minsk, Kiev and Altma Ata) and two others (St. Petersburg and Tiflis) were opened in 1993. In total there were 14 Goethe Institutes across Eastern Europe and the former USSR by the end of 1993. The demand for German language training in Eastern Europe has been considerable since 1989. For example, the Ministry of Education in Poland

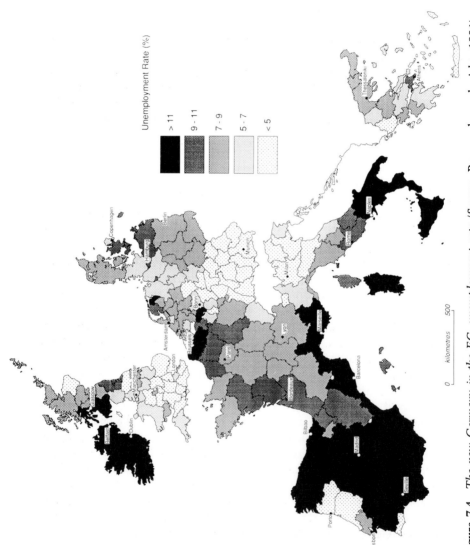

Figure 7.4 *The new Germany in the EC: unemployment rate (Source: Raumordnungsbericht, 1991)*

in 1991 advertised for 8000 prospective German teachers in recognition of the growing economic links (particularly labour movements) between the two countries.

The promotion of the German language has, however, suffered some set backs. Events in 1992, particularly neo-Nazi violence against foreigners, reduced the number of people visiting Germany to enrol on language courses run by the Goethe Institutes. In late November 1992, the president of the Goethe Institute reported that there was an 'enormous wave of antipathy' towards things German reflected in plummeting registrations for German language courses. The Goethe Institute was then forced to inform foreign students coming to Germany to learn the language that it could no longer guarantee their safety (*The Independent*, 27 November 1992).

The promotion of German trade with Eastern Europe and the former USSR and the substantial allocation of aid is also intended to stem possible large population flows from Eastern to Western Europe. Germany regards itself as in the frontline of population migration from Eastern Europe. Since 1989 the migration question has become one of the most pressing political issues in the new Germany.

POPULATION MOVEMENTS AND THE NEW GERMANY

In the 1980s between 12 000 and 40 000 East Germans (*Ubersiedler*) were allowed to leave the DDR each year in order to settle in West Germany. In 1989, following the events described in Chapter 4, 344 000 East Germans headed west to settle in West Germany, and in the six months before German economic and monetary union in July 1990, a further 239 000 followed. Some 20% of all *Ubersiedler* settled in Bayern in 1989–90, while a further 30% settled in Baden-Württemberg and Nordrhein-Westfalen. While there are problems of adjustment for East Germans in West Germany, attention since 1990 has focused upon the arrival in Germany of both thousands of ethnic Germans from Eastern Europe and the former USSR and asylum seekers who have limited or no knowledge of the German language.

The number of ethnic Germans (*Aussiedler*) living outside of Germany who are eligible for entry and residence in the country is difficult to determine, not least because heretofore those who have claimed even the most distant German ancestry have been able to gain German citizenship. A report in *Le Monde* in 1990 estimated that in Romania alone there were over 200 000 people who could apply for entry into Germany as ethnic Germans. The German government estimated in June 1992 that in the former USSR there were approximately 2.5 million ethnic Germans, with at least one million of them residing in Kazakhstan and a further 840 000 living in Russia (see Table 7.7). In total, some 3.4 million ethnic Germans are estimated to be living in the former USSR, Poland, Hungary, Romania,

Table 7.7   *Ethnic Germans in the former*
            USSR, 1989

Kazakhstan	957 000
Russian Federation	842 295
Kirgiziya	101 309
Usbekistan	39 809
Ukraine	37 849
Tadzhikistan	32 671
Moldova	7335
Turkmenistan	4434
Latvia	3783
Belorussia	3517
Estonia	3466
Lithuania	2058
Georgia	1546
Azerbaijan	748
Armenia	265
Total	2 038 603

Source: Bundesministerium des Innern, Bonn, 1992.

Czechoslovakia and Hungary according to recent calculations by the Bundesministerium des Innern (1992). This large number of ethnic Germans who may have the right of entry and admission into Germany is politically alarming. The possibility of ethnic unrest in the former USSR could potentially create large flows of ethnic Germans seeking permanent settlement in the new Germany.

During the period 1980–7 between 36 000 and 78 000 *Aussiedler* from Eastern Europe (mainly from Poland, the USSR and Romania) settled in West Germany. In 1988, a further 202 000 were admitted into West Germany causing particular difficulties for local labour and housing markets. Many of them arrived with little knowledge of German, wearing old-style peasant clothes and having idealised notions of some old pre-war Germany (Ardagh, 1991) (see Photograph 11).

The flow of ethnic Germans into Germany since German unification has continued largely unabated. Between the end of 1989 and 1991 well in excess of one million people entered Germany as *Aussiedler*. In 1991, 221 995 *Aussiedler* arrived in Germany, of whom 147 320 (66%) were from the former USSR. While their applications are processed, accommodation has to found by often hard-pressed local authorities.

Table 7.8 shows the number of *Aussiedler* settling in the individual *Länder* of Germany in 1991. Not surprisingly, 92% of all *Aussiedler* arriving in Germany in 1991 settled in the West German *Länder*. Nordrhein-Westfalen and Baden-Württemberg were the preferred destinations for *Aussiedler*, with

Photograph 11 *Ethnic Germans from the former USSR in a reception centre in Baden-Wurttemberg*. Many ethnic Germans have arrived in Germany since 1989. With few belongings, little knowledge of the German language and idealised views of life in modern Germany, their arrival has caused particular problems for the authorities

the former accounting for almost 30% of those arriving in Germany in that year. Pressure upon housing in both *Länder* was intense. For example, in the brown-coal-mining region west of Köln, where village resettlement schemes are taking place as a result of mining operations, properties in deserted villages have been used to house both *Aussiedler* and asylum seekers. In the former village of Garzweiler, ethnic Germans from the CIS were being housed in quickly constructed apartment blocks often shared with Romanian

Table 7.8   *Aussiedler arriving in Germany in 1991. Breakdown by Länder*

	Total	from	
		Poland	Former USSR
Nordrhein-Westfalen	63 747	18 570	42 116
Baden-Württemberg	36 617	3973	22 510
Bayern	34 232	3928	15 141
Niedersachsen	24 984	3647	20 672
Hessen	18 423	2458	14 486
Rheinland-Pfalz	12 385	1519	9965
Saarland	5037	632	3701
Schleswig-Holstein	3781	2031	1633
Bremen	3081	1227	1811
Hamburg	2612	717	1769
Sachsen	5297	223	4277
Thüringen	3809	268	3069
Sachsen-Anhalt	3027	310	2521
Brandenburg	2730	114	2134
Mecklenburg-VP	1905	308	1470
Berlin	328	204	45
Total	221 995	40 219	147 320

Source: Info-Dienst Deutsche Aussiedler, 1991.

and Yugoslavian asylum seekers (Photograph 12). Similarly in the *Land* capital, Düsseldorf, emergency housing has been constructed. This consists of 'container dwellings' which are one-bedroomed containers some 14 sq. metres in size and equipped with two bunk beds. Accommodation, albeit in very cramped conditions, is provided for four people. Between 1989 and 1991 container settlements of 20–40 units apiece were installed at 18 locations in the city. These container 'settlements' have become a permanent feature of the city's housing fabric, with some ethnic German families having already spent several years living in them (Glebe, 1994). In Baden-Württemberg former army barracks such as those at Rastatt have been selected as temporary housing for *Aussiedler*.

In an attempt to reduce some of the costs and pressures upon local authorities, the Ethnic Germans Admissions Act came into force on 1 July 1990. This Act requires those applying for residence in Germany as ethnic Germans to remain in their present home country while their application is being processed by the German authorities. By the end of 1991, approximately 500 000 applications for residence were made, and in the first 11 months of 1992 another 361 000. Between January and November 1992 a further 200 000 *Aussiedler* were allowed entry into Germany.

Consequently, since 1990 the German government has stepped up its

Photograph 12 *Village desertion brown-coal area, Garzweiler, Nordrhein-Westfalen.* The open-cast mining of brown coal in Nordrhein-Westfalen has required the demolition of many villages west of Köln. Many deserted properties have been used for the temporary accommodation of asylum seekers and ethnic Germans

financial support to those countries and regions in Eastern Europe and the former USSR where large numbers of ethnic Germans are known to live. The overriding aim of this support is to ensure that ethnic Germans remain in these settlement areas and at the same time retain their German cultural and language identity. Improving living conditions and promoting German language and culture are the focal points for German assistance to these areas. There are seven ways in which the German government hopes to achieve these aims:

* German clubs and meeting places (*Begegnungsstätten*);
* Publishing and distribution of local German newspapers;
* German radio and television programmes;
* Cultural events;
* School and youth club exchanges;
* Economic assistance to small businesses;
* Medical help.

Figure 7.5 shows the extent of these German-financed activities across the former USSR. Some 60 German clubs have been set up in the former USSR

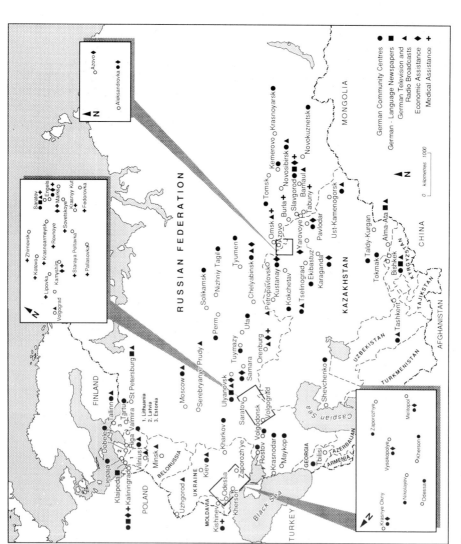

Figure 7.5 *German government assistance to German communities in the CIS, Georgia and the Baltic States, 1992* (*Source:* Government Office for Ethnic German Questions, Bonn)

and more are planned. Each club contains German books and magazines and a TV/video recorder with a collection of German films and language programmes. The clubs also offer training courses on agricultural issues, building and handicraft. Support for German-language newspapers is also given, in particular assistance towards setting up costs, printing and distribution as well as training for journalists. Nine German newspapers have been established in the former USSR, including the *Neues Leben* in Moscow, the *Nachrichten* in Uljanovsk, *Der Tropfen* in Bischkek and the *Deutsche Zeitung für Litauen* in Lithuania. Since October 1990, German TV and radio broadcasts to Eastern Europe and the former USSR have been increased and new stations and masts constructed. Ethnic Germans throughout the region can now tune into two half-hour programmes fortnightly, one on TV (known as 'Drehscheibe Europa') and another on radio ('Blickpunkt Europa') with each providing news, current affairs and documentary features. Cultural links between the new Germany and ethnic Germans in Eastern Europe and the former USSR are also maintained through various cultural programmes such as visiting orchestras, choirs and touring theatre companies. Since 1990 the German government has financed 74 such cultural programmes in the region. At school level, the German government has sponsored youth exchanges and supplied large amounts of German language teaching material.

On the economic and welfare front, German monies have gone towards assisting small economic ventures (for example, bakeries and butchers), particularly in areas where large ethnic German populations are settled. A large proportion of German aid for this purpose has therefore been directed towards the Volga region and northern Kazakhstan. Improving the welfare of ethnic Germans is to be achieved by increasing supplies of medications, drugs and instruments for local hospitals and district pharmacies. The Volga region has again been the main recipient of this aid.

However, the rate of migration of ethnic Germans to the new Germany is likely to depend upon other factors than the amount of German financial assistance to areas in which they are currently settled. The very generous rights of asylum in Germany, as defined by Article 16 of the Basic Law of 1949, have made the country an attractive destination for asylum seekers (see Table 7.9). Between 1990 and March 1992 over 636 000 people sought asylum in Germany. Since 1990, over 100 000 people from war-torn Yugoslavia and 76 000 from Romania have sought asylum in Germany. Internal disputes in the former USSR and Sri Lanka resulted in a further 11 000 people seeking asylum in Germany in 1991. The Federal Office for Recognition of Asylum Applications (Bundesamt für die Anerkennung von Asylbewerbern) is responsible for processing applications for asylum in Germany. They are assisted in this task by some 46 regional centres. Each of the *Länder* has to accept a given percentage of asylum seekers. For example,

Table 7.9   *Arrival of asylum seekers in Germany, 1989–91: country/region of origin*

	1989 Number	1989 %	1990 Number	1990 %	1991 Number	1991 %
Romania	3121	2.6	35 345	18.3	40 504	15.8
Former Yugoslavia	19 423	16.0	22 114	11.5	74 854	29.2
Turkey	20 020	16.5	22 082	11.4	23 877	9.3
Lebanon	6240	5.1	16 229	8.4	–	
Vietnam	984	0.8	9428	4.9	8133	3.2
Poland	26 092	21.5	9155	4.7	–	
Bulgaria	429	0.4	8341	4.3	12 056	4.7
Afghanistan	3650	3.0	7348	3.8	7337	2.9
Iran	5768	4.8	7271	3.8	8643	3.4
Palestine	2315	1.9	5723	3.0	–	
Total	121 318	100	193 063	100	256 112	68.5

Source: SOPEMI, 1992.

Hessen has to accept 7.4% of those people seeking asylum in Germany. Three reception centres have been created in Hessen—in Schwalbach, Giesen and since spring 1993 at Gelnhausen. This latter centre houses almost 1000 asylum seekers in former army barracks. With over 20 000 asylum seekers arriving each month in Germany, an almost intolerable burden has been placed upon regional and local authorities, whose responsibility it is to house, feed and, more recently, to protect them pending the outcome of their applications. In Hamburg, for example, 576 asylum seekers are being housed in 'floating accommodation' (*Wohnschiff*) in the harbour (*Frankfurter Allgemeine Zeitung*, 8 August 1992), while in Schleswig-Holstein, former brewery buildings and army barracks have been the temporary solution to asylum accommodation. The cost of housing and social security support (*Sozialhilfe*) for asylum seekers is considerable. For example, there were only 309 asylum seekers in the former border town of Helmstedt in Niedersachsen in 1991, yet over 2300 by August 1992, the majority of whom were from Romania. Pressures upon the local authority to find accommodation for them has been immense, resulting in the conversion of buildings or new temporary structures being hastily erected. In excess of DM2.3 million were spent on social security support for asylum seekers in Helmstedt in the first six months of 1992. In large metropolitan areas such as West Berlin the problem is of a much greater dimension, with 2300 people seeking asylum in 1988, some 16 000 in 1990, and a further 9800 in 1991.

The asylum issue has generated great public and political debate. A public-opinion survey commissioned by the Federal Ministry for Press and

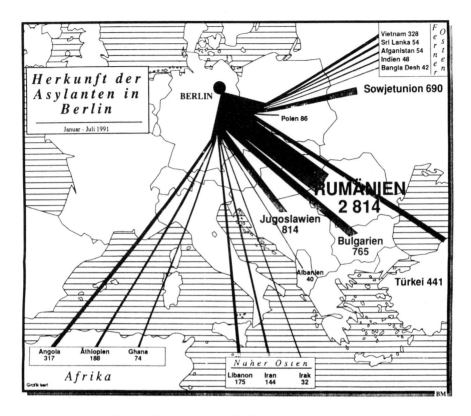

Figure 7.6 *Arrival of asylum seekers in Berlin*

Information and carried out in July 1992 revealed that while unemployment was regarded as the most important problem facing the new Germany by respondents in East Germany, the asylum issue and 'foreigners question' (*Ausländerfrage*) were the biggest worries for those surveyed in West Germany (reported in the *Magdeburger Volksstimme* newspaper on 28 July 1992). Some of the German press have portrayed the asylum question in less than subtle ways. For example, the Berlin newspaper *MorgenPost* on 11 August 1991 included a map of the origin of asylum seekers arriving in Berlin which was portrayed in a way that resembled a military invasion chart (see Figure 7.6).

The asylum question has been cited as one of the principal reasons for the outbreak of xenophobic violence that has engulfed Germany since 1990. Sporadic attacks against hostels and other centres for asylum seekers and resident Turkish workers have occurred in both the old and new *Länder*. In

1992 violence intensified, and many local authorities were forced to shunt bus loads of asylum seekers between cities and across *Länder* boundaries in search of 'safe' accommodation. In August 1992 one of the most serious outbreaks of violence against asylum seekers took place in the Baltic port of Rostock in Mecklenburg-Vorpommern. Rostock has been severely affected by the process of German unification with over 15 000 jobs lost in the shipbuilding industry and unemployment levels well in excess of 15%. In the Lichtenhagen district of the city, where the unemployment level had risen to 17%, stood an 11-storey apartment block with a bright sunflower mural (Sonnenblümenhaus). It was the home for Vietnamese workers who had been in the city even before German unification and for asylum seekers from Romania who, since 1991, had been arriving in Rostock at the rate of 70–80 daily. Although the block itself was designed to accommodate 320, there were twice if not three times that number living there by August 1992. Tensions between local residents and the asylum seekers were already running high following the murder of a Romanian asylum seeker in March of the same year (*Die Welt*, 25 August 1992). The attack on the hostel by an estimated 200 neo-Nazis in front of a crowd of over 1200 local people chanting '*Ausländer raus*' (foreigners out) received widespread political condemnation. The incident marked the beginning of more widespread and frequent attacks upon ethnic minorities in Germany, culminating in the fire-bombing of a house in the north German town of Mölln in November 1992 which caused the deaths of three Turkish people.

Against a background of growing alarm over neo-Nazi attacks on foreigners, the German government and opposition parties, after months of disagreement, finally agreed plans in early December 1992 to tighten regulations covering applications for asylum in the country (*Süddeutsche Zeitung*, 7 December 1992). In 1993 the Bundestag voted by a two-thirds majority in favour of changing the constitution to enable the German authorities to turn back asylum seekers entering from other European countries or from other countries in which it is judged that there is no political persecution. In addition, the processing of asylum applications is to be speeded up, thereby reducing the costs of housing asylum seekers in Germany.

Tighter policing of the German frontier with Poland and the former Czechoslovakia has also been instigated since 1991 in a major drive to reduce the entry into Germany of illegal migrants. Over three-quarters of those illegal immigrants in Germany in 1991 had entered the country from either Poland or Czechoslovakia. These trans-frontier regions are also the subject of economic cooperation programmes ('Euroregions') between Germany, Poland and the Czech Republic. Seven Euro-regions have been established along the Polish–German and Czech–German borders. These

Photograph 13 *Anti-racism poster in Dresden, Sachsen.* 'Christ a jew, your car Japanese, your Pizza Italian, your democracy Greek, your coffee Brazilian, your holiday Turkish, your arithmetic arabic, your script latin . . . and your neighbour only a foreigner?'

regions have been badly affected historically through population displacement as a result of war and suspicions over German territorial ambitions. Cooperation is envisaged between businesses on each side of the frontier, as well as the joint financing of projects (industrial, rural, tourism and environmental) of mutual benefit. The financial involvement of the EC is also expected under a new Community initiative known as 'Interreg'.

THE BONN–BERLIN DEBATE AND THE NEW GERMANY

German unification raised the issue of where the future capital of the country should be. As Chapter 1 described, there had been great debate in 1949 over the choice of capital for the Federal Republic. One of the main reasons for Bonn's selection was that its capital status would be provisional, i.e. until Berlin and Germany were reunited. However, over the last 40 years Bonn has not only served as seat of government and home of accredited embassies but has also symbolised the democratic nature of post-war West Germany. The *Einigungsvertrag* (Article 2) of 1990 categorically stated that the capital of the united Germany would be Berlin, though the question of the seat of parliament and government was to be resolved at a later date. This marked the beginning of a lengthy and what turned out to be an acrimonious debate over whether Bonn or Berlin would house the parliamentary and governmental offices of the new Germany.

Laux (1991) provides an excellent analysis of the 'Bonn versus Berlin' question (*Haupstadtfrage*). On 20 June 1991 members of the Bundestag debated the issue in a session lasting over 10 hours and including 107 oral and 105 written statements. With almost one-third of Bundestag members contributing, it was indeed one of the fullest debates in the Bundestag's history.

Proponents of Berlin as seat of parliament and government, argued three points:

(i)   the choice of Berlin would be an important step in achieving true political and social union of the two Germanies;

(ii) the economic and social development of the new *Länder* would best be achieved (in speed and effectiveness) by locating government offices in Berlin;

(iii) the choice of Berlin would not only demonstrate the Federal government's commitment to the new *Länder* but would recognise the changing European situation in which the new Germany found itself, i.e. as a bridge between Western and Eastern Europe.

Among politicians, Richard von Weizsäcker, the German President and Hans-Dietrich Genscher, the Foreign Minister, both championed Berlin. The Chancellor, Helmut Kohl, appeared less sure.

For those in favour of Bonn, arguments centred upon five issues:

(i)   Bonn symbolised democracy and respect for European integration (in contrast to Berlin which stood for military aggression, nationalism and conflict);

(ii) West German success since 1949 had been based upon the principle of federalism, with no single German city dominating the urban hierarchy. Berlin, if chosen, would become a powerful economic and political centre, not only creating an imbalance in the federal structure of the country but also hindering development in the new *Länder* as a whole;

(iii) the cost of moving the seat of government from Bonn to Berlin would run into billions of DM. There were other, more urgent, tasks in the new *Länder* to which this money could be better put;

(iv) Berlin having been divided for over 30 years was in need of substantial infrastructure investment. Government and parliament would not be able to function effectively under such conditions;

(v)   over 80% of employment in Bonn and its sub-region was in the service sector. Over 13 000 jobs were in government ministries, 10 000 in embassies and press offices and a further 24 000 directly linked to

Bonn's function as seat of parliament and government. Removing the parliamentary and government functions from Bonn would have major social and economic consequences upon the city and the Rhein region.

In the Bundestag debate 338 members voted in favour of Berlin while 320 favoured Bonn. Among the main political parties, 145 CDU members voted for Berlin and 123 for Bonn, while the SPD members cast a majority in favour of Bonn (126 votes and only 110 for Berlin). Laux (1991) has shown that the age of MPs was also significant in their voting decision, with younger members tending to vote for Bonn rather than Berlin. Geographically, MPs from western and southern constituencies (see Figure 7.7) tended to favour Bonn while those from northern and eastern regions preferred Berlin. There were some exceptions. For example, only a small majority of members from Baden-Württemberg preferred Bonn, most of the MPs from Hessen favoured Berlin, while those from the new *Länder* of Sachsen and Thüringen voted for retaining the seat of government in Bonn. The results reflected political associations, identities and antagonisms established over the course of centuries of German history.

Following the Bundestag debate, the Federal government together with the Berlin authorities drew up plans for the transfer of parliament to Berlin. The resolution of the Bundestag stated that in addition to the parliament, the core of government functions would be located in Berlin. There was no doubt that Bonn would be seriously affected by these moves. Consequently, the Federal government in collaboration with the *Länder* of Nordrhein-Westfalen and Rheinland-Pfalz agreed to draw up proposals under which Bonn would accommodate new institutions (both national and international) to compensate for the loss of the seat of parliament and government functions. Bonn's future development was to be based upon *three* roles—as the location for new functions in the fields of science, research and technology, and education; as a government centre for cultural policy; as a seat of international and European institutions.

The Federal government did not intend for Bonn to lose all its political functions to Berlin. Eight Federal ministries and some divisions of other ministries are to stay in Bonn. Agriculture, health, defence, and somewhat surprisingly environment were included in the list of those ministries to continue to occupy sites in Bonn. Some two-thirds of all ministry jobs are expected to remain or be created in Bonn. While 9600 ministry jobs will be transferred to Berlin, the Federal government has decided to relocate 16 Federal agencies to Bonn. These include the audit, vocational training, statistics, banking supervision and insurance offices. Ironically, many of these are being relocated from Berlin. In addition to these agencies, the Federal government intends to relocate in Bonn (again largely from Berlin) the following institutions: the German International Development Foundation,

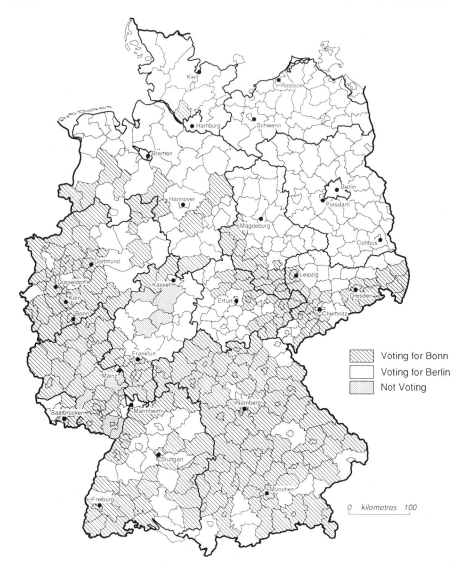

Figure 7.7 *The new Germany: voting trends (Bonn or Berlin) (Source*: Laux, 1991)

the German Development Service, the German Food Institute and the Max Planck Institute of Educational Research. About 7300 jobs are expected to be created in Bonn following these particular relocations.

The Federal government is also considering moving central and manage-ment offices of the German railways (Deutsche Bahn) to Bonn and has

Photograph 14   *Beethoven statue, Bonn.* Bonn's famous son. The development of
the city as a cultural centre for the Rhinelands is regarded as one of
the key ways in which Bonn can overcome some of the difficulties
caused by the loss of its capital city functions

approached the European Commission to have the European Centre for the
Advancement of Vocational Training (CEDEFOP) transferred from Berlin.
The Federal government has also approached the UN to seek a permanent
move of the headquarters of the UN Development Programme and UN
Population Fund to Bonn.

The development of Bonn as a science centre in the 1990s is to be based
upon the expansion of research and technology centres. Several projects are
envisaged to achieve this objective. A technical faculty is to be developed at
the University of Bonn comprising departments of biotechnology, environmental technology and a mathematics research centre. A European centre for
high-tech research in the field of strategic technology is also to be set up. In
addition, the Federal government intends to commission a study on the
creation of a science park in the Bonn region. It is expected that over 1500
new jobs will be created as a result of these initiatives.

The promotion of Bonn as a centre of cultural administration is an equally
important aim for the city's planners in the 1990s. Several projects are
intended including the establishment of a German music information centre
(based upon the idea of Bonn as the home of Beethoven (see Photograph
14)) and a European cultural research centre.

Bonn's proximity to the Brussels–Luxembourg–Strasbourg axis of the EC has prompted the Federal government to retain the European Commission bureau in Bonn and to press for new EC institutions to be located in the city. The possibility of a European central bank being housed in Bonn was also mooted, although the decision by EC governments in late 1993 to locate the EC's monetary institute in Frankfurt-am-Main has removed this possibility.

The decision by the Federal government to retain some of its political functions in Bonn and at the same time to develop the city in the 1990s as a centre for science, technology and cultural activities is not without considerable financial cost. It was announced in the Bundestag in May 1992 that the Federal government has allocated over DM212 million to developing Bonn's new functions.

The decision to move Germany's capital from Bonn also poses two major challenges for Berlin—how to manage its expected growth and how to unite the divided city. The tearing down of the Berlin Wall revealed the great contrast in conditions under which West and Ost Berliners had lived. In many respects Berlin has been selected as the capital of the new Germany at the very moment it is least able to take on the responsibility. It remains a divided city with economic and social conditions varying greatly between its western and eastern parts. For example, while 207 000 people were registered as unemployed in the city in early 1993 (13.8% of the workforce), the unemployment rate varied from 12.5% in West Berlin to 15.1% in Ost Berlin. There are, therefore, both opportunities and difficulties ahead for the city.

Controversy over the future development of Berlin has been intense. On the one hand are those who wish to see the city develop as a world metropolis linking Western and Eastern Europe, with architecture to match. On the other, is a conservationist lobby eager to protect the city from the high-rise office developments that have been constructed in West German cities such as Frankfurt-am-Main and Düsseldorf. These different viewpoints are no better expressed than in the debate over the future development of the Potsdamer Platz and Leipziger Platz, which in the 1920s and 1930s had been the heart of the thriving capital, yet in the post-war period were urban wastelands straddling the wall between the western and eastern sectors of the divided city (see Photograph 15). Now, plans are afoot to make this area the focal point of a massive development to establish a new commercial centre in Berlin. In 1990, Daimler-Benz, Sony, Asea Brown Boveri and Hertie/Wertheim, a German retail chain, purchased most of the site for development, with the Berlin authorities inviting 17 German and foreign teams of architects to tender for the design of the development. The most ambitious schemes were ruled out, eventual preference being given to a scheme proposed by a Berlin-based team which respects the conventional grid of old streets and blocks of buildings.

Photograph 15 *Potsdamer Platz, Central Berlin.* The demolition of the Berlin Wall has led to ambitious plans being proposed for the redevelopment of urban wastelands such as that at Potsdamer Platz

The modernisation of the central districts of Berlin is already well underway with building works stretching along many of the principal routeways between western and eastern parts of the city. Much of the redevelopment is being financed by the Federal government under the *Gemeinschaftswerk Aufschwung Ost* programme: for example, along Leipziger Strasse. The private banks are also heavily involved in certain urban redevelopment projects: for example, the Landesbank Berlin is financing the redevelopment of the Haus Alexander, a shopping, restaurant and office development scheme in Alexander Platz.

The central districts of the city are expected to become the primary location for government buildings. While some new constructions are planned, for example a library and conference centre on the Spree, it is hoped that many government ministries and offices will be able to occupy existing buildings. The residence of the Federal president is expected to be the Schloss Bellevue in Berlin's Tiergarten while the German Interior ministry is to take over the former SED Central Committee building (previously the Reichsbank).

The central role to be played by Berlin in the new Germany is also emphasised in the transport schemes planned to knit the two Germanies together physically (see Chapter 6). Berlin is to be a major hub of the transportation network in the new Germany, linking the country's major urban and industrial centres to each other and to similar agglomerations elsewhere in Western and Eastern Europe. The decision to move the seat of government and parliament to Berlin can only serve to increase the capital's role in the new Germany.

The removal of the seat of government from Bonn is expected to have a profound effect upon land prices in Berlin and add to the pressures upon the city's over-stretched housing market (Ellger, 1992). In February 1990, the West Berlin authorities agreed to allocate DM25 million for the promotion of urgent renewal measures in Greater Berlin, with additional funds provided by the authorities in Ost Berlin. Some 70 000 dwellings in Ost Berlin are regarded as in need of renewal, particularly buildings and blocks built before 1918 in the inner city areas of Mitte, Prenzlauer Berg and Friedrichshain. At the time of German unification in 1990, there remained over 40 000 dwellings in Ost Berlin with outdoor toilets.

It has been estimated that the united Berlin is currently short of over 100 000 dwellings, an estimate that takes a charitable view of many thousands of run-down flats in the eastern sector of the city. The provision of new housing is likely to be on green-field sites in neighbouring Brandenburg, and for this reason there is added urgency for the two states to cooperate on planning matters. There is general agreement that Berlin will increase its economic influence over neighbouring *Länder*, especially Brandenburg. While some have argued that an expanding Berlin will upset the delicate balance of the federal system in the country, in Brandenburg worries focus upon the immediate effects of the suburbanisation of the capital. Pressures for the fusion of Berlin with the *Land* of Brandenburg have become stronger since 1991 as the city has begun to exert its pull over the surrounding region. In late 1992, agreement was reached between representatives of the two *Länder* that Berlin and Brandenburg would merge by the end of the decade. Discussion has also taken place between the two *Länder* concerning cooperation over economic and regional planning. Development programmes were initiated in 1993 to deal with a range of issues emanating from the expected growth of Berlin including economic promotion in Brandenburg, regional transport improvements as well as airport construction, waste disposal and water supply and out of centre hypermarkets. Emphasis in the development plan is to be placed upon the concept of 'planning rings' (Figure 7.8). Three such rings have been designated, the first covering a radius of 40–60 kilometres from central Berlin to be linked by S-Bahn, the second to be known as Berlin's outer ring and a third within which development centres have been designated: for example Neuruppin, Frankfurt an Oder and Cottbus. These are expected to act as growth poles for surrounding areas of Brandenburg (Birkholz, 1993). The Berlin–Brandenburg agglomeration once formally merged will have a total population of 6.2 million making it the fifth largest *Land* in the new Germany and the third largest conurbation in Europe.

From 1995 Berlin will lose its favourable tax and Federal subsidy status (financial support by the Federal government for West Berlin was calculated to have reached £2000 per city resident in 1990). The two parts of the city are undergoing renewal schemes, while improving the transport links between the western and eastern parts of the city is still a high priority. The housing question is likely to remain a major problem for the city authorities as the city experiences the full effects of moving the seat of government from Bonn and taking on the capital city status measured in terms of civil servants, government officials, diplomats and journalists seeking accommodation and the growing likelihood of ever-increasing numbers of migrants from neighbouring *Länder* in search of employment.

CONCLUSIONS

The new Germany lies at the centre of Europe, and its geography makes it a central focus of European concerns. Germany, through its geographical location, economic power and history has a crucial role to play in the process of integration—not solely in the European Community but also in the development of relations between Western and Eastern Europe. As Gruner (1992) notes, 'the changes in Eastern Europe and the dissolution of the two political blocs have ended the unnatural divisions of both Germany

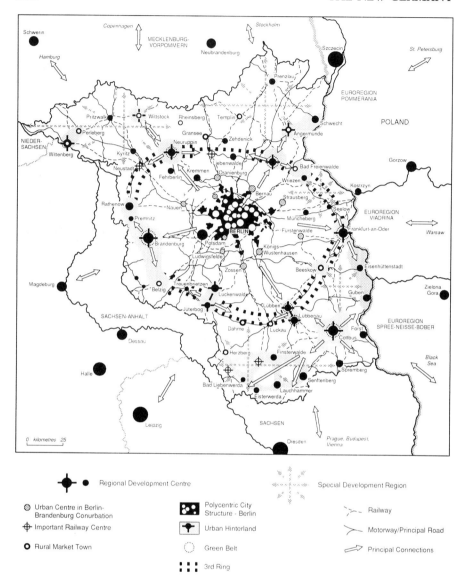

Figure 7.8 *Berlin and Brandenburg: development programme (Source:* Birkholz, 1993)

and Europe. They open up new perspectives for a unification of the continent based on what has already happened in Western Europe' (p. 219). In this chapter we have seen how the economic and social profile of Germany has been affected by the unification of West and East Germany and that these raise issues not only for Germans but also ones to which Europe as a whole must respond. German unification thus offers both major opportunities and challenges for Germany and Europe in the 1990s and beyond.

SUGGESTED FURTHER READING

Ardagh, J. (1991) *Germany and the Germans After Unification*. Penguin, London.

Ellger, C. (1992) 'Berlin: Legacies of division and problems of unification', *Geographical Journal*, **158** (1), 40–7.

Graff Kielmansegg, P. (1992) 'Germany—a future with two pasts' in D. Grosser (ed.), *German Unification. The Unexpected Challenge*. Berg, Oxford. 180–94.

Jones, P.N. and Wild, T. (1992) 'Western Germany's "third wave" of migrants—the arrival of the Aussiedler', *Geoforum*, **23** (1), 1–11.

Smyser, W.R. (1992) *The Economy of United Germany. Colossus at the Crossroads*. Hurst, London.

Stares, P.B. (ed.) (1992) *The New Germany and the New Europe*. Brookings Institution, Washington DC.

Thies, J. (1992) 'Germany—into turbulent waters', *The World Today*, **48** (8), 148–51.

Watson, A. (1992) *The Germans: Who Are They Now?* Methuen, London.

8 A conclusion that is just a beginning

Any interpretation of the processes associated with German unification and their effects must be sensitive to the speed at which policy makers were forced to act in 1989–90 and must appreciate the scale of the task that confronted them. There was no right or wrong way for managing German unification. It was a huge economic, political and social experiment whose results could not be predicted. Politicians responded to the demands of East Germans for unification with West Germany and at the same time saw great political advantage in championing the unification cause. There seemed to be no reason to disbelieve that one of the most successful economies in the world would not be able to cope with the demands placed upon it. However, it soon became all too painfully clear that the West German economy was not as healthy as it appeared—high wage costs, generous holiday provisions, pensions and social security schemes for workers had all contributed to the loss of global competitiveness of West German industry. Even in the more prosperous regions of West Germany such as Baden-Württemberg, economic weaknesses were beginning to appear. West Germans would, therefore, need to make more than minor sacrifices to accommodate East Germany. This fact did not feature in the euphoria engulfing the discussions over German unification. East Germans, meanwhile, had no doubt that unification would greatly improve their living standards, imagining that the range of material benefits and quality of life possessed by West Germans would soon be theirs also.

The effects of German unification upon the economy of the new *Länder* have been frankly catastrophic. The terms of monetary union have been the principal cause of the economic difficulties now affecting the East. Several senior financial officials in West Germany had warned of the dangers, but their advice went unheeded. The resulting collapse of the GDR economy after monetary union came so quickly that plans had not been drawn up— let alone implemented—on how to deal with it. Balfour (1992) argues that the Bonn government cannot be criticised for this, though many would dispute his position.

The Treuhandanstalt (THA) was given an almost impossible set of tasks, namely to privatise enterprises wherever possible and mediate their sale and to shut down those for which buyers could not be found. It has had to face East German anger and bitterness as whole sections of industry have been closed down or where sell-offs to West German investors have also led to the redundancy of workers. The financial costs of the THA's work have spiralled, as pressure has mounted for it to provide a life-line to those struggling enterprises in the East whose closure would create further local and regional crises. In this sense, priorities have had to change as the social and regional consequences of the THA's actions have taken on added importance. Moreover, the earlier declaration that property would be handed back to former owners on satisfactory examination of their claims hindered the Treuhandanstalt's activities. Compensation, rather than restitution, has been one of the lessons learnt from the unification process.

The costs of unification were seriously underestimated by the Bonn government. Privatisation of the East German economy, job creation schemes, retraining of workers, combating urban and rural deprivation, provision of new infrastructure such as roads, railways and hospitals, and environmental clean-up have required massive financial transfers from West to East. Bringing East German living standards up to those in the West has been a goal that has been difficult to achieve. Demands for East German wage levels to match those in the West, despite the critical differences in productivity, run the risk of jeopardising further the competitiveness of East German industry. Currently, of course, the new Germany is characterised by differences in wealth between its western and eastern *Länder*. East Germans may well be reflecting over what they have lost through German unification. Some may now question whether a liberal democracy is the best way to run their territory since at least under the socialist regime they had jobs and employment security, low rents, cheap foodstuffs (though a limited range) and favourable health, maternity and other social benefits.

Externally Germany must face a number of difficult challenges. In the European Community, Germany is expected to lead the process of European union, bear the brunt of the financial costs involved and act in unison with other Community member states. The possible enlargement of the EC in the mid-1990s to accommodate Austria and other European Free Trade Area (EFTA) participants is expected to emphasise further Germany's already strong links with these countries. Germany, too, has most to gain and lose from processes of change in Eastern Europe. The new Germany is in a commanding position to profit from trade and investment opportunities in Eastern Europe and the former USSR, yet cannot afford to take full responsibility for the costs of aid and development programmes in these countries. Moreover, ethnic unrest in Eastern Europe could result in large-scale migration westwards, with Germany being the most obvious destination, especially for ethnic Germans.

Unification, paradoxically, has so far been a most divisive experience for the Germans. It has not simply been a story of winners and losers (although the Bonn–Berlin debate has been cast in these terms) but rather another painful chapter in Germany's turbulent history. The German people will express their opinion on their own personal experience of unification in the elections planned for 1994. These may mark the beginning of a new stage in the development of the new Germany.

Bibliography

Abelshauser, W. (1984) *Der Ruhr-kohlenbergbau seit 1945: Wiederaufbau, Krise, Anpassung.* Verlag C.H. Beck, München.

Adomeit, H. (1982) *Soviet Risk Taking.* Allen and Unwin, London.

Albrecht, G. and Meincke, R. (1993) 'Entwicklungstendenzen im ländlichen Raum', *Praxis Geographie,* **23** (6), 18–23.

Alsop, R. (1992) 'The experience of women in Eastern Germany' in J. Osmond (ed.), *German Reunification: a Reference Guide and Commentary.* Longman, Harlow. 185–97.

Ardagh, J. (1988) *Germany and the Germans.* Penguin, London.

Ardagh, J. (1991) *Germany and the Germans After Unification.* Penguin, London.

Backer, J. (1978) *The Decision to Divide Germany.* Duke University Press, Durham, USA.

Balfour, M. (1982) *West Germany. A Contemporary History.* Croom Helm, London.

Balfour, M. (1992) *Germany. The Tides of Power.* Routledge, London.

Bark, D.L. and Gress, D.R. (1989) *A History of West Germany. Volume 1. From Shadow to Substance 1945–1963.* Basil Blackwell, Oxford.

Barsch, H. *et al.* (1993) 'Altlastenverdachtsflächen neben naturnahen Biotopen: Truppenübungsplätze der ehemaligen sowjetischen Streitkräfte in Brandenburg', *Geographische Rundschau,* **45** (6), 353–9.

Bentley, R. (1991) *Research and Technology in the former GDR.* Westview Press, Boulder.

Berentsen, W. (1981) 'Regional change in the GDR', *Annals of the Association of American Geographers,* **71** (1), 50–66.

Berentsen, W. (1984) 'Regional planning in Central Europe: Austria, the FRG, the GDR and Switzerland', *Environment and Planning C: Government and Policy,* **3**, 319–39.

Berghahn, V.R. (1987) *Modern Germany.* Cambridge University Press, Cambridge.

Bergmann, E. (1992) 'Räumliche Aspekte des Strukturwandels in der Landwirtschaft', *Geographische Rundschau,* **44** (3), 143–7.

Berlin Senatsverwaltung für Bau- und Wohnungswesen (1991) *Urban Renewal Berlin. Experience—Examples—Prospects.* Berlin.

Birkholz, K. (1993) 'Der räumlich-strukturelle Wandel in der Region Brandenburg-Berlin', *Geographische Rundschau,* **45** (10), 564–73.

Blacksell, M. (1981) *Post-War Europe: A Political Geography.* Hutchinson, London.

Blumenfeld, E. (1990) 'Unification is going too fast', *European Affairs,* **2**, 32–5.

Bradley-Scharf, C. (1984) *Politics and Change in East Germany. An Evaluation of Socialist Democracy.* Westview Press/Pinter, Boulder.

Breugel, I. (1993) 'Local economic development in the transformation of Berlin', *Regional Studies,* **27** (2), 155–9.

Breuilly, J. (ed.) (1992) *The State of Germany.* Longman, Harlow.

Brisou, S. (ed.) (1990) *Les Deux Allemagne 1984–1989.* La Documentation Française, Paris.

Buchner, H.J. (1990) 'Grundlagen, Konzeptionen und Probleme der Stadterneuerung in der DDR am Beispiel von Greifswald' in M. Domros *et al.*, *Festschrift für Wendelin Klaer zum 65 Geburtstag*. Mainz. 121–42.

Bulmer, S. (1989) 'The European Dimension', in G. Smith *et al.*, *Developments in West German Politics*. Macmillan, Basingstoke. 211–28.

Bulmer, S. and Paterson, W. (1987) *The Federal Republic of Germany and the European Community*. Allen and Unwin, London.

Bundesministerium des Innern (1991) *Aufzeichnung zur Ausländerpolitik und zum Ausländerrecht in der Bundesrepublik Deutschland*. Bonn.

Bundesministerium des Innern (1992) *Hilfen für Deutsche im Osten Europas*. Bonn.

Bundesministerium für Landwirtschaft (1992) *Agrarwirtschaft in den neuen Landern*. Bonn.

Bundesministerium für Verkehr (1992) *Verkehrsprojekte Deutsche Einheit*. Bonn.

Bundeministerium für Raumordnung (1991) *Raumordnungsbericht*. Bonn.

Bundesministerium für Wirtschaft (1992) *Wirtschaftliche Förderung in den neuen Bundesländern*. Bonn.

Burdick, C. (ed.) (1984) *Contemporary Germany. Politics and Culture*. Westview Press, Boulder.

Burtenshaw, D. (1974) *Economic Geography of West Germany*. Macmillan, Basingstoke.

Carlin, W. (1992) 'Privatisation in East Germany 1990–1992', *German History*, **10** (3), 335–51.

Carlin, W. and Mayer, C. (1992) 'Restructuring enterprises in Eastern Europe', *Economic Policy*, **15**, 312–52.

Childs, D. (1983) *The GDR: Moscow's German Ally*. George Allen and Unwin, London.

Childs, D. (1985) *Honecker's Germany*. George Allen and Unwin, London.

Childs, D. (1991) *Germany in the Twentieth Century*. Batsford, London.

Childs, D. and Johnson, J. (1982) *West Germany: Politics and Society*. Croom Helm, London.

Conradt, D.P. (1986) *The German Polity*. Longman, Harlow.

Conze, W. (1979) *The Shaping of the German Nation*. George Prior, London.

Craig, G. (1982) *The Germans*. Penguin, London.

Cuming, M. (1992) 'The confused role of the Treuhand', *German Monitor*, **25**, 25–40.

Dawson, A.H. (ed.) (1987) *Planning in Eastern Europe*. St Martin's Press, New York.

DDR (1988) *Statistisches Jahrbuch der DDR*. Berlin.

Debardeleben, J. (1985) *The Environment and Marxism–Leninism. The Soviet and East German Experience*. Westview Press, Boulder.

Dege, W. and Kerkemeyer, S. (1993) 'Der wirtschaftliche Wandel im Ruhrgebiet in den 80er Jahren', *Geographische Rundschau*, **45** (9), 503–9.

Dennis, M. (1988) *GDR. Politics, Economics and Society*. Pinter, London.

De Zayas, A.M. (1979) *Nemesis at Potsdam: the Anglo–Americans and the Expulsion of the Germans*. Routledge, London.

Dickinson, R.E. (1953) *Germany: A General and Regional Geography*. Methuen, London.

Diemer, G. and Hoffmann, H. (1990) *Blickpunkt DDR*. Olzog Verlag, München.

Die Regierung der Bundesrepublik Deutschland (1992) *Hilfen für Deutsche in der GUS, Georgien und den baltischen Staaten*. Bonn.

Dloczik, M. *et al.* (1990) *Der Fischer Informationsatlas Bundesrepublik Deutschland*. Fischer Taschenbuch Verlag, Frankfurt-am-Main.

Dyson, K. (1977) *Party, State and Bureaucracy in West Germany*. Sage, London.

Dyson, K. (1981) 'The politics of economic management in West Germany', *West European Politics*, **4** (1), 35–55.

Dyson, K. (1989) 'Economic Policy' in G. Smith *et al*. *Developments in West German Politics*. Macmillan, Basingstoke. 148–64.

Edinger, L.J. (1986) *West German Politics*. Columbia University Press, New York.

Edwards, G.E. (1985) *GDR Society and Social Institutions*. Macmillan, Basingstoke.

Ehlers, E. (1988) 'Die Agrarlandschaft der Bundesrepublik Deutschland und ihr Wandel seit 1949', *Geographische Rundschau*, **40** (1), 30–41.

Elkins, T.H. (1988) *Berlin: The Spatial Structure of a Divided City*. Methuen, London.

Ellger, C. (1992) 'Berlin: Legacies of division and problems of unification', *Geographical Journal*, **158** (1), 40–7.

Ernst, E. (1993) 'Länderneugliederung in Deutschland', *Geographische Rundschau*, **45** (7–8), 446–58.

European Commission (1990) *The European Community and German Unification*. Brussels.

European Commission (1991) *Community Support Framework 1991–1993 for the New Lander*. Luxembourg.

European Commission (1992a) *Socio-Economic Situation and Development in the Neighbouring Countries of the Community in Central and Eastern Europe*. Brussels.

European Commission (1992b) *The ERDF in 1990*. Brussels.

European Parliament (1990) 'The impact of German unification on the EC', *Research and Documentation Papers*, Working Document 1, Luxembourg.

Feld, W. (1981) *West Germany and the European Community. Changing Interests and Competing Policy Objectives*. Praeger.

Fischer Welt Almanach (1990) *Zahlen. Daten. Fakten*. Fischer Taschenbuch Verlag, Frankfurt-am-Main.

Foucher, M. (1993) *Fragments d'Europe*. Fayard, Paris.

Francisco, R.A. and Merritt, R.L. (eds) (1985) *Berlin between Two Worlds*. Westview Press, Boulder.

Frick, D. (1991) 'City development and planning in the Berlin conurbation', *Town Planning Review*, **62**, 37–49.

Fritsch-Bournazel, R. (1988) *Confronting the German Question. Germans on the East–West Divide*. Berg, Oxford.

Fulbrook, M. (1991) *The Fontana History of Germany 1918–1990. The Divided Nation*. Fontana, London.

Gatzweiler, H.P. (1992) 'Neue Aufgaben für die Raumordnungspolitik in Deutschland', *Geographische Rundschau*, **44** (3), 136–8.

Glaessner, G.J. (1992) *Der Schwierige Weg zur Demokratie. Vom Ende der DDR zur Deutschen Einheit*. Westdeutscher Verlag, Opladen.

Glebe, G. (1994) 'Düsseldorf: economic restructuring and demographic transformation' in H.D. Clout, *Europe's Cities in the 1980s and Beyond*. Netherland Geographical Studies, Amsterdam.

Graff Kielmansegg, P. (1992) 'Germany—a future with two pasts', in D. Grosser (ed.) *German Unification. The Unexpected Challenge*. Berg, Oxford. 180–94.

Gransow, V. (1989) 'Colleague Frankenstein and the pale light of progress—life conditions, life activities, and technological impacts on the GDR way of life', *International Journal of Sociology*, **18** (3), 194–209.

Grass, G. (1990) *Deutsche Lastenausgleich. Wider das dumpfe Einheits gebot. Rede und Gespräche.* Luchterhand Verlag, Frankfurt-am-Main.

Graubard, S.R. (1991) (ed.) *Eastern Europe..Central Europe..Europe.* Westview Press, Boulder.

Green, T. (1959) 'West German city reconstruction', *Sociological Review,* 7, 231–44.

Grimm, F. (1991) 'Geographische Aspekte der Situation und Perspective der Kreisstädte und Kreise in den mittel und ostdeutschen Ländern' *Ber. z. dt Landeskunde,* 65 (1), 83–105. Trier.

Grosser, A. (1971) *Germany in Our Time.* Pall Mall Press, London.

Grosser, D. (ed.) (1992) *German Unification. The Unexpected Challenge.* Berg, Oxford.

Grotewold, A. (1973) 'West Germany's economic growth', *Annals of the Association of American Geographers,* 63, 353–65.

Gruner, W. (1992) 'Germany in Europe: the German question as burden and as opportunity' in J. Breuilly (ed.), *The State of Germany.* Longman, Harlow. 201–24.

Hadju, J. (1983) 'Post-war development and planning of West German cities' in T. Wild, *Urban and Rural Change in West Germany.* Croom Helm, London. 16–39.

Hagedorn, K. *et al.* (1992) 'Transformation of socialist agriculture in Eastern Germany—concepts and experiences', *Report of a Joint ECE/FAO Workshop,* Godollo, Hungary, 22–6 June. United Nations Economic Commission for Europe.

Hall, D. (1990) 'Planning for a united Germany', *Town Planning Review,* 58, 19–28.

Hamilton, F.E.I. (1975) *Poland's Western and Northern Territories.* Oxford University Press, Oxford.

Harder, E. (1991) 'Rahmen Bedingungen Künftiger Wirtschaftlicher Entfaltung' in Sachsische Landeszentrale für Politische Bildung. *Sachsen: Land im Aufbruch.* Dresden. 40–5.

Heineberg, H. (1988) 'Die Stadt im westlichen Deutschland', *Geographische Rundschau,* 40 (1), 20–9.

Heinrich, R. and Wiegandt, C.C. (1991) 'Altlasten-Restriktion für die räumliche Entwicklung in den neuen Bundesländern', *Raumforschung und Raumordnung,* 4, 209–17.

Heinzmann, J. (1991) 'Strukturwandel altindustrialisierte Regionen in den neuen Bundesländern—Bedingungen und Probleme', *Raumforschung und Raumordnung,* 2-3, 100–6.

Heisenberg, W. (1991) *Die Vereinigung Deutschlands in europäischer Perspektive.* Nomos Verlagsgesellschaft, Baden-Baden.

Helbrecht, I. and Pohl, J. (1993) 'München zwischen Expansion und Kollaps?', *Geographische Rundschau,* 45 (4), 238–43.

Helm, J.A. (1989) 'Structural change in the Ruhr valley: what price social peace?' in P. Merkl (ed.), *The Federal Republic of Germany at Forty.* New York University Press, New York. 193–212.

Hendriks, G. (1991) *Germany and European Integration: The Common Agricultural Policy: An Area of Conflict.* Berg, Oxford.

Hennings, K.H. (1982) 'West Germany' in A. Boltho (ed.), *The European Economy. Growth and Crisis.* Oxford University Press, Oxford. 472–501.

Henrichsmeyer, W. (1990) 'Anpassungsprobleme und Perspektiven der DDR Landwirtschaft', *Agrarwirtschaft,* 39 (8), 233–4.

Herles, H. (1991) *Die Haupstadt-Debatte.* Bouvier Verlag, Bonn.

Herrmann, H. (1992) 'Ursachen und Entwicklung der Ausländerbeschäftigung', *Informationen zur politischen bildung*, 237 (4), 4–7.

Hewitt, K. *et al.* (1993) 'Städte nach dem Krieg: Aspekte des Wiederaufbaus in Deutschland', *Geographische Rundschau*, 45 (7–8), 438–67.

Hoffmann-Lange, U. (ed.) (1991) *Social and Political Structures in West Germany*. Westview Press, Boulder.

Hohmann, H-H. (ed.) (1982) *The East European Economies in the 1970s*. Butterworth, London.

Hohn, C. (1990) 'Wie weiter nach der Wende? Stadtplanung in der ehemaligen DDR zwischen Kontinuität und Kontrasten', *Geographische Rundschau*, 42 (11), 604–12.

Hohn, U. and Hohn, A. (1993) 'Gross siedlungen in Ost Deutschland: Entwicklung, Perspektiven und die Fallstudie Rostock-Gross Klein', *Geographische Rundschau*, 45 (3) 146–52.

Hönsch, F. (1992) 'Der Leipziger SüdRaum—eine Region im Wandel', *Geographische Rundschau*, 44 (10), 592–9.

Hooper, A.J. (1988) 'Planning versus the control of development in West Germany', *Town Planning Review*, 59, 183–206.

Hubatsch, W. (1967) *The German Question*. Herder Book Center, Marburg.

Hughes, M. (1988) *Nationalism and Society: Germany 1800–1945*. Edward Arnold, London.

Immler, H. (1971) *Agrarpolitik in der DDR*. Köln.

Info-Dienst Deutsche Aussiedler (1992) *Zahlen. Daten. Fakten*. Bonn.

Innenministerium des Landes Mecklenburg-Vorpommern (1993) *Städtebauförderprogramm*. Schwerin.

Inotai, A. (1992) 'Economic implications of German unification for Central and Eastern Europe', in P.B. Stares (ed.), *The New Germany and the New Europe*. Brookings Institution, Washington DC. 279–301.

InterNationes (1992) *On the Path to German Unity. Chronology of Events 1989–1991*. Bonn.

Irmen, E. (1990) 'Die räumliche Entwicklung in der BRD in den 80er Jahren', *Geographische Rundschau*, 42 (7), 432–7.

Jeffries, I. (1992) 'The impact of reunification on the East German economy', in J. Osmond (ed.), *German Reunification: A Reference Guide and Commentary*. Longman, Harlow. 152–9.

Jeffries, I. and Melzer, M. (eds) (1987) *The East German Economy*. Croom Helm, London.

Johnson, N. (1983) *State and Government in the Federal Republic of Germany*. Pergamon, Oxford.

Jones, A. (1990) 'New directions for West German agricultural policy', *Journal of Rural Studies*, 6, 9–16.

Jones, A. (1991) 'Impact of the EC's set-aside programme. Response of farm businesses in Rendsburg-Eckernförde (Germany)', *Land Use Policy*, 8, 108–23.

Jones, A. *et al.* (1992) 'Gründe für eine Beteiligung am EG-Flächenstillegungsprogramm. Anhaltspunkte aus Trier-Saarburg und Rheinland-Pfalz', *Landbauforschung-Volkenrode*, 3, 176–92.

Jones, A. *et al.* (1993) 'Farm household adjustments to the EC's set-aside policy. Evidence from Rheinland-Pfalz', *Journal of Rural Studies*, 9 (1), 65–80.

Jones, A. and Budd, S. (1991) *The European Community. A Guide to the Maze*. Kogan Page, London.

Jones, A. and Budd, S. (1994) *The European Community. A Guide through the Maze*. Kogan Page, London. Fifth edition.

Jones, P.N. and Wild, T. (1992) 'Western Germany's "third wave" of migrants—the arrival of the Aussiedler', *Geoforum*, **23** (1), 1–11.

Karaganov, S.A. (1992) 'Implications of German unification for the Former Soviet Union', in P.B. Stares (ed.), *The New Germany and the New Europe*. Brookings Institution, Washington DC. 331–64.

Karger, A. and Werner, F. (1982) 'Die sozialistische Stadt', *Geographische Rundschau*, **34** (11), 519–28.

Keiderling, G. (1982) *Die Berliner Krise*. Verlag das Europaische Buch, West Berlin.

Keithly, D.M. (1992) *The Collapse of East German Communism. The Year the Wall Came Down 1989*. Praeger, London.

Kohli, J. (1993) 'Wohnungspolitik und Wohnungswirtschaft in den neuen Ländern', *Geographische Rundschau*, **45** (3) 140–5.

Kohne, M. (1990) 'Erfolgsvoraussetzungen für LPGen', *Agrarwirtschaft*, **39** (9), 265–6.

Kommunalverband Ruhrgebiet (1992) *The Ruhr. The Driving Force of Germany*. Essen.

Kloss, G. (1976) *West Germany. An Introduction*. Macmillan, Basingstoke.

Knott, J. (1981) *Managing the German Economy*. Lexington, Columbus.

Kohl, W.L. and Basevi, G. (1980) *West Germany: A European and Global Power*. Lexington, Columbus.

Koves, A. and Marer, P. (1991) *Central and East European Economies in Transition*. Westview Press, Boulder.

Kratke, S. (1992) 'Berlin: the rise of a new metropolis in a post-Fordist landscape' in M. Dunford and G. Kafkalas (eds), *Cities, Regions and the New Europe*. Pinter, London. 214–39.

Krippendorf, E. and Rittberger, V. (eds) (1980) *Foreign Policy of West Germany*. Sage, London.

Krisch, H. (1985) *The GDR. The Search for Identity*. Westview Press, Boulder.

Laux, H.D. (1991) 'Berlin oder Bonn? Geographische Aspekte einer Parlamentsentscheidung', *Geographische Rundschau*, **43** (12), 740–3.

Leaman, J. (1988) *The Political Economy of West Germany 1945–1985*. Macmillan, Basingstoke.

Lebeau, R. (1989) *L'Allemagne fédérale: géographie économique*. Masson, Paris.

Leptin, G. and Melzer, M. (1978) *Economic Reform in East German Industry*. Oxford University Press, Oxford.

Leupolt, B. (1993) 'Entwicklung der Industrie in Berlin–Brandenburg', *Geographische Rundschau*, **45** (10), 594–600.

Liebert, U. and Merkel, W. (eds) (1991) *Die Politik zur deutschen Einheit*. Leske und Budrich Verlag, Opladen.

Littlechild, M.B. (1982) 'Regional policy in Germany', *Town and Country Planning*, **51** (5), 155–9.

Ludlow, P. (1991) 'Die deutsch-deutschen Verhandlungen und die "Zwei-Plus-Vier" Gespräche' in W. Heisenberg (ed.), *Die Vereinigung Deutschlands in europäischer Perspektive*. Nomos Verlagsgesellschaft, Baden-Baden. 17–28.

Markovits, A.S. (ed.) (1982) *The Political Economy of West Germany*. Praeger, New York.

Mayhew, A. (1970) 'Structural reform and the future of West German agriculture', *Geographical Review*, **60**, 54–68.

Mayhew, A. (1970) 'Agrarian reform in West Germany', *Transactions of the Institute of British Geographers*, **52**, 61–76.

Mayhew, A. (1973) *Rural Settlement and Farming in Germany*. Batsford.

McAdams, A.J. (1989) 'Inter-German Relations' in G. Smith *et al.*, *Developments in West German Politics*. Macmillan, Basingstoke. 229–45.

McCauley, M. (1983) *The GDR since 1945*. Macmillan, Basingstoke.

McCauley, M. (1986) 'Social Policy under Honecker' in I. Wallace (ed.), *The GDR Under Honecker*. GDR Monitor Special Series, Dundee. 3–19.

Meincke, R. (1993) 'Mecklenburg-Vorpommern', *Praxis Geographie*, 23 (6), 4–9.

Mellor, R.E.H. (1978) *The Two Germanies. A Modern Geography*. Harper and Row.

Mellor, R.E.H. (1992) 'Railways and German unification', *Geography*, 77 (3), 261–4.

Merkl, P. (1963) *The Origin of the West German Republic*. Oxford University Press, Oxford.

Merkl, P. (1989a) 'The German Search for Identity' in G. Smith *et al.*, *Developments in West German Politics*. Macmillan, Basingstoke. 6–19.

Merkl, P. (ed.) (1989b) *The Federal Republic at Forty*. New York University Press, New York.

Milward, A.S. (1984) *The Reconstruction of Western Europe 1945–1951*. Methuen, London.

Ministerium für Landwirtschaft (*Land* Brandenburg) (1992) *Agrarbericht*. Potsdam.

Ministerium für Umwelt des Landes Sachsen-Anhalt (1990) *Umweltbericht 1990*. Magdeburg.

Ministerium für Umwelt des Landes Sachsen-Anhalt (1991) *Umweltbericht 1991*. Magdeburg.

Moser, H. (ed.) (1992) *Berlin-Report: Eine Wirtschaftsregion im Aufschwung*. Gabler Verlag, Berlin.

Moreton, E. (ed.) (1987) *Germany between East and West*. Cambridge University Press, Cambridge.

Morgan, R. and Bray, C. (1986) *Partners and Rivals in Western Europe: Britain, France and West Germany*. Gower, Aldershot.

Munziger Archiv (1991) *Sachsen*. Dresden.

Murswiek, D. *et al.* (1991) *Die Vereinigung Deutschlands*. Gebr. Mann Verlag, Berlin.

Neuss, B. (1992) 'The European Community: How to counterbalance the Germans' in D. Grosser (ed.), *German Unification. The Unexpected Challenge*. Berg, Oxford. 136–49.

Nuhn, H. and Sinz, M. (1988) 'Industrial change and employment trends in the FRG', *Geographische Rundschau*, 40 (1), 68–78.

Osmond, J. (1992) *German Reunification: a Reference Guide and Commentary*. Longman, Harlow.

Padgett, S. and Paterson, W.E. (1991) *A History of Social Democracy in Post-War Europe*. Longman, Harlow.

Platzer, H.W. (1992) 'Die EG und das vereinigte Deutschland', *Sozialwissenschaftliche Informationen*, (1), 24–8.

Pommerin, R. (1989) *Von Berlin nach Bonn. Die Allierten, die Deutschen und die Hauptstadtfrage nach 1945*. Böhlau Verlag, Köln.

Pond, E. (1990) 'A wall destroyed: the dynamics of German unification in the GDR', *International Security*, 15, 35–66.

Priebe, H. (1980) 'German agricultural policy and the EC' in W.L. Kohl and G. Basevi (eds) (1980) *West Germany: A European and Global Power*. Lexington Books. 139–49.

Prufer, A. (1992) 'Pilotprojekt regionale Konversion in der Region Neuruppin', *Informationen zur Raumentwicklung*, 5, 343–50.

Richter, M. (1991) 'Sowjetische Besatzungszone Deutschlands (SBZ)', *Informationen zur politischen Bildung*, **231**, 2–9.

Ruppert, K. (1982) 'Raumstrukturen der Alpen', *Geographische Rundschau*, **34** (9), 386–9.

Rutz, W. (1991) 'Die Wiedererrichtung der östlichen Bundesländer', *Raumforschung und Raumordnung*, **5**, 280–6.

Rutz, W. et al. (1993) *Die Funf Neuen Bundesländer. Historisch begründet, politisch gewollt und künftig vernünftig.* Wissenschaftliche Buchgesellschaft, Darmstadt.

Sachsisches Staatsministerium für Wirtschaft und Arbeit (1992) *Der wirtschaftliche Wiederaufbau in Ostdeutschland—Beispiel Sachsen.* Dresden.

Sandford, G. (1983) *From Hitler to Ulbricht: The Communist Reconstruction of East Germany, 1945–1946.* Princeton University Press, Princeton.

Scharf, C.B. (1984) *Politics and Change in East Germany: an Evaluation of Socialist Democracy.* Pinter, London.

Scharf, C.B. (1989) 'Social policy and social conditions in the GDR,' *International Journal of Sociology*, **18** (3), 3–26.

Schmidt, I. (1990) 'Former GDR communities in radical change' *International Journal of Urban and Regional Research*, **14** (4), 667–75.

Schmidt, H. and Scholz, D. (1991) 'Die neuen deutschen Länder. Chancen und Probleme aus geographischer Sicht' *Bericht zum deutsche Landeskunde*, **65** (1), 65–82.

Schmoll, F. (1990) 'Metropolis Berlin? Prospects and problems of post-November 1989 urban developments', *International Journal of Urban and Regional Research*, **14** (4), 676–86.

Schneider, E. (1978) *The GDR.* Hurst, London.

Schnitzer, M. (1964) *East and West Germany. A Comparative Economic Analysis*, Praeger, New York.

Scholler, P. (1965) 'The division of Germany—based on historical geography?', *Erdkunde*, **19**, 161–4.

Schonfeld, R. (1992) 'Germany: Privatising the East', *The World Today*, 48 (8), 152–5.

Schroder, R. (1993) *Deutschland schwierig Vaterland: für eine neue politische Kultur.* Herder Verlag, Freiburg.

Schulz, M. (1993) 'Wohnbedingungen und innerstädtische Differenzierung in Ost-Berlin', *Geographische Rundschau*, **45** (10), 588–93.

Schulze, E. (1992) 'Städtebauliche Erneuerung der Städte und Dorfer in den neuen Bundesländern', *Informationen zur Raumentwicklung*, **6**, 457–72.

Selke, W. (1991) 'Raumordnungspolitische Aufbaustrategie für den Osten Deutschlands', *Informationen zur Raumentwicklung*, **11** (2), 747–54.

Shackleton, M. (1990) *Financing the European Community.* Pinter, London.

Siebert, H. (1991) 'German unification: the economics of transition', *Kiel Arbeitspaper nr 468a*, Kiel: Institut für Weltwirtschaft.

Simonian, H. (1981) 'France, Germany, and Europe', *Journal of Common Market Studies*, **19** (3), 204–19.

Simonian, H. (1985) *The Privileged Partnership: Franco–German Relations in the European Community, 1969–1984.* Clarendon Press, Oxford.

Sinnhuber, K. (1965) 'Eisenhüttenstadt and other new industrial locations in East Germany', *Festschrift für Leo Scheidl*, Universitat Wien.

Sinz, M. (1992) 'Europäische Integration und Raumentwicklung in Deutschland', *Geographische Rundschau*, **44** (12), 686–90.

Smith, A.H. (1983) *The Planned Economies of Eastern Europe.* Croom Helm, London.

Smith, E.O. (1983) *The West German Economy*. Croom Helm, London.

Smith, G. *et al.* (1989) *Developments in West German Politics*. Macmillan, Basingstoke.

Smyser, W.R. (1992) *The Economy of United Germany. Colossus at the Crossroads.* Hurst, London.

SOPEMI (1990) *Annual Country Reports—Germany.* OECD, Paris.

Sontheimer, K. and Bleek, W. (1975) *The Government and Politics of East Germany.* Hutchinson, London.

Sowden, J.K. (1975) *The German Question 1945-1973. Continuity in Change.* Bradford University Press, Bradford.

Spence, D. (1991a) 'Die Verhandlungen der Europäischen Gemeinschaft' in W. Heisenberg (ed.), *Die Vereinigung Deutschlands in europäischer Perspektive.* Nomos Verlagsgesellschaft, Baden-Baden. 29–54.

Spence, D. (1991b) 'Enlargement without accession: The EC's response to German unification', *RIIA Discussion Paper 36.* Royal Institute of International Affairs, London.

Stadt Duisburg (1991) *Landschaftspark Duisburg-Nord.* Duisburg.

Stares, P.B. (ed.) (1992) *The New Germany and the New Europe.* Brookings Institution, Washington DC.

Stiens, G. (1988) 'Raumordnung in der Bundesrepublik Deutschland', *Geographische Rundschau*, 40 (1), 54–9.

Stolper, W.F. (1960) *The Structure of the East Germany Economy.* Harvard University Press, Cambridge MA.

Strassburger, J. (1984) 'Economic system and economic policy: the challenge of the 1970s' in K. Von Beyme and H. Zimmerman (eds), *Policy Making in the GDR.* Gower, Aldershot. 109–43.

Szabo, S.F. (1992) *The Diplomacy of German Unification.* St Martin's Press, New York.

Thies, J. (1990) 'Be patient with Germany', *European Affairs*, 4, 22–3.

Thies, J. (1992) 'Germany—into turbulent waters', *The World Today*, 48 (8), 148–51.

Thomaneck, J.K. and Mellis, J. (1989) *Politics, Society and Government in the GDR. Basic Documents.* Berg.

Thurich, E. (1991) 'Die Sieger in Deutschland', *Informationen zur politischen Bildung*, 232 (3), 6–18.

Tilford, R.B. (ed.) (1975) *Ostpolitik and Political Change in West Germany.* Saxon House.

Treuhandanstalt (1991) *Privatisierung: Land und Forstwirtschaft.* Berlin.

Treuhandanstalt (1992) *Wegweiser und Zwischenbilanz.* Berlin.

Turner, H.A. (1987) *The Two Germanies since 1945.* Yale University Press, New Haven.

Turner, H.A. (1992) *Germany from Partition to Reunification.* Yale University Press, New Haven.

Usbeck, H. (1991) 'Flächennutzungsplanung und Stadtentwicklung in Leipzig', *Raumplanung* (Dortmund), 52, 5–8.

Verheyen, D. (1991) *The German Question. A Cultural, Historical, and Geopolitical Exploration.* Westview Press.

Von Beyme, K. and Zimmerman, H. (eds) (1984) *Policy Making in the GDR.* Gower, Aldershot.

Von Beyme, K. *et al.* (1992) *Neue Städte aus Ruinen. Deutscher Städtebau der Nachkriegszeit.* Prestel Verlag, München.

Wallach, H.G.P. and Francisco, R.A. (1990) *United Germany.* Praeger, New York.

Watson, A. (1992) *The Germans: Who Are They Now?* Methuen, London.

Weiland, S. *et al.* (1991) *9 November. Das Jahr danach. Vom Fall der Mauer bis zur ersten gesamtdeutschen Wahl.* Wilhelm Heyne Verlag, München.

Weiler, H. *et al.* (1990) *Wirtschaftspartner DDR.* Economica Verlag, Bonn.

Weiss, W. and Blauschmidt, C. (1990) 'Zur Bevölkerungsdynamik der Gemeinden in den Nordbezirken der DDR am Beispiel des Kreises Waren', *Petermanns geog mitt,* **134** (3), 189–92.

West German Embassy (Press and information Office) (1985) *Facts and Figures. A Comparative Survey of the FRG and GDR.* Bonn.

Wetzlaugk, U. (1993) 'Auf dem Weg zum Parlaments- und Regierungssitz', *Informationen zur politischen Bildung,* **240** (3), 27–34.

Wiese, B. and Zils, N. (1987) *Deutsche Kultur-Geographie.* Busse Seewald Verlag, Herford.

Wild, T. (1979) *West Germany. A Geography of its Peoples.* Longman, Harlow.

Wild, T. (ed.) (1983) *Urban and Rural Change in West Germany.* Croom Helm, London.

Wild, T. (1992) 'From division to unification: regional dimensions of economic change in Germany', *Geography,* **77** (3), 244–60.

Wilkins, H. (1981) *The Two German Economies.* Gower, Aldershot.

Windsor, P. (1969) *German Reunification.* Elek Books, London.

Woods, R. (1986) *Opposition in the GDR under Honecker 1971–1985.* Macmillan, Basingstoke.

Zarth, M. (1992) 'Regionale Auswirkungen des Truppenabbaus und der Rüstungskonversion', *Informationen zur Raumentwicklung,* **5**, 311–32.

Ziener, K. (1993) 'Wandel in der zentralörtlichen Gliederung Brandenburgs', *Geographische Rundschau,* **45** (10), 574–80.

Index

Index compiled by Caroline Sheard